THE LANCASHIRE
WITCH CRAZE

The Lancashire Witch Craze

*Jennet Preston and the
Lancashire Witches, 1612*

JONATHAN LUMBY

Carnegie Publishing, 1995

The Lancashire Witch Craze
Jonathan Lumby

First Edition
Published by Carnegie Publishing Ltd, 1995

Copyright © J. Lumby, 1995

Typeset in 11/13 Monotype Bembo by
Carnegie Publishing Ltd, 18 Maynard St, Preston, Lancs.
Printed in the UK by T. Snape & Co., Preston

British Library Cataloguing in Publication Data
A CIP record for this book is available from the British Library

ISBN 1–85936–025-4

Preface

THE inspiration for this book lies in the histories of Everton and of Melling produced by Mr E. E. Newton, MBE. Eddie proved that a community which delights in its history is thereby tickled into life and emboldened to face new ventures.

People from around Pendle have been generous. Kate Hooper and Anne Fellowes (née Nutter), descendants of those who were racked by the seventeenth-century witchcraft turmoils, gave encouragement. Constance and Don Nicholson entertained me at Newfield Edge; George and Myfanwy Bargh would speak of Greenhead, Myfanwy's family's home after the Nutter's time; and Christopher and Marion Hindley of Gisburne Park kindly allowed reproduction of the picture of Arnoldsbigging and Westby, painted for the Listers whose estate they now enjoy. Edith Peel first took me to Malkin Tower; she showed me Bulhole, Wheathead, Fence and other sites on the southern slopes of Pendle. Dorothy Taylor fed me with information about the Listers, while Bob (R. J.) Hayhurst opened his extensive library and print collection at Narrow Gates Mill, Barley, and shared his knowledge of the buildings of Pendle. The Rev. Alan Bailey, Vicar of Waddington, discussed the liturgical use to which James's spell may have been put in the medieval church, and The Rev. John Kelly of Lytham was a guide to by-ways of seventeenth-century hermetic lore and magic. Christine Thistlethwaite of Rimington and John Hartley of Whalley, the former a dialect poet and the latter a teller of whimsical stories, for me stirred a living flame from the embers of their region's history.

My daughter Laurie (Belinda) preferred a feminist critique of the early stages of the text; Julia Carnwath kept me in touch with late medieval academic studies.

I print later a bibliography as an expression of gratitude to scholars whose works have aided and enthralled me. Local history librarians at Clitheroe, Sue Holden and Laura Waterhouse, laid quick hands on books I have needed, and brought forth that treasure of the library, a first edition of John Webster's *The Displaying of Supposed Witchcraft*. Lancashire Record Office, the British Museum Reading Room, and Claremont in Leeds, the home of the Yorkshire Archaeological Society, made research a pleasure.

During these last months in the mountains of Meirionnydd, Eveline King, of Croesor, has typed and ordered my scribblings, and David Lea and Awel Irene have given to me and to my donkeys shelter, grazing and peace.

Thank you.

Llanfrothen
November 1994

For
Hannah
my daughter
and for
the people of Gisburn

Contents

Preface		v
List of Illustrations, Family Trees and Maps		xi
Chronicle of Events		xv
Events in 1612		xviii

1.	The Investigation	1
2.	The Silencing of Dissention	5
3.	Gisburn: Jennet's Homeland	7
4.	Thomas Potts' Chronology	12
5.	The Child of one Dodg-sonnes	17
6.	Over the Moors to Malkin Tower	19
7.	Questioning Alizon	21
8.	Death in Chester and Old Chattox	29
9.	Old Demdike and the Making of Pictures	35
10.	The Meeting at Malkin Tower	41
	1. Sources: Elizabeth, James and Jennet	41
	2. Upon Good Friday Last	42
	3. Roll Call	43
	4. Three Causes	45
	5. Naming of the Spirit	46
	6. Violence at Lancaster	49
	7. Killing of Master Lister	50
	8. Malign Magic or Herbal Healing?	51
	9. Night-flying	52
	10. The Great Assembly of Witches	57
	11. Romles-Moore	60

11.   Judge Bromley and Judge Altham   61
12.   The Dying Man's Railing and the Bleeding Corpse   66
13.   Wedding Traumas   70
14.   The Victimisation of Jennet   80
15.   James: Religious Scruples and Malign Magic   82
16.   The Little Wench and More of Chattox   89
17.   Spells   93
        1. Three Biters hast thou bitten   93
        2. *In Hoc Signum*   96
        3. Steck, steck hell doore   96
18.   Catholicism in Whalley Parish   102
19.   Grindletonianism   106
20.   Charmers and William Perkins   109
21.   Roger Nowell's Protestant Heritage   115
22.   The 7. in Lancashire   119
23.   Little Darrel's Tricks   125
24.   Thomas Lister and the Guilt of Schism   129
25.   Margaret Pearson of Padiham   134
26.   The Witches of Samlesbury   136
27.   The Unease of Henry Towneley   143
28.   Verdicts   149
29.   Coda: John Webster and Sir John Assheton   152

      Appendix 1
      T. Potts: *The Arraignement and Triall of Jennet Preston* 163
      Appendix 2
      Rental of Pendle Forest 1608/9   175

      Notes   183
      Bibliography   200
      Index   203

List of Illustrations, Family Trees and Maps

Illustrations

2   Title page from *The Arraignement and Triall* . . . by T. Potts, 1612. Reproduced by permission of the British Library.

8   Clitheroe Castle. From T. D. Whittaker *A History of the Parish of Whalley*, 4th edn, 1876.

10   Gisburn Hall. Sketch by Samuel Buck *c*.1720, from the collection of R. J. Hayhurst.

11   Grave monument in Gisburn churchyard.

13   Westby Hall in Craven. Sketch by Samuel Buck *c*.1720, from the collection of R. J. Hayhurst.

15   Title page from *The Wonderfull Discoverie* . . . by T. Potts, 1613. Reproduced by permission of the British Library.

25   The hanging of the Chelmsford witches, 1589. From a contemporary broadside.

27   Bulhole Farm in Goldshaw Booth. Photograph R. J. Hayhurst.

32   Greenhead Farm. From the collection of R. J. Hayhurst.

36   Witch with a cat. Woodcut.

37   Ferdinando, Earl of Derby.

39   Lancaster.

44   Under Pendle. From the collection of R. J. Hayhurst.

53   Night-flying of witches. Drawing by Knelling.

55   Frontispiece from *Pandaemonium* by R. Bovet, 1684. Reproduced by permission of the British Library.

58   A Witches' Sabbath. A sixteenth-century German woodcut.

62   Monument of Sir James Altham in Oxhey Chapel.

64   King James I of England.

74   Westby Hall and Arnoldsbigging, by Robert Griffier, *c*.1735. Reproduced by permission of Christopher Hindley of Gisburne Park.

79   The Parish Church of St Mary the Virgin, Gisburn. Photograph by R. J. Hayhurst.

85   Carr Hall, Barrowford in 1954. From the collection of R. J. Hayhurst.

99   A deathbed scene from the *Ars Moriendi* (*The Art of Dying*), a late mediaeval devotional work.

100   'The Seven Sorrows of Mary', a print published *c.*1530 by the Parisian François Regnault in a popular devotional primer.

104   Whalley Church. A pen drawing by Frank Greenwood published in *Lancashire Ways* by J. C. Walters, 1932.

112   Title page of *A Discourse* . . . by William Perkins, 1608. Reproduced by permission of the British Library.

116   Alexander Nowell, Dean of St Paul's. Portrait from Brasenose College, Oxford.

121   Cleworth Hall, Tyldesley, destroyed 1805. Engraved by N. G. Philips.

122   Magic circles:
      a) from *Newes from Scotland*, 1591.
      b) frontispiece of *Dr Faustus* by Christopher Marlowe, 1604, 1636 edn.

123   Title page of *A True Narration* . . . by John Darrel, 1600. Reproduced by permission of the British Library.

132   Cardinal William Allen.

135   The Pillory. Contemporary woodcut.

137   Samlesbury Hall. Sketch by the Rev S. J. Allen in the nineteenth century.

139   Lower Hall, Samlesbury.

140   Witches exhuming a corpse, from the *Compendium Maleficarum*, Milan, 1626.

145   Sir John Towneley and his family, 1601. Reproduced by permission of Towneley Hall Art Gallery and Museum, Burnley Borough Council.

146   Towneley Hall.

150   Hanging of witches. Frontispiece of *Englands grievance discovered* by R. Gardiner, 1655.

153   Browsholme.

158   Title page of *The Displaying of Supposed Witchcraft* by John Webster, 1677. Reproduced by permission of the British Library.

160   Sir Jonas Moore, engraved by T. Cross from a portrait by H. Stone, 1649. Reproduced by permission of the National Portrait Gallery.

196   Title page of *The Surey Demoniack* by John Carrington, 1697.

198   Title page of *The Surey Imposter* by Zachary Taylor, 1697.

Family Trees

23   Dendike and the Devices.

30   The Nutters of Greenhead.

33   Chattox and the Redfernes.

71   The Listers of Westby and Arnoldsbigging in the sixteenth and early seventeenth centuries.

73   The Hebers of Marton.

90   The Asshetons of Downham.

117   The Nowells of Read.

120   The Starkies of Huntroyd.

138   The Southworths of Samlesbury Hall.

144   The Towneleys of Carr Hall.

147   The Shuttleworths of Gawthorpe.

154–5   The Listers of Westby in the seventeenth and early eighteenth centuries.

The family trees of the Devices, Nutters and Redfernes were compiled solely from evidence within *The Wonderfull Discoverie*, those of the Listers from *Memorials of an Ancient House* and records of Gisburn Parish Church, and those of other families largely, though not exclusively, from the genealogies within the histories of Whalley and of Craven by T. D. Whittaker.

Maps

xiv   From Christopher Saxton's map of Lancashire, published in *Christopher Saxton's 16th Century Maps*, ed. W. Ravenyhill, Chatsworth Library, 1992.

9   Thomas Jefferys' Map of Yorkshire, 1772. Reproduced by permission of the Yorkshire Archaeological Society.

20   Pendle Forest.

31   Christopher Greenwood's Map of Lancashire, 1818. Reproduced by permission of the County Archivist, Lancashire Record Office, Preston.

130   From the map of Lancashire drawn for Lord Burghley, in the custody of the Public Record Office, London (SP 12/235).

Chronicle of Events

All the dates given in the trial evidence should be treated with caution.

1577   Alice Lyster named by Archbishop Sandys as a Catholic recusant.

1580   George Dobson 'resigned' as Vicar of Whalley.

1583   Fr John Nutter executed.

1585   Purported exorcisms by the Jesuit William Weston.

1586   Margaret Clitheroe pressed to death.

1587   William Allen created Cardinal.

1587   15 May
        William Preston married Jennet Balderston in Gisburn Church.

1588   Spanish Armada. Cardinal Allen calls on Catholics to co-operate with invaders.

c.1592 Demdike first met Tibb in a stone-pit in Goldshey ('about twenty years past').

1592   Thomas Lister junior born.

1594   Death of Ferdinando, Earl of Derby, attributed to witchcraft.

c.1594 Robert Nutter believed he was being bewitched by Chattox and Redferne ('eighteen or nineteen years ago').

c.1595 Robert Nutter died at Candlemas, 2 February.

1595   John and Ann Starkie bewitched.

c.1595 Christopher Nutter died at Maudlintide, 22 July, saying he was bewitched.

1596   John Darrel feigned dispossession of Thomas Darling.

1597   March
        Edmund Hartley hanged for bewitching the Starkie household.

1597   Publication of Daemonologie by King James VI of Scotland.

c.1598 Chattox gave her soul to 'a thing like a Christian man' ('fourteen or fifteen years ago').

1598   Trial of John Darrel before the High Commission.

1598   Thomas Lister senior inherited the estate on death of his father.

*c.*1598	Spirit like a brown dog sucked at Demdike. She was stark mad for eight weeks ('after six years').
1600	12 June John Rigby hanged, drawn and quartered.
*c.*1600	Chattox took teeth from skulls in Newchurch churchyard ('twelve years ago').
1600	26 July Fr Robert Nutter executed at Lancaster.
*c.*1601	Linen and oatmeal stolen by Chattox's daughter Elizabeth from Malkin Tower ('about eleven years ago').
*c.*1601	John Device died when he stopped paying Chattox ('about eleven years ago').
1602	Death of Alexander Nowell, Dean of St Paul.
1603	Reissue of *Daemonologie* by James, now King of England.
1606	The Gunpowder Plot.
*c.*1606	Hugh Moore of Pendle died, blaming Chattox for bewitching him ('six or seven years ago').
*c.*1606	Chattox's altercation with John Nutter's son. A cow died ('about six years ago').
*c.*1606	Chattox's bewitching of James Robinson's newly tunned drink ('about six years ago').
1607	Feb (before 8th Feb) Marriage of Thomas Lister junior to Jane Heber.
1607	8 Feb. Burial at Gisburn of Thomas Lister 'mort apud Braswell'.
1608	Publication of William Perkins *A Discourse* . . .
1608	John Robinson alias Swyer died after Elizabeth Device made a picture ('four years ago' - or 'three years ago' according to James).
1608	20 Feb. Jane, widow of Thomas Lister senior died.
1609	Elizabeth and James became witches, according to Jennet ('for the space of three years').
1610	Roger Nowell High Sheriff of Lancashire.
1610	Lent. John Duckworth dies after disagreement with James ('Lent last one').
1610	Maundy Thursday. James to communion at Newchurch. Met hare on return ('Sheare Thursday was two years').
1610	James had altercation with Mistress Ann Towneley of Carr Hall ('within two or three days after'). Ann Towneley died 'within two weeks'. (Jennet Device said it was 'about a year ago'.) James met dog in Newchurch.
1610	James saw Redferne, his wife and daughter with pictures.

1610   Chattox accused of bewitching the ale of John Moore of Higham.
        John Moore's son John died half a year after.

1610   (c) Anne Nutter died after laughing at Chattox ('about two years
        ago').

1610   (c) Richard Baldwin of Weathead Mill fell out with Demdike.
        His daughter died a year later.

1610   (c) Demdike changes milk into butter ('about two years ago').

1610   (c) Alizon took a familiar. Alizon met a Black dog in John
        Robinson's close in Roughlee ('about two years ago').

1610   Summer
        'Fancie' came to Chattox 'like a bear, gaping'.
        Chattox last saw 'Fancie' ('Thursday last year but one, next before
        Midsummer').

1610   Sept. Thomas Dodgson of Bolton by Bowland baptised.

1611   April. Thomas Dodgson buried.

c.1611 Richard Baldwin's daughter died 'after languishing a year'.

1611   29 June. 'about St Peters Day last' Henry Bulcock claimed Alizon
        had bewitched his child.

1612   John White of Eccles publishes *The Way to the True Church* . . .

Events in 1612

4 Jan.	William, infant son of Thomas Lister of Westbie, buried in Gisburn Church.
18 March	Alizon Device met the pedlar John Law in Colne-Field.
21 March	Abraham Law, John Law's son, received letter in Halifax.
c.23 March	Alizon encountered a black dog in a close in Newchurch ('About five days after').
c.27 March	James saw a brown dog come from Demdike's house ('a month ago').
29 March	Abraham Law took Alizon to his father in Colne. Alizon confessed.
30 March	Roger Nowell at Read examined Abraham Law and Alizon. Alizon imprisoned.
c.30 March	James heard shrieking at Malkin Tower ('two or three days later').
2 April	A black cat lay on James ('three days later').
2 April	Roger Nowell at Fence examined Demdike, Chattox, John Nutter, Margaret Crooke and James Robinson.
4 April	Demdike, Chattox, Anne Redferne and Alizon sent to Lancaster gaol.
c.6 April	Jennet Preston's first trial in York (within four days of Malkin Tower meeting).
9 April	Maundy Thursday. James Device stole a wether from John Robinson of Barley.
10 April	Good Friday at noon. Gathering at Malkin Tower.
15 April	Robert Holden examined William Alker about Jane Southworth of Samlesbury.
21 April	According to James, his Spirit appeared for the last time, asking for his soul ('Tuesday next before his apprehension').
27 April	Roger Nowell and Nicholas Bannister at Fence examined Elizabeth, James and Jennet Device.

5 May	Roger Nowell, Nicholas Bannister and Robert Holden heard statement from the Constable, Henry Hargreaves.
19 May	William Sandes (Mayor), James Anderton and Thomas Covell (coroner and gaoler) examined Chattox and James Device.
12 July	Sir Thomas Gerrard examined all the witnesses in the case against Isabel Roby of Windle.
27 July	Trial of Jennet Preston in York, followed by her hanging.
7 August	Robert Holden examined John Singleton (and, probably, Grace Sowerbutts) about the Samlesbury allegations.
9 August	Nicholas Bannister examined Jennet Booth to take evidence against Margaret Pearson of Padiham.
15 August	Nicholas Bannister made his will.
16 August	Judges Bromley and Altham arrived in Lancaster.
17 August	Assizes in Lancaster opened.
18 August	Chattox, Elizabeth Device and James Device tried and found guilty.
	Anne Redferne tried for murder of Robert Nutter and found not guilty.
19 August	Trial of the Samlesbury Witches. Case adjourned.
	Anne Redferne tried for the murder of Christopher Nutter and found guilty.
	Alice Nutter and Katherine Hewitt tried and found guilty.
	Samlesbury Witches found not guilty.
	John Bulcock, Jane Bulcock, Alizon Device, Margaret Pearson, and Isabel Roby of Windle tried and found guilty.
	The following sentenced to death: Anne Whittle (alias Chattox), Elizabeth Device, James Device, Anne Redferne, Alice Nutter, Katherine Hewitt, John Bulcock, Jane Bulcock, Alizon Device, Isabel Robey.
	The following sentenced to be pilloried and imprisoned: Margaret Pearson.
20 August	Public Hanging in Lancaster.
	The Arraignment and Trial. Published in 1612.
16 Nov.	Potts writes dedication to *The Wonderfull Discoverie*.

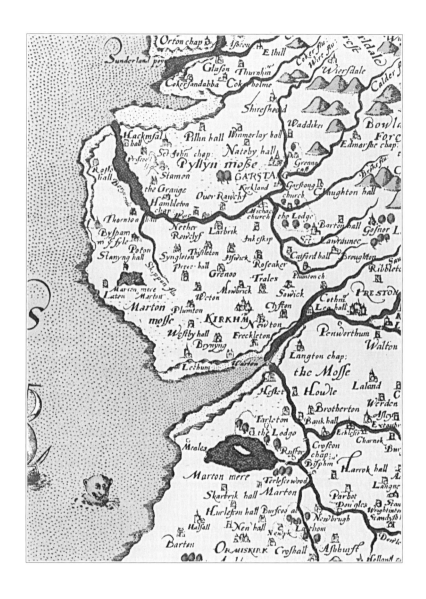

From Christopher Saxton's Map of Lancashire, 1577. The map shows Gisburn, Bracewell, Grindleton and Mitton in Yorkshire; Downham the seat of the Asshetons, Read the home of the Nowells, Altham the home of the Bannisters, Stoneyhurst, Samlesbury (Samsburye) Hall, Towneley, and, on the coast, Rossall the home of the Allens.

Further south, near Ormskirk, is Lathom the seat of the Earls of Derby, and Tildesley near Leigh where Nicholas Starkie's family lived. Hoghton Tower, Horrock Hall the home of John Rigby, and Eccles near Manchester enter our story. New Church in Pendle marks the site around which much of our drama was enacted.

The Investigation

When Master Lister lay upon his death-bedde, hee cried out in great extremitie; Jennet Preston lays heavy upon me, Preston's wife lays heavy upon me; helpe me, help me: and so departed, crying out against her.[1]

So died one of the leading gentleman in the West Riding, Thomas Lister of Westby Hall, Gisburn. The year was 1607. The scene at Lister's death-bed had been desperate. Anne Robinson told the Assize Court in York in 1612 that the stricken man had been intensely agitated about Jennet Preston. Anne said that Thomas Lister:

cried out to them that stood about him; that Jennet Preston was in the House, look where she is, take holde of her; for Gods sake shut the doors, and take her, shee cannot escape away. Look about for her and lay hold of her, for she is in the house: and so cried very often in his great paines.

In the city of York in July of 1612 Jennet Preston of Gisburn was hanged for the murder by witchcraft of Thomas Lister.

Later in that same year a fifteen-page booklet entitled *The Arraignement and Triall of Jennet Preston, of Gisborne in Craven in the Countie of Yorke* was published in London. This book is our main source. Its author was Thomas Potts, a lawyer.

Thomas Potts gave this reason for publishing the account of Jennet's witchcraft: 'I think it necessary not to let the memorie of her life and death die with her.' He intended to 'satisfie the world how dangerous and malitious a witch this Jennet Preston was, How unfit to live.'[2] The vigour of his language and that of those he quoted—he wrote within a year of the publication of the King James Bible—makes the reading of his booklet a delight, although the tale it unfolds may evoke pity and outrage.

At the end of 1612 Thomas Potts lodged in Chancery Lane,

THE ARRAIGNEMENT AND TRIALL OF IENNET PRESTON, Of GISBORNE IN CRAVEN, in the Countie of Yorke.

At the Afsifes and Generall Gaole.
Deliuerie holden at the Castle of Yorke
in the Countie of Yorke, the xxvij. day of
Iuly laft paft, *Anno Regni Regis* IACOBI
Angliæ, &c. Decimo, & Scotiæ
quadragefimo quinto.

Before
Sir IAMES ALTHAM *Knight, one*
of the Barons of his Maiefties Court of Exchequer;
and Sir EDVVARD BROMLEY Knight, another of
the Barons of his Maiefties Court of Exchequer;
his Maiefties Iuftices of Affife, Oyer and Terminer,
and generall Gaole-Deliuerie, in the Circuit
of the North-parts.

LONDON,
Printed by W. STANSBY for IOHN BARNES, and
are to be fold at his Shoppe neere Holborne Conduit. 1612.

Thomas Potts, Clerk to the Circuit, published in 1612 his account of
Jennet Preston's trial.

London. Some months earlier he had served as Clerk to the Justices of Assize on the Northern Circuit, so had recorded the evidence submitted at the trial of Jennet Preston. Potts had access to the depositions presented to the court, accounts of the interrogations of four witnesses which had been written by a Lancashire magistrate, Roger Nowell of Read. To construct his booklet Potts prefaced Nowell's writings with an introduction of passion and panache, though not always of clarity. He then interspersed other comments, probably relying in great part on the speeches in court of the prosecuting magistrate, Thomas Heber.

Three hundred and eighty years have elapsed since Jennet's trial. This book today casts an ironic eye over what Thomas Potts wrote. It treats with scepticism the evidence which in its own day convinced a jury. It seeks to reveal the influences and assumptions which dictated the way that Potts and the magistrates perceived and recorded the story of Jennet Preston. So it considers the bias, the corruption even, of the magistrates as they pursued the charge against her. Had fewer years passed we would call this a work of investigative journalism. We wish to establish whether justice was done in the York Assizes of summer 1612. Was the trial a trumped up affair? Was Jennet Preston framed? If so, by whom? And why?

If we unearth the answer to these questions we will be able to re-evaluate the famous story of the Pendle Witches, those seven women and two men who were brought to trial in Lancaster a month after Jennet's trial in York, and who, before a judge on the same Circuit and on evidence supplied in large part by the same magistrate, were likewise condemned to death.[3] About the Lancaster trial Thomas Potts was to write a further book, *The Wonderfull Discoverie of Witches in the Countie of Lancaster*. This second book is similar in structure to his Jennet Preston booklet, but over ten times as long.

Detailed consideration of the proceedings in Lancaster is outside the scope of this volume, though to follow the story of Jennet Preston we must tell the story of Chattox and Demdike and of the other Pendle witches amongst their families and friends. Were those whom Jennet met at Malkin Tower a witches coven? Or a religious sect? Were they persecuted old crones? Or the wise-women and -men of the neighbourhood?

Common both to Jennet's trial and to that of the Lancastrians is the question: How far did the Puritan beliefs, or the religious ambivalence, of the gentry and magistrates of the Lancashire and Yorkshire border dispose those justices to believe that witchcraft was rife and that witches must be exposed and condemned? What matrix of assumptions, what grid of preconceived ideas, did the accusers impose on the events they recorded?

The Silencing of Dissention

M ANY of Jennet's contemporaries believed that she had been
wrongfully condemned, indeed maliciously accused.

The jury at Jennet Preston's trial 'spent the most part of the day
in consideration of the evidence against her.'[4] Did the jurors themselves have misgivings? Outside the court people were outraged at
the death sentence. Potts, despite his intentions, provides us in his
introduction with evidence of this indignation. So stung was he by
the slighting of the legal profession by the common people that he
retaliated by berating even the bereaved husband of the unfortunate
Jennet:

> You that were husband to this Jennet Preston, her friends and
> kinsfolk . . . have not been sparing to devise so scandalous a
> slander out of the malice of your hearts as that she was maliciously
> prosecuted.[5]

Jennet's friends were claiming that 'her life [had been] unjustly
taken away by practise.' Attend carefully to Pott's phrase. The word
'practise' in the early seventeenth century meant 'scheming' or
'trickery' or 'plotting'; Potts uses 'practise' four times with this sense
when he writes about the trial of the Samlesbury witches at Lancaster. So Jennet's kinsfolk in saying that there had been 'practise'
were alleging that the magistrates had intrigued to engineer her
death. They were alleging corruption, a serious charge indeed.

The friends of Jennet told how Jennet even on the scaffold had
made no confession; this was evidence, they were asserting, that
'she died an innocent woman'. These friends sought to exonerate
Jennet, irreversible though her sentence had been. Hence they
impugned the system of justice which had hanged her, impugned
the magistrates, the judges, the court of which Potts was the servant.
Potts disparages this popular clamour as being like witchcraft itself;
he calls these claims:

charmes of imputations and slander, laid upon the Justice of the Land, to clear her that was justly condemned and executed for her offence.

But for all Potts' disdain of Jennet's friends' 'idle conciepts', he lets fall that what they were saying had plausibility, that it was 'able to seduce others.'[6]

To confute the critics of the court Potts writes urgently. His booklet *The Arraignement and Triall* . . . was published in London within weeks of the end of her trial in York. Likewise after the Lancaster trial Potts lost no time in penning *The Wonderfull Discoverie* . . . The printer W. Stansby, in a note correcting some errors, pleads that the printing was 'a worke done in great haste at the end of a Tearme'.[7]

Potts concludes his account of Jennet's trial with a prayer which plainly shows the hidden agenda that impelled his writing:

> God grant us the long and prosperous continuance of those Honourable and Reverend Judges, under whose government we live in these North parts: for we may say, that God Almightie hath singled them out and set them on his seat, for the Defence of Justice. And for this deliverance, let us pray to God Almightie, that the memorie of these worthie Judges may be blessed to all posterities.[8]

Thomas Potts, obsequious to those on whom he relied for patronage, is transparently biased. In writing of Jennet's trial he wished to silence criticism of the judiciary.

Gisburn: Jennet's Homeland

J ENNET PRESTON was of 'Gisborne in Craven in the Countie of
Yorke'.

The marriage of William Preston to Jennet Balderston is recorded
in the Register of Gisburn Parish Church. It took place on 10 May
1587. If Jennet had been eighteen years old at her wedding (many
were younger), she would have been thirty-eight years old at the
time of the tragic death of Thomas Lister, and forty-three years old
at her trial. Even in the seventeenth century an old crone was the
stereotype of a witch; it seems likely, however, that Jennet was in
the prime of life.

Jennet's husband may have been a little older. Thomas Potts
called him 'Old Preston', though that was when William attended
the Lancaster trials.[9] By then he would have been bowed by the
grief of bereavement and aged by the tension of the previous months.
William's baptism may be that recorded in the Gisburn Parish
Register in 1564: 'William son of Henry Preston'. The date
is whimsical: 'the day following', the previous date being '30th
February'.

Gisburn, Jennet's home township, lies between Clitheroe and
Skipton. The village stands half a mile back from the steep banks
of the River Ribble which gathers its waters in the limestone valleys
around Settle to the north and which near Gisburn turns its broad
but shallow course to flow south-westward to the Lancashire coast
at Preston. The east-west road, more than the river, shaped the
village. This route was anciently important, for it allowed access
through the Craven gap in the long line of the Pennine hills. It thus
linked the valley of the Ribble with Airedale, Lancashire with Yorkshire beyond the hills, the de Lacy's castle at Clitheroe with the
seat of the Cliffords at Skipton. Along this route in 1648 was to
march the army of Oliver Cromwell in some haste from Yorkshire

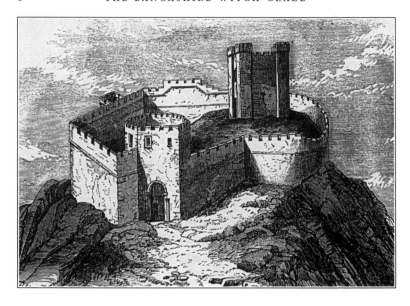

Clitheroe Castle had been the seat of the De Lacys,
within whose Honour lay the Forest of Pendle.

to engage The Duke of Hamilton's Scottish force in the decisive
battle of Preston. Cromwell spent the night in Gisburn at the
sympathetic Lister home.

Pendle Hill, a long bulk like a basking whale, lies to the south
of Gisburn, though obscured from the village centre by the incline
of the immediate valley. But climb for 400 yards up the Burnley
Road, and down a drive to the right, and you come to Westby
Hall or Arnoldsbigging,[10] the seat till the eighteenth century of the
Listers, whence you can see both Pendle Hill and the long westward
valley which leads past the ancient Cistercian Abbey of Salley (or
Sawley) to Clitheroe and beyond. Since boundary changes in 1974
all this area has been within Lancashire, but previously Gisburn,
Rimington, Sawley and the Forest of Bowland to the north of the
Ribble lay in the Craven area of the West Riding of Yorkshire,
while Clitheroe, Downham, Pendle Hill and all to the south of the
hill lay as now in Lancashire.[11] That Gisburn was in Yorkshire in
1612 is significant for our story; Jennet's trials on the charge of
witchcraft would be held not in Lancaster but in York.

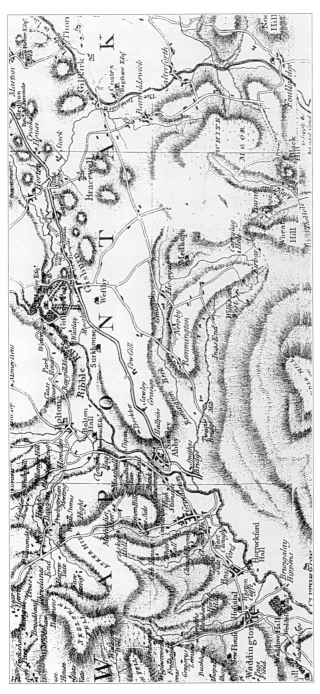

Jeffreys' Map of Yorkshire was published in 1771, before a turnpike road had been constructed south from Gisburn. The map shows Westby, the home of the Listers in the seventeenth century; Gisburn Park, formerly Lower Hall, to which the Listers moved; Cow Gill, the home of Leonard Lister; Marton Hall, the home of the Hebers; Bracewell Church, the place of the wedding; Grindleton; Coates Hall; Sawley Grange and Gisburn Hall. Malkin Tower, being in Lancashire, is not marked; it would be by the 'k' of Black Hill.

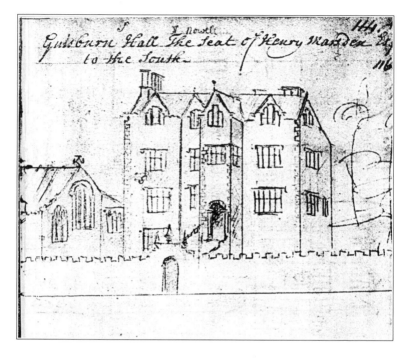

Gisburn Hall, home of the Marsdens, stood to the east of Gisburn Church.
Sketch by Samuel Buck about 1720.

From Gisburn a road runs south through Middop. It climbs
through the pass by Greystone Moor and then descends to Blacko
and thence to Burnley or Colne. This present road was built by a
Turnpike Trust in the late eighteenth century. Jennet would have
travelled by a different route to Malkin Tower, as she does in our
history. The old pack-horse track she knew runs along the ridge
top to the east of the present road. It almost ascends Weets Hill
then drops to Colne, skirting to the east of Blacko Hill. For much
of its way Jennet's route is now a near-forgotten track.

Nearly all the houses in modern Gisburn have been built since
Jennet's day. Along the main street only Snowhill, a fine house to
the south, and the church, with its wide squat tower and generous
interior, remain much as Jennet would have known them. The
church, originally a Norman one, had been largely rebuilt less than
a century before Jennet's time to incorporate pillars and masonry

from the dissolved abbey at Sawley. Gisburn Hall, a noble Jacobean house then inhabited by Henry Marsden, Member of Parliament for Clitheroe, stood on the site now occupied by Gisburn Vicarage. The Listers' rising prosperity in the seventeenth century allowed their purchase from the Marsdens of the Lordship of the Manor, the Rectory of the Church and finally of their house, which they razed to the ground. The Marsdens moved to Wennington Old Hall.

A monument popularly held to mark the grave of Jennet Preston.

In Gisburn Churchyard today you may find an iron grave monument reputed to mark the burial-place of Jennet Preston, a pleasant fancy inspired by the design it bears of a widow leaning over an urn or cauldron. In fact Jennet's corpse from the gibbet would have been buried in York; the monument is not so early.

Thomas Potts' Chronology

THOMAS POTTS' account of Jennet's trial is printed on pages 163–174. Those who read Potts' introduction frequently misconstrue the sequence of events to which he alludes.[12] We need to distinguish between two Thomas Listers, father and son, and to realise that Jennet was convicted of murdering the former and of planning, unsuccessfully, to murder the latter. It was the son Thomas Lister, whom Potts calls 'Master Lister now living', who testified against Jennet in court in 1612. It was the father Thomas Lister who died amidst such agitated cryings four years earlier.

Lest we be unwary, it is salutary to glance at the misreadings in modern guides to Jennet's story. In other respects their works are admirable, but not when they tell of Jennet Preston and the Listers.

G. B. Harrison, the editor in 1929 of *The Trial of the Lancashire Witches* (Peter Davies, London, 1929) in which he reprinted the text of *The Wonderfull Discoverie . . .*, mistakenly conflates the two Thomas Listers; he would have us believe that a Mr Lister died between the Malkin Tower meeting and the trial.[13] Rachel Hasted in *The Pendle Witch Trial* (published by Lancashire County Council Library Committee, 1987) compounds this error. She realised that a Thomas Lister died four years before the trial, so she calls unreliable the witnesses at the trial for claiming that this same murder (as she thought it) was planned at Malkin Tower four years after it had actually occurred. Her confusion is extreme. Other commentators have followed them. However the story that Thomas Potts intends is correctly told in that dependable study *The Trials of the Lancashire Witches* by Edgar Peel and Pat Southern (Hendon Publishing, Nelson 1969).

You will notice that Jennet was twice arraigned on charges of witchcraft; she was tried in York at both the Lent and at the Summer Assizes of 1612.

'Westby Hall in Craven, The Seat of Tho. Lister Esq'.
Sketch by Samuel Buck about 1720.
Jennet Preston 'had access to his house, kind respect and entertainment'.

If events are placed in the order of occurrence, this is the story that Potts unfolds:

1. Jennet lived 'neare Master Lister of Westbie'.

2. Jennet was treated with generosity by this gentleman, Mr Thomas Lister of Westby Hall, who was the main landowner in Gisburn. Potts says she 'had access to his house, kind respect and entertainment; nothing denied her that she stood in need of'. Thomas Lister's kindness to Jennet was well-known: 'which of you that dwelleth near them in Craven but can and will witness it?'

3. However Jennet, despite these favours—'the grace and goodness bestowed upon her'—began to bewitch her benefactor—'to work this mischief, according to the course of all witches.' By witchcraft she murdered him. This happened, says Potts, 'four years since'. Church records confirm this; Thomas Lister did die in February 1607 (or 1608 if one reckons, as is the modern custom, that the year begins in January).

4. Thomas Lister junior, the elder son of the murdered one,

now master of Westby, at first showed Jennet many kindnesses—'the reliefe she had at all times with many other favours'.

5. Jennet, ungrateful, then bewitched the property of Thomas Lister junior 'who in a short time received great losse in his goods and Cattel by her meanes.'

6. Jennet was thus suspected of witchcraft, arraigned at the instigation of Thomas Lister junior and tried at the Assizes in York in Lent 1612 before the judge Lord Bromley on the charge, surprisingly, of murdering 'a child of one Dodg-sonnes'. She was acquitted by a merciful jury.

7. Four days after her acquittal in York, Jennet went to a great assembly of witches at Malkin Tower to seek the malign aid of the witches in a vengeful plan to murder Thomas Lister junior who had prosecuted her—to bring about 'the utter ruin and overthrow of the name and the blood of this Gentleman.'

8. Jennet was returned by the magistrates to York. She was indicted in the July Assizes at York on the charge of having murdered Thomas Lister senior those four years before—'for that shee felloniously had practised, used, and exercised divers wicked and devilish arts called Witchcrafts, Inchantments, Charmes, and Sorceries, in and upon Thomas Lister of Westby in Craven . . . and by the force of the same witchcrafts felloniously the said Thomas Lister had killed.'[14] Other charges relating to the Malkin Tower meeting were also brought against her. She was found guilty and executed.

In 1613, the year following the publication of *The Arraignment and Triall of Jennet Preston . . .*, the same publisher, John Barnes of Holborne in London, brought out *The Wonderfull Discoverie of Witches in the Countie of Lancaster*, Potts' similar account of the trial of the Lancashire witches. At the end of this larger work Barnes sensibly bound the fifteen-page booklet about Jennet Preston which he had recently published. He retained the old title page of the Jennet Preston booklet; it is still dated 1612 whereas the title page of the main part of the new book, '*The Wonderfull Discoverie . . .*', is dated 1613. This combined printing is the one that survives.[15]

This accident of printing has caused Jennet's story to be treated, when it has been noticed, as an appendix to the main story of the Lancashire witches. However when we read Jennet's narrative as, for the most part, a distinct tale its significance is enhanced.

THE
WONDERFVLL
DISCOVERIE OF
WITCHES IN THE COVN-
TIE OF LAN-
CASTER.

With the Arraignement and Triall of
Nineteene notorious WITCHES, at the Affizes and
generall Gaole deliuerie, holden at the Castle of
LANCASTER, *vpon Munday, the fe-*
uenteenth of August last,
1612.

Before Sir IAMES ALTHAM, and
Sir EDWARD BROMLEY, Knights; BARONS of his
Maiesties Court of EXCHEQVER: And Iustices
of Affize, Oyer *and* Terminor, *and generall*
Gaole deliuerie in the circuit of the
North Parts.

Together with the Arraignement and Triall of IENNET
PRESTON, *at the Affizes holden at the Castle of Yorke,*
the feuen and twentieth day of Iulie last past,
with her Execution for the murther
of Master LISTER
by Witchcraft.

Publifhed and fet forth by commandement of his Maiefties
Iuftices of Affize in the North Parts.

By THOMAS POTTS *Efquier.*

LONDON,
Printed by *W.Stansby* for *Iohn Barnes,* dwelling neare
Holborne Conduit. 1613.

Thomas Potts published in 1613 his account of the trial of the Pendle Witches.

Jennet's was the earliest of the witch trials in the whole Pendle-Craven witch persecution of 1612. It preceded, was not subsequent to, the other trials. The historical value of Jennet's story resides in this: first, that the trial of Jennet Preston by Judge Altham in York established in the Northern Circuit a pattern of trial and conviction later to be followed, tragically, by Judge Bromley in the Lancaster trial; and second, that from as early as 1607 allegations against Jennet had preoccupied the gentry and magistrates so that her story did much to generate in the gentry of Pendle and Craven those obsessions which in 1612 were to embroil all the Lancashire witches. If one would learn why Craven and Pendle Forest should have become the arena for the most intense witch persecution in England apart from the Hopkins persecution in East Anglia in 1644–5, the clues lie in the tale of Jennet Preston.

The Child of One Dodg-sonnes

THE trial of Jennet Preston in the Lent Assize of 1612, her first
trial, had unexpected features. Sadly we have no full account
of this trial, only Pott's allusions to it in his introduction. There
we see that Jennet was accused of one thing only: 'the murder of
a child of one Dodg-sonnes'. It is curious that the charge Jennet
faced did not derive from what Potts said had provoked her trial,
namely, that people had grown to suspect she was a witch because
of the loss to Thomas Lister of 'goods and Cattel'. At her later trial,
moreover, Jennet was condemned for having murdered Thomas
Lister senior in 1607. Why at her first trial was she not charged
with murdering Lister, if she was known to have committed this
act? Why was another charge brought? [16]

We have little to inform our speculations.

Thomas Lister junior instigated the accusation against Jennet at
the Lenten Assizes. Even in 1612 he was but twenty or twenty-one
years old. In later years Lister junior served as a magistrate, but at
the time of the York trials his youth precluded him from that office.
Thomas Heber of Marton, Lister's close neighbour amongst the
Yorkshire gentry, was we may assume, the prosecuting magistrate
in this first trial in April, as in the second trial in July. Yet when
Jennet was acquitted she was clear that it was Lister (not, as it might
have been, either Heber or the Dodgsons) who had 'borne malice
unto her, and had thought to have her put away at the late Assizes
at Yorke';[17] revenge for this malice was said to have been her
motive for afterwards seeking the aid of those at Malkin Tower to
kill Lister junior.

Lister's purpose was to be rid of Jennet, but, we shall see, he
did not wish to create scandal. Though privately he might be
claiming that Jennet had killed his father in 1607, he had cause to
evade legal scrutiny of his family's tragedy, of its griefs, jealousies

and deceptions. Lister wished to appear disinterested while destroy-
ing Jennet. This aim was thwarted by her acquittal.

Who was the 'child of one Dodg-sonnes' whom Jennet was
accused of murdering? We have no sure evidence. Dodgsons of
Padiham appear in the testimony concerning Margaret Pearson, one
of the witches tried at Lancaster. This Margaret Pearson was accused,
on bizarre and flimsy evidence, of having caused the death of the
mare of 'one Dodgeson of Padiham'. However in the case against
Jennet the child was unlikely to have been a Dodgson from Padiham,
for Dodgsons abounded in and around Jennet's own parish of
Gisburn.[18]

Between 1575 and 1675 in Gisburn Church forty-eight baptisms
were recorded with the surname spelt 'Dodshon' or 'Dodgshon',
and about twenty burials. Where abodes of Dodgsons are given in
the registers they are consistently 'of Newsholme' or 'of Paythorne',
two hamlets within the parish on the north side. Unfortunately, in
the burial register as we scan backwards from 1612 we find no
Dodgson child later than 19 March 1598 when 'Johes filius Henrici
Dodshon'—John the son of Henry Dodshon—was buried. In this
period about half the deaths that must have occurred in the Parish
are not recorded.

The parish of Bolton-by-Bowland borders on Gisburn and on
the Lister estate. In that parish's register for 1610 is recorded the
baptism of:

Thomas, the sonne of Edward Dodgson
bapt the xth daie of September.

Seven months later among the burials of 1611 is found:

Thomas, the sonne of Edward Dodgsonne,
buried the xiiijth daie of Aprill.

This would be a good candidate for 'the child of one Dodg-sonnes'.[19]

We do not know how or why Jennet was said to have killed
the Dodgson child. Perhaps the father of a child that had died was
a retainer or servant of Thomas Lister junior. Lister would readily
have insinuated to him that Jennet had bewitched the young one
and should be prosecuted.

In the event the evidence against Jennet did not persuade the
jury. Jennet was acquitted, and returned home to Gisburn.

Over the Moors
to Malkin Tower

THOMAS POTTS tells the next part of the story: 'This wicked and bloud-thirstie Witch was no sooner delivered at the Assizes holden at Yorke in Lent last past . . . but upon the Friday following, being Good-Friday, shee rode in hast to the great meeting at Malking-Tower, and there prayed aide for the murther of M. Thomas Lister.'[20] Jennet went to an assembly of witches at Malkin Tower. This was established in court by written testimonies sent to York by Lancashire magistrates Roger Nowell and Nicholas Bannister. These statements had been gathered from three members of the family who lived at Malkin Tower, Elizabeth, James and Jennet Device.

Malkin Tower, the Device's home, stood isolated on the South-eastern slopes of the moors by Blacko Hill. Its site is not far from the old Gisburn-Colne road. There is today a farm called Malkin Tower. Above it is a field wall which contains a stretch of more perfect masonry; this is probably all that remains of the home of Demdike and the Devices. The dwelling must have been simpler than 'Tower' implies, for the Devices scratched a living from casual work, from begging and, others maintained, from stealing. But more significantly, so Roger Nowell had discovered, the older members of the family functioned as witches.

The Device family had suffered in the month that had passed. Jennet Preston can have known little of their plight, for during those same weeks Jennet had been waiting to go to York, had probably been in custody, and had faced her trial in the York court-room for the alleged murder of the Dodgson child. There had been much to preoccupy her. But when she returned to Gisburn, relieved that she was still alive and was now free, news of the Device's misfortunes will have reached her. Without delay, and this reveals her energy, she took her foal and rode in haste over the moors to Malkin Tower.[21]

We must, though, leave Jennet at the door of Malkin Tower so that we can tell what happened to the Devices to occasion her visit. In doing so we retell the story that Jennet was to learn as she entered Malkin Tower. The evidence we use is that presented at the Lancaster trial, but the magistrates' depositions, at least in outline, were available at Jennet's own second trial in York to show what company she had kept.

We enter here upon a similar and concurrent tragedy.

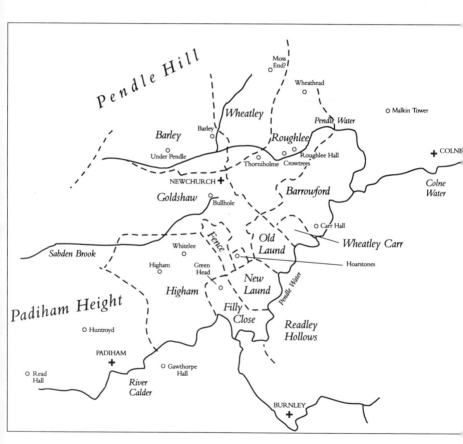

The Booths of the Forest of Pendle.

Questioning Alizon

ELEVEN days before Jennet Preston rode to Malkin Tower, on
30 March 1612, Alizon Device, the teenage daughter of that
house, had been taken to Read Hall at the instigation of a cloth-dyer
of Halifax, Abraham Law. Alizon was the daughter of Elizabeth
Device; she was the sister of James, 'a labourer', and of the nine-
year-old Jennet Device. Read Hall, to the south west of Pendle
Hill, was the home of the magistrate Roger Nowell. Probably
Alizon Device and Abraham Law were accompanied on the journey
by the constable, Henry Hargreaves.[22]

Abraham Law, the man from Halifax, was intent on complaining
to Nowell that by witchcraft Alizon had caused his father to have
a seizure. Alizon and he did not disagree about what had occurred.

John Law, Abraham's father, was a travelling pedlar. The youthful
Alizon on 18 March had met the pedlar near Colne. She had begged
pins from him. John Law had refused her, at which Alizon had
been resentful. She felt angry. That very moment, by fateful mis-
chance, John Law had fallen down to the ground, strangely lame.
The pedlar believed that Alizon had caused his affliction, indeed
days later he openly stated from his couch in an inn that 'the hurt
he had in his lamenesse was done unto him by Alizon Device, by
witchcraft'. Alizon, whose sweet and fragile nature disposed her to
accept blame when accused, begged John Law's forgiveness, kneel-
ing before him in the ale-house in Colne. The lamed man generously forgave. His son, though, sought justice.[23]

John Law, the pedlar, had suffered from a stroke; a modern
reader sees this clearly. Law 'lay in Colne speechlesse, and had the
left side lamed all save his eye'. After a few days he 'had something
recovered his speech, and did complaine that hee was pricked with
Knives, Elsons and Sickles'. Five months later at Lancaster he came
to the court-room 'not well able to goe or stand, being led thither

by his poore sonne Abraham Law'. Previously he had been 'a verie able sufficient stout man of Bodie, and a goodly man of Stature', but, it was observed,

> by this Devilish art of Witchcraft his head is drawne awrie, his Eyes and face deformed, His speech not well to be understood; his Thighes and Legges starke lame: his Armes lame especially the left side, his handes lame and turned out of their course, his Bodie able to indure no travell.

Law's emotions were unrestrained, as in those who suffer strokes. Speaking in court he was to weep tears in great passion, but then, when Alizon again was on her knees before him, with charming fickleness he 'freely and voluntarily' forgave her.[24]

Roger Nowell the magistrate will have been disquieted when he heard Law's tale. But what his inquiries further elicited from Alizon will have alarmed him.

It was a cruel irony that John Law should suffer a seizure in the presence of that very person, Alizon Device, for it happened that Alizon and her family were vulnerable to charges of witchcraft. Alizon's grandmother, Elizabeth Southerns, the grandam of Malkin Tower, was a village healer who practised magic, not always benignly. The grandmother healed animals and people, and cursed them; she made potions and images; towards dogs and cats she was affectionately disposed, a trait considered curious in those days. People resorted to her at her home and called her out to heal their animals even though she was eighty years old and a bit senile; no doubt in earlier years she had been more active.

This grandmother, Elizabeth Southerns, was known as 'Demdike' or 'Old Demdike'. She shared her home, Malkin Tower, with her widowed daughter, Elizabeth Device, and with her grandchildren, Alizon, James and the nine-year-old Jennet. Over the years the old lady had initiated her family into the mysteries of her lore so that for them traditional village witchcraft was something of a family occupation, a cottage industry. A reputation for strange power was an asset too to those who otherwise sought money through begging. In these respects the role which Demdike fulfilled in early seventeenth-century Pendle was similar to that played in modern times by traditional gypsies, or by practitioners of new-age alternative therapies.

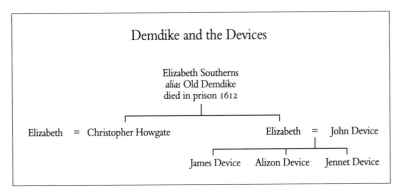

Demdike and the Devices

Elizabeth Southerns
alias Old Demdike
died in prison 1612

Elizabeth = Christopher Howgate   Elizabeth = John Device

James Device   Alizon Device   Jennet Device

Roger Nowell had heard the allegations of Abraham Law. He now turned to Alizon. The girl was awed by the surroundings of the Jacobean country house at Read and charmed, perhaps, by the cultured man in his late fifties absorbed by her talk. What was the chemistry between Roger Nowell and Alizon Device? Alizon talked freely and generously; one imagines they were unaccompanied. As she chattered, Alizon seems to have been unaware of the danger in which she and her family were placed.

Nowell had read widely about witches; Alizon could speak from experience about healing witchcraft, her family's craft.

Nowell's concept of witchcraft was that of the learned man; he had read King James, the *Malleus Malificarum*, Perkins. As he asked Alizon about her family's practices, Nowell was thirsting to learn about the Faustian compact with the devil, about the selling of one's soul, about the erotic enormities of witches' sabbaths and about the sensual intimacies of animal familiars. Alizon meanwhile was musing about the friendships and the misunderstandings of village people, about the small life of a hill community and about bits of sympathetic magic here and there which might have worked—who knows?—and which won one person or another a reputation as a wise-woman or -man. The paradigms in Nowell's mind were those anecdotes about witches which had swirled round the Western foothills of the Alps in the late fifteenth century and which, under the influence of the Inquisition, had crystallized into the doctrine of witchcraft as the ultimate heresy. But Alizon and her family were involved in a simpler reality that did not answer to Nowell's expectations. From this mismatch evolved the tragedy.

Alizon, her family and their colleagues were to be crushed between the mill-stones of two different perceptions of the nature of witch-craft.

What Alizon and others of the Pendle witches said when Nowell interrogated them we have in a form that has undergone changes. First Nowell will have asked questions, probably in a very informal way. He then wrote up the answers as though they were continuous statements or confessions that had been made to a formal court; this obscured the question and answer structure of the spoken word. Then at the Assizes each person arraigned was tried separately, so the court produced for each those parts of each statement that were relevant to that person. Potts in *The Wonderfull Discoverie . . .* as in *The Arraignment and Triall . . .* serves them in this disjointed form; the statements come piecemeal and are often duplicated. With study however we can reverse this process and can guess the sequence of Nowell's questioning.

Alizon confirmed to Nowell the story of the laming of John Law. Obviously the poor girl believed that her anger had caused his seizure, that such a cause could produce such an effect. She had been reared after all in a family that cherished its reputation for occult powers.

It seems a black dog had been with Alizon at the fateful time; John Law, the pedlar, was to speak at Alizon's trial of the dog that had stood over his stricken body 'with very fearefull fierie eyes, great teeth, and a terrible countenance, looking him in the face'. Law, a kind and fair man, was to make no claim that the hound was a devilish apparition. Nowell, however, in his interview with the girl, acquired a different understanding. He wrote that Alizon had confessed that she first had met this dog about two years before in Rough Lee, that it had spoken to her desiring her soul, that as she sat down it 'did with his mouth (as this examinate then thought) sucke at her breast, a little below her Paps, which place did remaine blew halfe a yeare next after', and that it had been this dog that had suggested to her, speaking 'in English' that she ask it to lame the pedlar.[25]

Poor Alizon! She may have tried for a moment the immature tactic, that of Eve in blaming the snake, of passing responsibility away from herself to an animal. She then found herself entangled by

Nowell's obsessed questioning. Nowell from his reading would expect a witch to have just such an animal familiar. He would presume too that the familiar would intimately suck her flesh.

One familiar sucks Joan Prentis; others surround her. She and two others were hanged for witchcraft in Chelmsford, Essex in 1589.

That witches leagued themselves with imps and devils was believed throughout western Europe; that the imp or devil might take the shape of an animal, usually of a cat or a dog, but sometimes of a toad, a hare or an insect, was a peculiarly English notion, but well attested by case-law. The Witchcraft Statute of 1604 had reinforced the idea that witches leagued with imps, for Parliament had made it a felony to 'consult with, covenant with, entertain, employ, feed, or reward any evil or wicked spirit'. William Perkins, the influential Cambridge theologian, considered a 'true proof' of witchcraft the confession, or the testimony by two good witnesses,

> that the partie hath intertained a familiar spirit and had conference with it in form or likeness of a mouse, catte or some other visible creature.[26]

Nowell would know of all this; these preconceptions directed his inquiries.

Other members of the Device family, and Chattox, would later tell Nowell that they too conversed with animals. Nowell records that they, like Alizon, spoke of giving their souls to these familiars and of allowing themselves to be sucked in intimate parts. Repeatedly, obsessively, Nowell must have asked those whom he interviewed what pet animals they had, how they embraced them, and about the moment, significant for him, when they first took in a stray dog, or, for the familiars sometimes took a human form, first developed an affection for a stranger.

When Demdike, Chattox or James Device sensed that disclosures they had unwisely made jeopardised their safety, they, like Alizon, may have welcomed Nowell's prompting that some animal, not themselves, was responsible for the mischief of which they had spoken. Little would they imagine that this in Nowell's mind would but confirm their own diabolical wickedness and would give to him evidence that they had entertained imps, evidence that merited the penalty of death.

Conversation cannot have been easy. The ear of the cultured Nowell would not be attuned to the unschooled dialect of Alizon and later of the others, nor would they easily comprehend him. When Nowell posed questions they, diffident, callow youths or mumbling eighty-year-olds, seem to have blustered, bragged and then to have placated their questioner with nods and assents. Did Nowell loosen their tongues with wine from his cellar?

Those examined would not have been able to check what Nowell deposed as their evidence. It is unlikely that he read it to them or even composed it while they were present. Rarely do we detect a Lancastrian inflection. The witnesses may never have known how Nowell interpreted their shrugs and grunts.

Alizon had admitted that she associated with a familiar. That will have enkindled Roger Nowell. He, the youthful girl before him, would know that it was his duty as magistrate to examine the intimate place of the familiar's sucking.

The conversation had turned to Old Demdike. Alizon spoke with pride about her grandmother's mystic abilities. She told how the old lady had once turned 'a Pigginfull of blew Milke' into butter while still in bed, and how John Nutter of Bulhole, amongst others, had called her to cure a sick cow of his—though this seems not to have been a success, for next morning the cow was dead. A more eerie story concerned Demdike's falling out with Richard Baldwin of Wheathead Mill. 'About 2 yeeres agoe' the miller would not let Demdike on his land. Because the old lady was 'blind' (which may mean very weak of sight) the children then at Demdike's request had led her out after dark 'about ten of the clocke in the night', had left her for an hour, and had fetched her in again. The next day Baldwin's daughter had taken ill. She had languished for a year, and then died.[27]

Alizon talked freely about an associate and rival of her grandmother's, another witch of similar great age named Anne Whittle

Bulhole farm in Goldshaw Booth was the home of John Nutter. Two of his cows died; one, it was said, bewitched by Chattox, one by Demdike.

but known as Chattox. Eleven years ago, one of Chattox's daughters, she said, had stolen linen and oatmeal from Alizon's own home, Malkin Tower. More seriously, Alizon said that her late father, John Device, had paid protection money to Chattox, fearing her, and that when about the same time he had ceased to pay, he had died. Alizon recounted too how her friend Anne Nutter, daughter of an Anthony Nutter, had once laughed innocently but that Chattox had misconstrued the joke as impertinent; she had threatened Anne who three weeks later had duly died.[28]

Alizon retold yet more stories about Chattox. Two years previously, she said, John Moore of Higham, a gentleman, had accused Chattox of bewitching some ale. Chattox had resented the accusation and so had made 'pictures', little figurine images used for casting spells, which Demdike had later told Alizon were of John

Moore's son. The lad, also called John, took ill and died. While the boy had been languishing Alizon 'saw Chattox sitting in her owne garden, and a picture of Clay like unto a child in her Apron; which this Examinate espying, Anne Chattox would have hidde with her Apron.'

Another Moore, Hugh Moore of Pendle, had accused Chattox of bewitching his cattle, Alizon said. Chattox, put out again, had vowed revenge. Hugh Moore took ill. He died after half a year, claiming on his death-bed that Chattox had bewitched him.[29]

Alizon told how another cow of John Nutter's met its end. Six years before, Elizabeth, a daughter of Chattox's, had begged milk from John Nutter at Bulhole and had taken it to her mother in the field. Chattox had churned it with two sticks in the can, but John Nutter's son, seeing this, had been angry (perhaps he considered it acceptable to beg milk to slake one's thirst, but unacceptable to beg milk to make the luxury item of butter). Young Nutter kicked over Chattox's can, whereupon John Nutter's cow became sick. It expired after four days.[30]

In all then Alizon had told Nowell of five human deaths that had followed the anger, resentment or curses of the old ladies; one after Demdike's dark musings, and, according to those hearsay tales, four after Chattox's anger. Nowell had learnt about the expiry of two cows, about the pedlar's seizure, and about Alizon's black dog. He began his writing of Alizon's 'confession' with these words:

> She saith, That about two yeares agone, her Grandmother, called Elizabeth Sothernes, alias Dembdike, did (sundry times in going or walking together, as they went begging) perswade and advise this Examinate to let a Divell or a Familiar appeare to her, and that shee, this Examinate would let him suck at some part of her; and she might have and doe what shee would.[31]

That served to define what Alizon's black dog really was. Here was evidence of Alizon's compact with the devil.

Nowell imprisoned Alizon, this trusting girl. Elizabeth, her mother, if she had not accompanied her daughter to Read, will soon have learnt the news, for Nowell arranged that Alizon's grandmother, Old Demdike, and Old Chattox too, should appear before him in Fence three days later.

Death in Cheshire,
and Old Chattox

D EMDIKE and Chattox, both in their eighties according to Potts, appeared before Roger Nowell in Fence on 2 April. Three others also arrived to give Nowell evidence. They were John Nutter of Higham Booth, his sister Margaret Crooke and their friend, James Robinson. It is probable that this John Nutter was he of Bulhole, one cow of whose had succumbed to Demdike, one to Chattox. Nowell will have sought him out for comment.[32] In fact the story that he and his sister and friend told was much more serious. They claimed that Chattox and Anne Redferne, Chattox's married daughter, had long ago killed Robert Nutter, who was brother to John and to Margaret. John Nutter began this story of his brother's bewitching. Eighteen or nineteen years before he, John, had been travelling on the road from Burnley with his brother, Robert, and his father, Christopher. He had heard brother Robert tell their father that he suspected he was being bewitched by both Chattox and Anne Redferne; presumably in some way Robert was not feeling fit. 'I pray you cause them to bee layed in Lancaster Castle', he pleaded. His father had dismissed the idea: 'Thou art a foolish Ladde, it is not so, it is thy miscarriage'. But Robert had wept and had insisted that if he returned, for he was about to go away with his master Sir Richard Shuttleworth, he would 'procure [Chattox and Anne] to bee laid where they shall be glad to bite Lice in two with their teeth'.[33]

John's sister, Margaret Crooke, continued the narrative. It had been Whitsuntide when this had happened. Robert had become ill a week later and had died at Candlemas. While he was ill 'he did a hundred times at the least say, That the said Anne Redferne and her associates had bewitched him to death'. By next Maudlintide their father Christopher had fallen sick too, had languished until

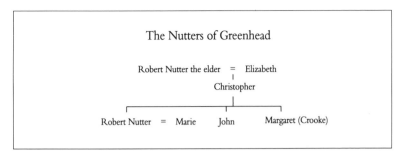

The Nutters of Greenhead

Michaelmas, and then had died, saying many times that he was bewitched, though not naming anyone.[34]

James Robinson then told Nowell that he had lodged with John and Robert's grandfather, Robert Nutter the elder, presumably as a servant at their family home of Greenhead.[35] He confirmed that Robert had believed himself bewitched and said that he had heard Robert threaten Thomas Redferne, Anne's husband, telling him that when he returned from Wales 'he would get his Father to put the said Redferne out of his house, or he himselfe would pull it downe'. (The home that the Redfernes and Anne's mother, Old Chattox, shared must have stood in the lands of Greenhead.) Robinson said that Robert Nutter 'never came back againe, but died before Candlemas in Cheshire as he was comming homeward'.[36]

Robinson went on to assert that Chattox and Anne Redferne 'are commonly reputed and reported to bee Witches'. Then he told a story of only six years before. He had engaged Chattox for three days to card wool with his wife in his house. After Chattox had dipped into the 'newly tunned drinke' (fermenting beer), the drink had been spoiled for two whole months.[37] Robinson does not explain why he and wife allowed Chattox into their home if her repute was as ill as he claimed.

Nowell then questioned Chattox herself. Potts was later to describe her:

> a very old withered spent & decreped creature, her sight almost gone
> . . . her lippes ever chattering and walking: but no man knew what.[38]

The old lady began shrewdly enough. She placed the late Robert Nutter in a less favourable light. It seems he had deserved the enmity of the Redfernes, for Chattox told how Robert 'did desire

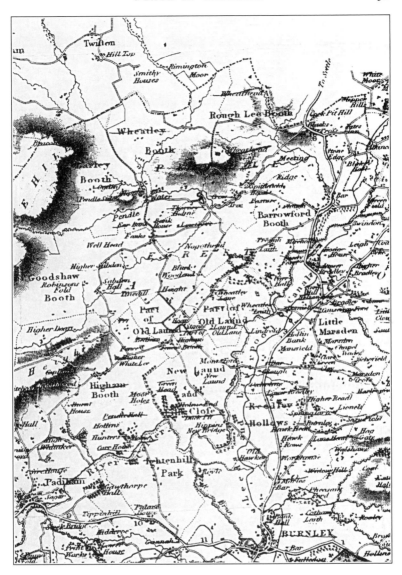

Christopher Greenwood's Map of Lancashire of 1818 shows the divisions of
Pendle Forest: Goldshaw (Goodshaw) Booth, Barley Booth, Wheatley Booth,
Rough Lee Booth, Barrowford Booth, Old Laund, New Laund and (Filly)
Close (with Greenhead, the home of the Nutters), Reedley Hollows and
Higham Booth. Malkin Tower (not marked) would be in the top right-hand
corner of Barrowford Booth.

Greenhead Farm. Here, Chattox and Anne Redferne were said to have
bewitched to death both Robert Nutter and his father, Christopher.

her Daughter, one Redferns wife, to have his pleasure of her, being
then in Redferns house'. Anne Redferne had refused his amorous
advances, whereupon Robert Nutter, humiliated, had ridden off
'saying in a great rage, that if ever the Ground came to him, shee
should never dwell upon his Land.' Chattox's familiar, in human
form, enters the story, for Nowell records Chattox saying that she
then 'called Fancie to her who came to her in the likenesse of a
Man in a parcell of Ground called The Laund'[39] and she asked
Fancie to 'revenge her of the sayd Robert Nutter'.

Chattox added further information. Much earlier than all this,
she said, the Nutter's grandmother, old Robert Nutter's wife, had
besought her and two other women now dead to kill that same
grandson, young Robert, so that 'the Women their Coosens might
have the Land'.[40] Chattox and the other two had consented to 'get
young Robert Nutter his death', but Thomas Redferne, her son
in law, had dissuaded them. One supposes that the cousins favoured
by a murderous grandmother were some other of her grandchildren,
probably the children of either John or his sister Margaret who had
raised the whole story.[41]

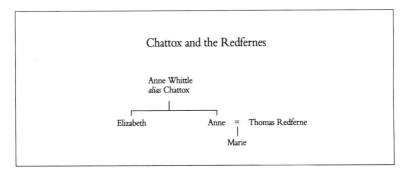

Had John Nutter and his sister by then left the house in Fence where Nowell was interviewing? We should have liked to know how they responded to Chattox's disclosure of a dark side to their family history.

Nowell now wished the old lady to confirm by confession Alizon's story that she, Chattox, had caused the deaths of the two children, the son of John Moore, and the daughter of Anthony Nutter, Anne, the one who had laughed. Chattox, wily in her verbosity, talked not of the death of children but only of the death of cows. A cow belonging to each family had died, she admitted, each bitten by 'Fancie', who appeared in one case 'in the likenesse of a browne Dogge' and in the other case 'like a man'. About the Moore's unpalatable ale Chattox confirmed that there had been resentment, but her story was that the ale had been 'forspoken or bewitched' before ever she arrived and that she had been called to amend it. She gave the words of the charm she used.[42]

Chattox was cajoled by Nowell into telling of the first giving of her soul. Nowell recorded that she had given her soul fourteen or fifteen years before to 'a thing like a Christian man' who had been seeking it for four years. At the time she had been in her own house. Afterwards 'the Devill . . . in the shape of a Man said to this Examinate: Thou shalt want nothing; and be revenged of whom thou list'.

The devil asked her to call him by the name 'Fancie'.[43]

We have met Fancie, Chattox's familiar, four times now; three times as a man and once as a brown dog. Another manifestation that Chattox spoke of suggests that she was then slipping deeper into paranoia:

. . . In Summer last, save one, the said Devill, or Fancie, came upon this Examinate in the night time: and at diverse and sundry times in the likenesse of a Beare, gaping as though he would have wearied this Examinate. And the last time of all shee . . . saw him, was upon Thursday last yeare but one, next before Midsummer day, in the evening, like a Beare, and this Examinate would not then speake to him, for which the said Devill pulled this Examinate downe.[44]

What were these familiars really?

Like Chattox's, Demdike's familiar first appeared in the form of a male human-being: 'in the shape of a boy'. This leads us to speculate about Nowell's methods of eliciting these 'admissions'. Did he ask the ladies about those to whom they had 'given their souls'? Did they in response to his prompting babble first about the loves of their long-lost youth, their 'fancy' men, and then about pet animals on whom in age they lavished their love? Or is there a quite different explanation? Was the 'thing like a Christian man' whom Chattox said asked for her soul some religious enthusiast of long ago, a pietist, Puritan or even Catholic, who sought from her religious commitment—the giving of her soul—and offered to her the promise of salvation?

Undoubtedly Demdike, the Devices and Chattox had animals that accompanied them and whom they called by pet names. This was true even of the young man James and of Alizon. As beggars they probably traded on this peculiarity, so that the dog at the foot, or even a tame hare, was to them as a monkey to an organ-grinder or as Toby to Punchinello. They may at times have told their dogs to do their bidding, to give to someone who harassed them a vicious bite.

It is likely that Nowell, intent on his case, misconstrued the chattering mumble of innocent revelations.

Old Demdike and the
Making of Pictures

She was a very old woman, about the age of Foure-score years, and had been a Witch for fiftie yeares'.[45]

So wrote Thomas Potts. He never saw Demdike, for before the trial she had died in Lancaster gaol. Demdike's home was Malkin Tower. To her Roger Nowell now turned. Nowell recorded what Demdike said about her first meeting with the 'Spirit or Devill'. The devil was 'in shape of a boy' and she encountered him near a stone-pit at Gouldshey 'about twentie yeares past'. The boy was in motley; 'the one halfe of his Coat blacke, and the other browne'. He promised her gain, and said that his name was Tibb. Demdike was 'contented to give her Soule to the Spirit', but not until five or six years later did Tibb suck her, and then he was

in the likenes of a browne Dogg, forcing himselfe to her knee, to get blood under her left Arme: and she being without any apparrell saving her Smocke, the said Devill did get blood under her left arme.[46]

That had been a Sunday morning; she had a sleeping child on her knee and had herself been slumbering. She had cried out:

Jesus save my Child; but had no power, nor could not say, Jesus save herself.

Hearing her words, the dog vanished, and 'this Examinate was almost starke madd for the space of eight weeks'.[47]

Nowell must then have asked Demdike about the death of the miller's daughter. Demdike's story differed a little from that which her grand-daughter, Alizon, had told, and is more realistic. 'A little before Christmas last' Alizon had led Demdike to Richard Baldwin's mill. Demdike had wished to claim payment owed by Baldwin to her daughter Elizabeth who had worked at the mill-house. Baldwin had not welcomed the grandmother and grandchild. He had shouted:

> Get out of my ground, Whores and Witches, I will burne the one of you, and hang the other.

Tibb had appeared, whether in human or animal form we are not told; he suggested avenging this insult. Demdike admitted that she said to Tibb: 'Revenge thee eyther of him, or his'. Tibb went off but she had never since seen him.[48]

When Nowell asked Demdike what she knew about the much-discussed death of Robert Nutter, the old lady talked freely further to incriminate Chattox. Potts commented on this edge of malice when either Chattox or Demdike spoke of the other. Chattox was, he wrote,

> always opposite to old Demdike: For whom the one favoured, the other hated deadly; and how they envie and accuse one an other, in their Examinations, may appeare.[49]

Six months before Robert Nutter had died, Demdike said, about midsummer she had been near the Chattox/Redferne home. There Demdike had seen Chattox and her daughter Anne Redferne sitting either side of the ditch 'within three yards of the East end of the house'. They had 'two Pictures of Clay or Marle lying by them'; Anne was making a third one. Tibb, who accompanied Demdike 'in the shape of a black Cat', told her that these pictures were those of: 'Christopher Nutter, Robert Nutter, and Marie, wife of Robert Nutter'. Tibb was then offended, we read, because Demdike did not turn aside to help in this image-making; Tibb had pushed Demdike into the ditch, which 'shed the Milke which this Examinate had in a Can or kit'. Tibb had then changed form into a hare which walked silently along with her for 'about a quarter of a mile.'[50]

Witch with a cat—a woodcut used to illustrate the nineteenth-century reprinting of *The Arraignement and Triall* . . .

The making of models or images, 'pictures' as they are called

Ferdinando, Earl of Derby. A patron of Shakespeare, he died in 1549 at Lathom after a wax image of him had been found in his room.

in *The Wonderfull Discoverie* . . ., was a common technique of malignant magic. Wax dolls with pins stuck in them have survived. Tudor aristocrats felt threatened by this technique. A Southwark man, Stephen Kylden, was imprisoned for making images of both the Lord Treasurer and the Earl of Leicester, and images made of the Earl of Essex were spoken of at the infamous murder trial in 1616 of his former wife, Frances Howard, Countess of Somerset. Closer to Pendle, Ferdinando, Earl of Derby, had died from violent and corroding vomiting in 1594 at his seat in Lathom near Ormskirk, Lancashire. During his illness, in his Lordship's chamber

> . . . was found . . . a little image made of wax, with hairs of the colour of his in the belly of it, which occasioned many and various speculations, conjectures and constructions concerning the nature, meaning and effects thereof.[51]

The wax image had been curiously spotted, and soon after spots had appeared on the sides and belly of the distempered nobleman. The finder of the image, a Mr Halsall, innocently reacted in the worst possible way—he threw the puppet into the fire. A Dr Hacket was later hanged up by the wrists and tortured as a wizard for having made the image and caused his Lordship's suffering.

There is much evidence that Chattox, Demdike and their families made magical images. James Device, when interrogated on 27 April, said that he had shown the Constable, Henry Hargreaves, where to dig up a picture; it had been buried 'about halfe a yard over in the earth' near the west end of Malkin Tower.[52]

Demdike explained to Nowell that

> . . . the speediest way to take a mans life away by Witchcraft, is to make a Picture of Clay, like unto the shape of the person whom they meane to kill, & dry it thorowly: and when they would have them to be ill in any one place more than an other; then take a Thorne or Pinne, and pricke it in that part of the Picture you would so have to be ill: and when you would have any part of the Body to consume away, then take that part of the Picture and burne it. And when they would have the whole body to consume away, then take the remnant of the sayd Picture, and burne it: and so thereupon by that meanes, the body shall die.[53]

Demdike does not here admit to doing this herself. She was describing a method, as had the divine William Perkins. What Perkins wrote, published in 1608, reveals why the picture at Malkin Tower which James unearthed should have been buried. He described the witch's technique thus:

Lancaster Castle. Here the Pendle witches were imprisoned for four months, and the Assizes which condemned them were held. The witches were hanged outside the city.

> . . . to draw the picture of a child or maid or other creature in clay, or waxe, and to burie the same in the ground, or to hide it in some secret place, or to burn it in the fire, thereby intending to hurt or to kill the partie resembled. Againe, to make an impression into the said picture, by pricking or gashing the heart or any other place, with intent to produce dangerous or deadly pains to the same parts.[54]

The interrogation of Demdike and Chattox was over. The old women did not return home; Roger Nowell committed them to the dreadful gaol of Lancaster Castle to await the Assizes. He committed to gaol also Anne Redferne, Chattox's daughter, who, if she had also been at Fence, had discreetly said nothing for Nowell to record. More likely the constable apprehended her at home. In gaol they would join Alizon.[55]

On 27 April, three and a half weeks later, the magistrates Roger Nowell and Nicholas Bannister were to gain further information about the witches. That interrogation occurred after the Malkin Tower meeting which Jennet Preston had ridden in haste to attend. Now that the stories of Jennet Preston and of the Devices have merged, we will look at what the magistrates learned concerning the gathering at Malkin Tower.

We had left Jennet Preston about to enter the house on the moor, about to learn what we have just recounted.

The Meeting at Malkin Tower

1. *Sources—Elizabeth, James and Jennet*

At Malkin Tower Jennet Preston's host was Elizabeth Device. Elizabeth's old mother, Demdike, former ruler of the household, was now in gaol so Nowell designates Malkin Tower in James' statement as 'this Examinate's mothers house'.[56]

Thomas Potts described Elizabeth as she appeared at her trial. He was unflattering:

> This odious Witch was branded with a preposterous marke in Nature, even from her birth, which was her left eye, standing lower than the other; the one looking downe, the other looking up, so strangely deformed, as the best that were present in that Honorable assembly, and great Audience, did affirme, they had not often seene the like.[57]

Was Elizabeth as unprepossessing as that? After all, she had married; her husband had died eleven years before, as Alizon had told. Elizabeth had been taunted too 'with having a Bastard child with one Seller'; presumably that child was Jennet Device who in 1612 was nine years of age. A family with surname Seller farmed a holding close to Malkin Tower.[58] Elizabeth it seems was not odious to every unbiased observer.

What happened at her home, Malkin Tower, on Good Friday of 1612?

Our source is an interrogation which took place 'in the home of James Wilsey of Pendle' seventeen days after the Malkin Tower meeting.

Elizabeth had been summoned, and also her son James and her nine-year-old daughter Jennet Device. Potts prints short extracts from their testimony in *The Arraignement and Triall . . .*, but fuller versions in *The Wonderfull Discoverie . . ..*

Roger Nowell wrote the statements. Nicholas Bannister, another magistrate, had this time joined him.

Nowell must have been informed that, despite his committal to gaol of Demdike and Alizon, there had been a strange concourse at their home. He wished to know more. It is clear from the way he wrote up his evidence that he suspected that there had been a witches' sabbath.

In the days before this interrogation James Device had co-operated with the constable, Henry Hargreaves. Accompanied by Hargreaves James had travelled to Gisburn to identify 'the wife of one Preston' as one present—'to see whether shee was the woman that came amongst the said Witches, on the said last Good Friday'. The constable had also persuaded James to show him the place near to the west end of Malkin Tower where his grandmother had buried the picture, and James had even helped Hargreaves to dig it up. While digging they also unearthed there four human teeth; James explained that twelve years before in Newchurch churchyard Chattox had taken eight teeth from three skulls and had given these four to Demdike.[59]

Hargreaves, whom James assisted, was probably a farmer fulfilling a year-long manorial obligation to act as constable, an office responsible to the magistrate. James may have assumed that he could confide in him. Perhaps he believed that the reward for disclosure would be leniency for his family and his own immunity. By conversation with Hargreaves, James' tongue had been loosed; he was to supply Nowell and Bannister with damning evidence.

2. *Upon Good Friday Last*

The Malkin meeting took place on Good Friday, 10 April in the year 1612 at 'twelve of the clocke in the day-time'.

The holiness of the day would interest Nowell. Potts wrote of it with a heavy irony:

> Upon Good-fryday they met, according to solemne appoyntment, [and] solemnized this great Feastivall day according to their former order, with great cheare, merry company, and much conference.[60]

Good Friday's catholic ceremonies, forbidden in the previous decades by the new Protestantism, had been etched on people's consciousness. In a Parish Church before the Reformation on Good Friday a cross was unveiled above the rood screen or on the chancel steps. During solemn chanting of the 'Reproaches', parishioners crept unshod, on their knees, to kiss that cross's foot. Afterwards a crucifix and a pyx containing a consecrated host would be buried in linen cloths in a 'sepulchre' in the chancel, where until Easter a continuous watch was kept and many candles burnt.

Devotion in the North clung late to that old religion. Even midway through Elizabeth's reign Archbishop Grindal of York complained that on Good Friday 'some certeyn persons go barefooted and barelegged to the churche, to creepe to the crosse'.[61]

Puritans too observed Good Friday with great solemnity. The day was heavy with mourning.

It happened that the meeting at Malkin Tower took place during those hours when the faithful recalled Christ's hanging upon the cross. Nowell seems to have had a hunch that the meal at Malkin Tower was a parody of the eucharist. He cajoled the nine-year-old Jennet Device to describe what was eaten. She complied, saying

> That the persons . . . had to their dinners Beefe, Bacon, and roasted Mutton; which Mutton (as this Examinates said brother said) was of a Wether of Christopher Swyers of Barley: which Wether was brought in the night before into this Examinates mothers house by the sayd James Device . . . and in this Examinates sight killed and eaten.[62]

Was Nowell implying ritual significance in the slaughtering of a lamb at the season of the death of the 'Lamb of God'?

James had already admitted that he had filched the sheep on Maundy Thursday and killed it:

> That upon Sheare-Thursday last, in the evening, he stole a Wether from John Robinson of Barley, and brought it to his Grand-mother's house, old Demdike, and there killed it.[63]

3. Roll Call

Who attended the gathering at Malkin Tower? The nine-year-old Jennet Device told Nowell 'there was about twentie persons, whereof only two were men'. In *The Wonderfull Discoverie . . .* we can collect their names from the depositions of James Device, of

One Tree Farm, Under Pendle, the home of Jennet Hargreaves. She attended
the meeting at Malkin Tower but escaped prosecution.

Jennet Device, of Elizabeth Device (who mainly confirmed James' list), and from a list with slight omissions that Potts made.[64] There were four men—Jennet had probably excluded her brother and uncle when she counted. Twenty seems an accurate count, though Potts writes of 'many more, which being bound over to appear at the last Assizes, are since that time fled to save themselves'.

When Jennet Preston entered Malkin Tower these are the people she met: Elizabeth Device, the daughter of old Demdike, who now owned Malkin Tower; James Device, son of Elizabeth; Jennet Device, the nine-year-old daughter of Elizabeth; Christopher Howgate of Pendle who was a son of Demdike, uncle of James and Jennet; Elizabeth Howgate, his wife; Jennet Hargreaves, wife of Hugh Hargreaves of Under Pendle; Christopher Hargreaves, also called 'Christopher Jackes' of Thorniholme; Elizabeth Hargreaves, his wife; John Bulcock of Moss End; Jane Bulcock, the mother of John; Alice Nutter of Roughlee (also called by the Devices 'Dick Myles wife' and 'the mother of Myles Nutter'); Alice Gray of Colne; Katherine Hewitt of Colne, known as 'Mouldheels'; Anne Cronkshaw of Marsden; Grace Hay of Padiham; and, according to Elizabeth Device, 'two women of Burneley Parish, whose names the wife of Richard Nutter doth know'.

4. *Three Causes*

Roger Nowell wrote that James gave three 'causes' why these people met at Malkin Tower, reasons explained to him by his mother. They were:

a.   for the naming of the Spirit which Alizon Device . . . had;

b.   to free Demdike, Alizon, Chattox and Anne Redferne from Lancaster Castle 'killing the Gaoler at Lancaster, and before the next Assizes to blow up the Castle there'; and

c.   to respond to Jennet Preston's plea that they should avenge the malicious treatment of her by Thomas Lister junior by killing Lister and his uncle.

Elizabeth later confirmed to Nowell some of this, but not all. Nowell wrote that Elizabeth

also confesseth, in all things touching the Christening of the Spirit, and the killing of Master Lister of Westbie, as the said James Device hath before confessed; but denieth of any talke was amongst them the said Witches, to her now remembrance, at the said meeting together, touching the killing of the Gaoler, or the blowing up of Lancaster Castle.[65]

Elizabeth's testimony was shortened when presented at the trial of Jennet Preston. The court at York was not told that Elizabeth had refuted what James had said about planning to kill the gaoler and to blow up the Castle.

James' three 'causes' for the Malkin Tower gathering each merit our attention.

5. Naming of the Spirit

The first intention of which James spoke was:

> for the naming of the Spirit which Alizon Device, now Prisoner at Lancaster, had, but did not name him, because shee was not there.

Was Alizon's imp or familiar to be named at Malkin Tower? Was that 'the Spirit'? Nowell clearly means us to assume so. The 'Naming of the Spirit', he envisaged, would have been some sort of initiation ceremony. Nowell knew that Alizon had an animal companion, the 'Black Dogge' which in John Robinson's close in Rough Lee two years before had desired Alizon 'to give him her Soule' and 'did with his mouth (as this Examinate then thought) sucke at her breast, a little below her Paps'. Alizon, though, said that she had not seen the dog since the sucking until the pedlar's seizure near Colne, and subsequently but once, 'five days next after', while she was begging in Newchurch, but then she would not speak to it; 'Sithence which time this Examinate never saw him'. In fact a mere week was to elapse before her interrogation and arrest by Nowell.[66]

Was this black dog which Alizon had sometimes met on her begging journeys to be give a name at a special occult ceremony? There are factors which make us doubt this.

No ceremony was required to reveal what the familiars of other Pendle witches were called. Demdike at her first meeting with a 'Spirit or Devill in the shape of a Boy' had 'demanded his name? and the Spirit answered, his name was Tibb'. Chattox when she encountered 'the Devill then in the shape of a Man' had no need to ask, for 'the Devill . . . commaunded this Examinate to call him by the name of Fancie'. James Device had a spirit, a brown dog, who did 'ever after bid this Examinate to call it Dandy'. (His young sister in her evidence to the court said Dandy was a black dog.) Elizabeth Device had a brown dog named Ball, but we do not learn how he came by this name.[67]

Affectionate names for familiars appear in other witch trials in the sixteenth and seventeenth century. At Fewston in Yorkshire Margaret White had a cat, white and spotted with black, named Inges; Jennet Dibb had a black cat called Gibbe; and Margaret Thorpe had 'a bird, yellow of colour, about the bigness of a crow—the name of it is Tewhit'; and a 'strange woman' had a spirit in the likeness of a white cat called Fillie. That was in 1622. In Essex in 1645 Mary Hockett was accused of entertaining 'three evil spirits in the likeness of a mouse, called Littleman, Prettyman and Daynty'. Named familiars abound, but in no other cases save one do we learn of a ceremonial 'naming of a Spirit'.[68]

The one instance of a familiar being 'christened' comes in *Newes from Scotland*, the account of the examination in 1591 before King James VI of the school-teacher John Cunningham, alias Dr Fian, and his accomplices.[69] By witchcraft, it was alleged, Fian and his fellow witches had attempted to drown the King by raising a storm as he sailed home to Scotland with his Danish bride. Agnis Thompson, one of the accused, confessed to a nursery rhyme scenario—to having sailed in a sieve with a cat into the midst of the sea to arouse the tempest. First she had christened the cat:

> She confessed that at the time when his Majestie was in Denmarke, she . . . tooke a Cat and christened it, and afterwards bound to each part of that Cat, the cheefest partes of a dead man, and sevarall joynts of his bodie and that in the next night following the said Cat was conveied into the midst of the sea by all those witches sayling in their riddles.

Agnis made this confession, and others, after grievous tortures allowed by Scottish law. She

> had all her hair shaven of, in each part of her bodie, and her head throwen with a rope according to the custome of that

Countrye, beeing a paine most greevous, which she continued almost an hower.

The poor woman then, unsurprisingly, cracked and 'confessed whatsoever was demanded of her.'

Roger Nowell would have read *Newes from Scotland*. This story of the christening of a cat, it happens, is more likely to have shaped Nowell's preconceptions than to provide real evidence of an occult tradition in England of the baptising by witches of their familiars.

James Device's phrase was 'naming of the Spirit'. Elizabeth in her deposition calls the intention of the Meeting at Malkin Tower the 'Christening of the Spirit'. Was Nowell muddled as he tried to force what he had heard to fit the incongruous model of what he had read? Had Elizabeth been trying to explain to him that they planned to baptise Alizon—that the young lady was to be initiated into a Christian group through the ceremony of adult baptism? Was 'The Spirit' of which Elizabeth spoke either the Holy Spirit or Alizon's own inner spirit?

Baptism in the Spirit was all important for Anabaptists, for Seekers, and for similar radical Christian groups. Spirit-baptism, they held, symbolised and accompanied the inrush of God's grace that established one as a member of the elect. If this were the context, then the intended 'Christening of the Spirit' would have been a short ritual to mark Alizon's reception into the inner life of a group of Seekers. Would so Christian a meaning be compatible with the other practices of Alizon's family—with the village witchcraft, the making of Pictures, the cursing of the miller, the healing of animals? We must defer decisions about this until we have noticed other signs of the religious, or irreligious, persuasion of those at Malkin Tower.

If, as James and her mother said, Alizon was intended to be the focus of a ritual, then the Malkin Tower meeting must have been planned before she was arrested, and probably before she had met the pedlar on 30 March. In the event the gathering at the Device's home, whatever its original intention, became a response to the immediate predicament into which Demdike and Alizon had been plunged. Neighbourly concern will have brought along others like Jennet Preston who might not have planned to attend for the ritual.

6. *Violence at Lancaster*

The second 'cause' which James gave for the Malkin Tower meeting was

> for the deliverie of his Grand-mother [Demdike], this Examinates
> sister Alizon, Anne Chattox,and her daughter Redferne: killing the
> Gaoler at Lancaster; and before the next Assizes to blow up the
> Castle there; to that end the aforesaid Prisoners might by that meanes
> make an escape and get away. All which this Examinate then heard
> them conferre of.[70]

James' mother, Elizabeth, we have seen, denied that the witches
intended to kill the gaoler or to blow up the castle 'thereby to
deliver old Dembdike her mother'. Perhaps she realised that such
disclosures would enrage the court which her mother and daughter
would face, for that court would be held within Lancaster Castle
itself and in the presence of the gaolor, Thomas Covell, who was
also a coroner and former Mayor of Lancaster. A jury of Jacobean
gentry would fear violent public disturbance. The Gunpowder Plot
had been uncovered only eight years before. Thomas Potts dedicated
The Wonderfull Discoverie . . . to Thomas Knyvet, Lord Eskrick, the
man who had led the lanterned band into the cellars of Parliament
where among the barrels of explosives they had apprehended Guy
Fawkes and his accomplices.[71] Lancaster Castle itself had known
violence. It had been stormed late in Henry VIII's reign by a certain
John Lawrence and a mob of two hundred in an attempt to free
two of his servants.[72]

Those who met at Malkin Tower, however, were powerless
people. They could not seriously have entertained taking the castle
by force. Of what then had James spoken to cause Nowell to record
it in this way?

At Malkin Tower the friends of the Devices must have arrived
aggrieved about the plight of Demdike and Alizon. How could
they free them? How could they save them from the gallows?
Would they survive three months in that ghastly gaol? Could food
or clothing be taken to help them? Who could advise?

Why! Jennet Preston! She would have much to teach. Only four
days before Jennet had been tried for witchcraft in York and had
been acquitted. The same judge who had presided at her trial would

try Demdike and the others. A message to Jennet's home in Gisburn produced a prompt response. It is a measure of Jennet's resilience and kindness that, so recently returned to Gisburn, she rode 'in haste' over the moors to help as best she could.

Twenty friends consulted at Malkin Tower about ways to free Demdike, Alizon, Chattox and Anne Redferne. Someone, if only wistfully, was bound to suggest direct action. Later James was cajoled to divulge to Nowell those hot words. Nowell it was who chose to regard them as a 'cause' of the meeting, as though the destruction of the castle was what the conclave had assembled to plan.

7. *Killing of Master Lister*

The third reason given for the Malkin Tower meeting relates particularly to Jennet Preston. James is said to have attested

> that there was a woman dwelling in Gisborne Parish, . . . who there came, and craved assistance of the rest of them that were then there, for the killing of Master Lister of Westby; because, as she then said, he had borne malice unto her, and had thought to have put her away at the last Assizes at Yorke; but could not. And then this Examinat heard the said woman say, that her power was not strong enough to doe it her selfe, being now lesse than before-time it had beene.[73]

James, pressed by Nowell to implicate everyone at Malkin Tower, was later more explicit. Nowell wrote that James testified that he

> heard all give their consents to put the said Master Thomas Lister of Westby to death: and after Master Lister should be made away by witchcraft, then all the said Witches gave their consents to joyne altogether to hancke Master Leonard Lister, when he should come to dwell at the Sowgill, and so put him to death.[74]

Leonard Lister was uncle of Thomas Lister junior and brother of the Thomas Lister whom Jennet was accused of having murdered in 1607. Born at Westby and baptised in Gisburn Church in 1575, Leonard married Anne Loftus of Coverham Abbey, Yorkshire, in 1600. By 1612 they had a seven-year-old daughter, Alice, a three-year-old son, George, and a two-year-old, Elizabeth. Their home was Cowgill, written 'Sowgill' by Potts. Genealogical works, such as *Memorials of an Ancient House*, a study of the Listers, ascribed Leonard to 'Cowgill in the parish of Dent', near Sedbergh. This was a mistake. In fact Cowgill, Leonard's home, was a farmhouse to the west of Westby, in the parish of Gisburn, clearly shown on the Thomas Jefferys' map of Yorkshire of 1772. This location, but not Dentdale, was convenient for the witches to waylay him. The antagonism of those at Malkin Tower suggests that Leonard had colluded with his nephew Thomas in accusing Jennet of witchcraft.[75]

The word 'hancke' meant originally to bind up, as with a hank of cord. It was used figuratively of the binding or constraining of a person by the spells of witchcraft; a person so bound by spells was said to be 'in hancke'.

At Malkin Tower Jennet Preston will have told the throng about her own trial and acquittal, and about the victimisation that had preceded it. The injustices she disclosed, and we have still to reveal the main part of them, will have evoked their indignation. They will have talked of restitution and revenge. When these wild words were later reported to Roger Nowell, he would be disposed to misconstrue them as a definite murderous plan, for Jennet, whose own death had been planned by the gentry, had every cause to wish revenge. She was, Nowell would think, a danger to his class.

Nowell conceived that Jennet had gone to Malkin Tower to seek help of other witches in her plan to kill Thomas Lister junior and Leonard Lister. But why should she need this help? Thomas Lister, after all, was claiming that unaided she had killed his father by witchcraft. The reconciliation of this incongruity was achieved by a comment in James' evidence: 'that her power was not strong enough to doe it her self, being now lesse than before-time it had beene'. Nowell could easily elicit such a statement from the bemused James, or write in such an explanation.[76]

8. *Malign Magic or Herbal Healing?*

What more happened at Malkin Tower? Young Jennet Device 'accused John Bulcock to turne the Spitt there'. He roasted the stolen mutton. It may have been by the fire-side then that James overheard John Bulcock and Jane Bulcock his mother

confesse . . . that they had bewitched, at the new-field Edge in

Yorkshire, a woman called Jennet, wife of John Deyne, beside her Reason and the said Womans name so bewitched, he did not hear them speak of.[77]

Newfield Edge is a farm in Middop close to Jennet Preston's route to Malkin Tower. By the last dozen words James means that he had deduced that the demented person of whom James spoke was Jennet Deyne. James also told that Katherine Hewitt 'alias Mouldheeles' and Alice Gray

did confesse amongst the said Witches at their meeting at Malkin Tower aforesaid, that they had killed Foulds wifes child, called Anne Foulds, of Colne: and also said, that they had then in hanck a child of Michael Hartleys of Colne.[78]

What were these conversations at Malkin Tower really about? Were the Bulcocks and Alice Gray and Katherine Hewitt boasting, as Nowell assumed, about the efficacy of their malign magic? Or had James not grasped the import of the conversations at Malkin Tower? Or was Nowell misunderstanding James? Is it possible that at Malkin Tower the Bulcocks and Alice Gray and Katherine Hewitt had been but exchanging news of the condition of some whom they had been seeking to cure? We cannot be certain, for the evidence is strong that the Devices and Demdike sought by occult means to heal some, but also to harm others. Alice Gray was acquitted at Lancaster; Katherine Hewitt and the Bulcocks were found guilty. They were hanged.

9. *Night-flying*

Jennet Preston rode to Malkin Tower on a foal, and, after the meeting, Jennet and other visitors left on horseback and were gone. The facts as James told them are banal. Roger Nowell, however, strained to conform James' evidence to fit his inflamed preconceptions. Nowell believed that witches fly through the air to their sabbath meetings, and that for this night-flying either they would be transformed into beasts, or would mount devilish familiars. So Nowell has James describing Jennet's foal as a 'Spirit':

Prestons wife had a Spirit with her like unto a white Foale, with a blacke-spot on the forehead.

The night-flying of witches was described in many continental manuals of witchcraft. Drawing by Knelling.

This is repeated later; Jennet

> brought the Spirit with her, in the shape of a white Foale, as aforesaid.

The departure of the witches is described yet more mysteriously. What Nowell wrote as James' evidence was this:

> That all the Witches went out of the house in their own shapes and likenesses, and they all, by that they were forth of the doores, were gotten on horse-backe like unto Foales, some of one colour, some of another, and Prestons wife was the last; and when she got on horse-backe, they all presently vanished out of [James'] sight.[79]

After leaving the house, Nowell implies, the witches did not retain their own shapes, but were transmuted for their journey.

The pattern to which Nowell sought to match his witness's evidence is in chapter 4 of King James' *Daemonologie* where the King told of the magical flight of witches to their 'unlawful convention'. Witches could be

> carryed by the force of the Spirite which is their conducter, either above the earth or above the Sea swiftlie, to the place where they are to meet.

King James reported that, in 'their comming to their conventions' witches may be 'transformed in the likeness of a little beast or foule'.[80]

Nocturnal flying had become an established part of Continental witchcraft belief. Night-flying women, 'ladies of the night', were held to ride out in cavalcades of wild abandon with the goddess Diana or to cluster around Herodias. The notion, rooted in paganism, had not always been officially sanctioned. In the tenth century the church, far wiser then than later, had concluded that stories of night-flying had no basis in fact and that women who told that they engaged in such escapades were suffering from devilish delusion. In A.D. 906 Abbot Regino of Prüm compiled a list of base superstitions to be eradicated in his archdiocese, among them he wrote:

> One mustn't be silent about certain wicked women who become followers of Satan, seduced by the fantastic illusion of the demons, and insist that they ride at night on certain beasts together with Diana, goddess of the pagans, and a great multitude of women; that they cover great distances in the silence of the deepest night; that

The frontispiece of *Pandaemonium* by Richard Bovet, 1684. One witch rides through the air; another witch and the friar stand within magic circles.

they obey the orders of the goddess as though she were their mistress; that on particular nights they are called to wait on her.[81]

Regino's tenth-century judgement was codified in the *Canon Episcopi*, believed by the medieval church to have issued from the Council of Ancyra in 314. Thereby it became a heresy to assert that night-flying was anything other than the delusions of dreamers. Nevertheless, fifteenth-century ecclesiastical courts once more considered tales of nocturnal rides to be facts. In 1430 Joan of Arc was asked by the judges at Rouen whether she knew anything of those who 'went or travelled through the air with the fairies.' Joan said she had done nothing of that sort, but had heard of it; she knew it took place on Thursdays and that it was a 'sorcerie'.

Two Dominican Inquisitors, Jakob Sprenger and Heinrich Kramer published in 1486 the *Malleus Maleficarum*, a baleful encyclopaedia of demonology endorsed by a Papal Bull. These Dominicans upturned the *Canon Episcopi*, rule of orthodoxy though it was. Night-flying by witches occurred not in imagination only, they averred, but 'bodily and phantastically, as is proved by their own confessions'. Priests and others had seen the phenomenon with their own eyes; Sprenger and Kramer retailed their lies. They explained the technique whereby witches flew:

> Now the following is their method of being transported. They take the unguent which, as we have said, they make at the devil's instruction from the limbs of children, particularly of those whom they have killed before baptism, and anoint with it a chair or a broomstick; whereupon they are immediately carried up into the air, either by day or by night, and either visibly or, if they wish, invisibly.[82]

Through torture Continental investigators elicited many 'confessions' of night-time flying and other transvection. This occult transport, it was held, gave witches access to massive assemblies at the devil's behest. 'Nothing so venturesome can be found in English records', writes C. L'Estrange Ewen, 'and the few references to leaving the ground are little better than uncorroborated statements of demented and hysterical people.' No allegation of flying in England predates Nowell's attempt to represent as magical the transport to and from Malkin Tower. Despite King James' *Daemonologie*, later references to flying witches are mostly village burlesque, as, for instance, the allegation in a Cambridgeshire court in 1647 that 'old Stanguidge' had been carried over Shelford steeple upon a black hog and had torn his breeches on the weathercock.[83]

10. *The Great Assembly of Witches*

Before Malkin Tower never had it been alleged that witches had gathered in England for ritual meetings. The notion of a witches sabbath at which the devil presides was a foreign one. However Nowell, and Potts following him, described the Malkin Tower meeting in heightened language to suggest a sabbath. Potts, having told of the imprisonment of Demdike, Chattox, Alizon and Anne Redferne in Lancaster gaol, continued:

> heere they had not stayed a weeke, when their Children and Friendes being abroad and at libertie, laboured a speciall meeting at Malking Tower in the Forrest of Pendle, upon Good-fryday, within a weeke after they were committed, of all the most dangerous, wicked, and damnable Witches in the County farre and neere.

It was 'the great Assembly of Witches at Malking Tower'; 'a solemne meeting at Malkyn-Tower of the Ground Witches of the Counties of Lancaster and Yorke'; 'the Feast at Malking-Tower, at the great Assembly of Witches'; and 'this Feast and solemne meeting at Malking Tower of this hellish and devillish band of Witches, (the like whereof hath not been heard of)'.[84]

The evidence which Nowell had been able to gather was thin compared with the enormity which he presumed had been perpetrated. The concept of the witches' sabbath may be illustrated by the sentence pronounced by a reverend Inquisitor on a group of women charged at Avignon in France in 1582. 'Brother Florus', the Inquisitor, listed for the women's benefit their crimes, which included blasphemy, infanticide, cannibalism and sexual perversion:

> In the common synagogue of witches, sorcerers, heretics, conjurers and devil-worshippers, you did kindle a foul fire and after many rejoicings, dancings, eating and drinking, and lewd games in honour of your president Beelzebub the Prince of Devils in the shape and appearance of a deformed and hideous black goat, you did worship him in deed and word as very God and did approach him on bended

A witches' sabbath—a German print. Witches arrive through the air; they are
embraced by incubi; familiars are present, and a witch kisses the 'foul and
beastly posterior' of the devil in the form of a goat.

knees as suppliants and offered him lighted candles of pitch; and
(fie, for very shame!) with the greatest reverence you did kiss with
sacrilegious mouth his most foul and beastly posterior; and did call
upon him under the name of the true God and invoke his help; and
did beg him to avenge you upon all who had offended you or denied

your requests; and taught by him, you did wreak your spite in spells and charms against both men and beasts, and did murder many new-born children, and with the help of that old serpent Satan, you did afflict mankind with curses, loss of milk, the wasting sickness, and other most grave diseases. And your own children, many of whom with your own knowledge and consent, you did with those magic spells suffocate, pierce, and kill, you finally dug up secretly by night from the cemetery, where they were buried, and so carried them to the aforesaid synagogue and college of witches: there you did offer them to the Prince of Devils sitting upon his throne, and did draw off their fat to be kept for their use, and cut off their heads, hands, and feet, and did cook and stew their trunks, and sometimes roast them, and at the bidding of your aforesaid evil Father did eat and damnably devour them. Then adding sin to sin, you, the men, did copulate with Succubi, and you, the women, did fornicate with Incubi: moreover, in most bitter and icy connexion and foul coitus with demons you did commit the unspeakable crime of buggery.[85]

On the Continent the authorities used painful devices to force confessions: the strappado, the heated chair, vices for arms and legs, thumbscrews. Hundreds therefore confessed to partaking in sabbaths. Witch-hunts would sweep through a town, sometimes taking fifty or many more lives as one person's confession implicated another. In Wolfenbüttel in Brunswick in 1590 an observer wrote: 'The place of execution looked like a small wood from the number of stakes.' In an area of South-western Germany, modern Baden-Württemberg, between 1561 and 1670 records show that 3229 people were burned for witchcraft. In all on the Continent some 100,000 witches were executed from the fifteenth to the seventeenth century. The fantasies of Brother Florus' judgement, or the fantasies in Roger Nowell's mind, were such as lead to holocaust.[86]

Nowell, believing stories of sabbaths, must have been tantalised. Evidence of enormities, he would believe, was just eluding his grasp. His questioning had produced no trace of the presence of the devil, nor of obeisance to this Prince of Darkness, nor of sexual excess with imps. However Nowell moulded such material as he had—the feast, the holy day, the 'naming of the Spirit', the exit on horseback—to suggest that the Malkin Assembly was a satanic sabbath.

11. *Romles-Moore*

The witches arranged to reconvene on 'that day twelve-month' when Jennet Preston 'promised to make them a great feast' at her home in Gisburn. If they had occasion to meet earlier, they would 'upon Romles-moore' (or 'upon Romleyes Moore' as Potts transcribes it elsewhere).[87] Rombalds Moor stretches south-east from Skipton, a distance of a dozen miles east of Malkin Tower. It is a distant location for a future meeting. Twelve months hence is likewise a far-off time. Neither is convincing when those at Malkin Tower wished to give immediate help to their friends in Lancaster Castle. Perhaps Nowell wished to insinuate that the Malkin Tower group met with a regularity that parodied true religion and that flying to distant sabbaths was part of their wicked practice. James, discerning no significance in Nowell's probing, would have placated his questioner with nods of assent.

Our assessment of the Malkin Tower gathering is that it was first convened for 'the Christening of the Spirit', possibly a religious purpose. The meeting came to have immediate importances, for those who met responded to the incarceration of Demdike, Chattox, Alizon Device and Anne Redferne. Amongst those present were wise-women in the local community, but the gathering was no witches sabbath. The magistrates, Nowell and Bannister, projected upon the meeting their own elaborate expectations; they represented the gathering as being like a sabbath. Jennet Preston went to Malkin Tower to help others who were facing a crisis similar to that from which she had just emerged.

Lest it be thought that this interpretation presumes too much on the duplicity of the Lancashire and Yorkshire gentry, we return to a closer study of Jennet Preston. Did she really kill Thomas Lister senior? In her case do we have definite evidence that she was framed by the local gentry?

Judge Bromley and
Judge Altham

As we return to the specific charges against Jennet Preston of Gisburn, we do well to take the measure of the judges who tried her.

The judge who had presided over Jennet's first trial at the Lent Assizes in 1612 was 'Lord Bromley'. Sir Edward Bromley lived at Shifnal Grange in Shropshire. A nephew of Lord Chancellor Bromley, he had been created one of the Barons of the Exchequer in 1610. He and the jury he directed acquitted Jennet of the Dodgson charge at the Lent Assizes at York; perhaps the evidence against her was quite insufficient. Four months later that same judge was to preside over the trials in Lancaster.

Jennet's misfortune was that the judge for her second trial was Sir James Altham. Altham, born in Essex of a Yorkshire family, had been elected an MP for a Sussex seat in 1589. In 1606 he was appointed a Baron of the Exchequer, and the following year at Chelmsford Assizes had condemned a woman to death for witchcraft.[88]

The temper of Sir James is apparent from a famous case that had just engaged him. He was one of the judges whose opinion had been taken by the Lord Chancellor, Sir Thomas Egerton, Lord Ellesmere, upon the case of 'two blasphemous heretics', the last in England who were sentenced to death solely on grounds of heresy. It is worth summarising what occurred.

The two were Anabaptists and Seekers: Bartholomew Legate of Essex, who had for a time been in the Netherlands, and Edward Wightman a draper of Burton on Trent. Legate held that there was no true church, and would not be until there was a new revelation by 'miraculous prophets'. Christ, he believed was 'a meere man, as

Sir James Altham's monument in the chapel which he built
in 1612 at Oxhey Place, Watford. Sir James was the judge who presided
at the trial of Jennet Preston.

were Peter, Paul or I, onely borne free from sinne.' In Scripture
Christ was termed God not from 'his essence but his office.'
Wightman, like Legate, was a Seeker. He condemned infant baptism,
held that 'Christianity is not truely sincerely and wholly professed
and preached in the Church of England but onely in parte', and

believed that he himself, Wightman, was the future Prophet and Comforter foretold in the Bible. James I interested himself in both men. Intrigued by Legate, he engaged him in debate on several occasions. Wightman rashly delivered a manuscript of his writings to His Majesty. The King then lost patience and was content that the two be tried for heresy, Legate before a Consistory Court in London, Wightman in Lichfield where crowds gathered daily in the Lady Chapel of the Cathedral. Found guilty of heresy, both were handed over to the secular power. By the King's letter the Lord Chancellor was required, with doubtful legality, to issue a writ 'de heretico comburendo' for their execution. Those desiring this end were satisfied that Sir James Altham was selected to give Egerton his opinion on the legality of this, for Altham was said to be more favourable to the death sentence than Lord Coke would have been.

The writ was duly issued. Bartholomew Legate was burned at Smithfield on 18 March 1612 amid a vast 'conflux of people . . . He was comely and swarthy, fluent and confident, excellently skilled in the Scriptures and in character very unblameable.' He had refused to recant. Wightman similarly would retract nothing: 'I have made my sayd Answers, and I doe & will stand to them.' He was burned at Lichfield during April 1612, just three months before Jennet's second trial.[89]

We shall meet other Seekers as our tale develops. The fate of Wightman and Legate shows the cost implicit in that discipleship.

Sir James Altham, whom Jennet faced in July, was a judge whose hard line was known even to the King, who had engaged in a famous case, and who for recommending the death penalty on a religious charge had received, he believed, His Majesty's approbation. We may presume that Sir James, elated as he was by royal approval of his lack of the quality of mercy, was eager to condemn Jennet.

The influence of Judge Altham upon Judge Bromley, through conversations in the travelling coach and over dinner tables in York, Kendal and Lancaster, and above all through the example of his condemnation of Jennet Preston must be reckoned as a cause of the tragic outcome at Lancaster. Judge Bromley, before he served with Judge Altham, had not to our knowledge convicted any witch

King James I (1603–1625). His book *Daemonologie*, published in 1597, stimulated the prosecution of witches. Later he encouraged the courts to expose the deceptions of Puritan 'exorcists'.

to death. However at Lancaster he was to pass sentence of death on the ten 'witches' and later still was to continue a condemner of witches. In 1614, again at Lancaster, Bromley condemned to death one Cicilia Dawson of Walton-le-Dale, convicted of bewitching to death a certain Elena Moldinge of Hoghton, and of having 'wasted' George Harrison of Curedale and Thomas Wynckley.[90]

Bromley is mentioned in March 1617 in the diary kept by Nicholas Assheton, squire of Downham.

Then all to Lancaster . . . Judge Bromley, Judge Denham
xi executed.[91]

The Dying Man's Railing and
the Bleeding Corpse

A T Jennet Preston's second trial in York 'Master Heyber' was
the magistrate who acted as prosecutor. Thomas Heber, aged
forty five, lived in the hall at Marton in Craven. Potts, writing of
Heber's conduct of the prosecution of Jennet, calls him:

> one of his Majesties Justices of Peace in the said Countie, having
> taken great paines in the proceedings against her; and being best
> instructed of any man of all the particular points of Evidence
> against her.[92]

In court Heber called on Thomas Lister junior and Anne Robinson 'and others' to attest to the words that, four years before,
Thomas Lister senior had cried out on his deathbed: 'Jennet Preston
lays heavie upon me . . .'[93]

When Judge Altham instructed the jury he asked them to 'observe' that railing at a witch by an afflicted man.[94] In trials for
witchcraft in the sixteenth and seventeenth centuries evidence of
the crying out of the victim is common. Rarely is it so dramatic.

The prolific Puritan divine of Cambridge University, William
Perkins, whose *A Discourse of the Damned Art of Witchcraft*, published
in 1608, influenced the Pendle magistrates, was cautious about
death-bed railing. Perkins believed such railing was not in itself a
proof of witchcraft; he called it a 'presumption' that should lead a
magistrate to make special inquiries. Perkins wrote:

> If a man being dangerously sicke and like to die upon suspition will
> take it on his death that such a one hath bewitched him, it is an
> allegation . . . which may move the Judge to examine the partie, but
> it is of no moment for conviction. The reason is, because it was but
> the suspition of one man, and a mans own word for himself, though

in time of extremitie, when it is likely he will speak nothing but the truth, is no more force than another mans word against him.[95]

It seems that Judge Altham attributed a greater moment to the railing of a dying man than did Perkins.

The next strange piece of evidence was held by the learned judge to be 'of more consequence than all the rest'. It was

that Jennet Preston being brought to the dead corps, they bled freshly.

Potts states that Anne Robinson and Thomas Lister, 'with many other witnesses', gave the macabre evidence. What they testified to was this:

That Jennet Preston . . . being brought to M. Lister after he was dead, and layed out to be wound up in his winding-sheet, the said Jennet Preston comming to touch the dead corpse, they bled fresh bloud presently, in the presence of all that were then present.[96]

Potts explains that this bleeding of a corpse

hath ever been held a great argument to induce a Jurie to hold him guiltie that shall be accused of murther, and hath seldome or never, fayled in the Tryall.[97]

He was correct; there was good authority.

The King of England, for instance, believed just that—that a murdered corpse when touched by the murderer bled. King James had written and published *Daemonologie* in 1597, before he ascended the English throne; the book had been reissued since. In it the King referred incidentally but clearly to bleeding corpses:

. . . in a secret murther, if the deade carcase be at any time thereafter handled by the murtherer, it wil gush out of bloud, as if the blud wer crying to the heaven for revenge of the murtherer, God having appoynted that secret super-naturall signe, for tryall of that secrete unnaturall crime.[98]

We know that Potts had read King James' book on witchcraft for, in discussing the case of Isabel Robey, tried at Lancaster, he begins a sentence with a rhetorical question: 'What hath the Kings Majestie written and published in his *Daemonologie* . . .?'[99]

William Shakespeare draws on the phenomenon of bleeding

corpses in *Richard III*, Act 1, Scene 2, written in 1593. Lady Anne standing before the open coffin of Henry VI, berates the Duke of Gloucester whom she holds responsible for the King's death:

> . . . See, see! dead Henry's wounds
> Open their congeal'd mouths and bleed afresh.
> Blush, blush, thou lump of foul deformity,
> For 't is thy presence that exhales this blood
> From cold and empty veins, where no blood dwells;
> Thy deed, inhuman and unnatural,
> Provokes this deluge most unnatural.
> O God! which this blood madest, revenge his death;
> O earth! which this blood drink'st, revenge his death;
> Either heaven with lightning strike the murderer dead
> Or earth, gape open wide, and eat him quick
> As thou dost swallow up this good king's blood
> Which his hell-governed arm hath butchered.

Even Reginald Scot and Sir Francis Bacon, writers in general sceptical about witchcraft, believed that corpses would bleed at a murderer's touch.[100] The great Clitheroe schoolmaster pamphleteer, metallurgist and doctor, John Webster, normally cool in his judgements, cites precedents to establish that 'the bleeding or cruentation of the bodies of those that have been murthered . . . by prepense malice' is 'absolutely true de facto, and there is something more than ordinary in it'.[101]

The unlearned concurred. In 1636 it was alleged that Joan Elderson of Newton-in-Makerfield in Lancashire, a suspected witch, had stayed away from the funeral of two children for fear that, if she had been made to touch the corpses, her murder of them would be revealed. In Somerset in 1613 a murderer fled rather than touch a corpse.[102]

Michael Dalton in *The Countrey Justice, containing the Practice of Justices of the Peace out of their Sessions*, a handbook for magistrates published in London in 1643, thirty years after Jennet's trial, regards a corpse's bleeding in the presence of a suspected party as proof specifically of murder by witchcraft.[103]

When Thomas Lister junior and Anne Robinson testified that the corpse of Thomas Lister senior bled as Jennet touched it, they presented evidence acceptable to a seventeenth-century court. Judge

Altham in commending this evidence did not offend the medical
or forensic understanding of his day. However we have twentieth-
century questions to ask. Can we trust the veracity of the two
witnesses who claimed with their own eyes to have seen the corpse
of Thomas Lister senior gush with blood at the touch of Jennet
Preston? Or do we discern a collusion to deceive?

Wedding Traumas

WHERE did Thomas Lister senior die? The Court in York will have assumed that he died in his home, Westby in Gisburn. The scene as related appears domestic. It was 'in great extremitie, upon his death-bedde' that Lister died. Anne Robinson 'and others' referred to 'them that came to visit him during his sicknesse'. Their narrative included a 'house' in which Lister was alleged to have cried out against Jennet: 'Looke about for her, and lay hold on her, for she is in the house'.[104]

But Thomas Lister did not die at Westby. The court was misled.

The registers of Gisburn Parish Church normally do not reveal the place of death of those being buried. For Thomas Lister it happens that an exception was made. The Burial Register for 1607/8 has this entry:

> Thomas Lister, Ar: de Westbie
> Mort apud Braswell   Octavo die Februarii

It records that on 8 February Thomas Lister, esquire, of Westby, was buried and that he had died at Bracewell. Bracewell is the parish to the west of Gisburn.

The mystery deepens. What took Thomas Lister to Bracewell? Why was the Bracewell location of Lister's death concealed from the murder trial?

Historians frequently fling such questions to the skies, not expecting, after these years, to receive an answer. However, a glance into the Parish Registers of Bracewell Church uncovers an astonishing secret. *Bracewell Marriage Register* for 1607 records this:

> Feby [illegible] Thomas Lyster Sonn of Tho Lyster gent was married
> with Jane daughter of Mr heaber of Marton.

Here is the marriage in Bracewell of Thomas Lister junior. The date in February is illegible, but the entry which follows happens

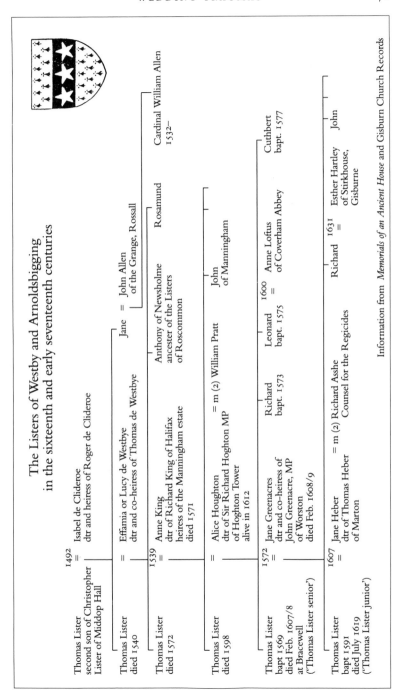

The Listers of Westby and Arnoldsbigging
in the sixteenth and early seventeenth centuries

Thomas Lister
second son of Christopher
Lister of Middop Hall
1492 = Isabel de Clideroe
dtr and heiress of Roger de Clideroe

Thomas Lister
died 1540
= Effamia or Lucy de Westbye
dtr and co-heiress of Thomas de Westbye

Jane = John Allen
of the Grange, Rossall

Thomas Lister
died 1572
1539 = Anne King
dtr of Richard King of Halifax
heiress of the Manningham estate
died 1571

Anthony of Newsholme
ancester of the Listers
of Roscommon

Rosamund

Cardinal William Allen
1532–

Thomas Lister
died 1598
= Alice Houghton
dtr of Sir Richard Hoghton MP
of Hoghton Tower
alive in 1612

= m (2) William Pratt

John
of Manningham

Thomas Lister
bapt 1569
died Feb. 1607/8
at Bracewell
('Thomas Lister senior')
1572 = Jane Greenacres
dtr and co-heiress of
John Greenacre, MP
of Worston
died Feb. 1608/9

Richard
bapt. 1573

Leonard
bapt. 1575

1600 = Anne Loftus
of Coverham Abbey

Cuthbert
bapt. 1577

Thomas Lister
bapt 1591
died July 1619
('Thomas Lister junior')
1607 = Jane Heber
dtr of Thomas Heber
of Marton

= m (2) Richard Asshe
Counsel for the Regicides

Richard
1631 = Esther Hartley
of Stirkhouse,
Gisburne

John

Information from *Memorials of an Ancient House* and Gisburn Church Records

to be for 8 February, so the marriage took place in the first week
of February. In Bracewell, we see, in the very same week, Thomas
Lister the son was married and Thomas Lister the father died.[105]

Who was Thomas Lister junior marrying? Why! He was marrying
the daughter of Thomas Heber, the daughter of that very magistrate
who, on Lister's behalf, four years later would prosecute Jennet for
witchcraft. No wonder they worked in harmony!

Consider again the sequence of events that first week of February
1607/8. Had Thomas Lister senior died in the days before his son's
marriage—had he died, for instance when visiting Bracewell Church
to prepare for the wedding—the wedding would have been postponed
until after the funeral. So the facts force us towards a dramatic scenario.

Sir Richard Tempest, whose hall stood close to Bracewell
Church, probably had offered to house the festivities. The gentry
families of Craven and Pendle assemble at Bracewell Church for
the wedding of the heir of the Listers. Tenants and villagers from
Gisburn and Marton look on. Thomas Owtinge, the Vicar of
Bracewell, probably officiates. The marriage ritual proceeds. Then
there is consternation. In the midst of this company, either in the
church or at the festivities that follow, the bridegroom's father,
Thomas Lister the elder, owner of great estates, is struck down by
a seizure. He is lifted to a couch or bed, surrounded by family and
by guests, by the solicitous and by the inquisitive. Laughter turns
to tears. Lister cries out, embarrassingly, and cries out again. There
is frantic perplexity as the life of the bridegroom's father ebbs away.
Thomas Lister senior was but thirty-eight years old.

The bridegroom, Thomas Lister junior, was sixteen years of age.
It was not uncommon amongst the Lancashire and Pennine gentry
for marriages of the young to be arranged by parents, for in this
way families forged alliances and bound settlements. We do not
have details, as we should like, of the marriage settlement between
Thomas Lister and Jane Heber. Although Jane was the eldest child
of Thomas Heber and his first wife, Eleanor, she was not heir to
the Heber estate, for she had a twelve-year-old brother, Thomas.
Nevertheless a dowry to consolidate a larger contiguous landholding
would have been valuable to the Listers. By the shrewdness of their
marriages from generation to generation the Listers established
wealth and influence.

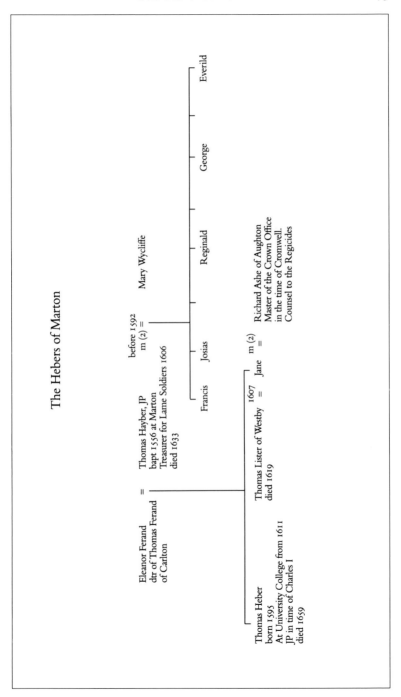

The Hebers of Marton

Eleanor Ferand
dtr of Thomas Ferand
of Carlton

=

before 1592
m (2) =

Thomas Hayber, JP
bapt 1556 at Marton
Treasurer for Lame Soldiers 1606
died 1633

Mary Wycliffe

Francis   Josias

Reginald   George   Everild

Thomas Lister of Westby
died 1619

1607
=

Jane

m (2)
=

Richard Ashe of Aughton
Master of the Crown Office
in the time of Cromwell.
Counsel to the Regicides

Thomas Heber
born 1595
At University College from 1611
JP in time of Charles I
died 1659

Westby Hall and Arnoldsbigging, by Robert Griffier, about 1735.
Pendle Hill rises to the left. Arnoldsbigging was then being demolished to
provide stone for the refurbishment of the Lower Hall. At Westby, resentment
towards Jennet Preston was bred.

Thomas Lister's own wife, the bridegroom's mother, also a Jane, was daughter and heiress of John Greenacres of Worston, one of the two first Members of Parliament returned for the borough of Clitheroe.

The strange circumstances of the death of Thomas Lister were concealed from the court that tried Jennet Preston. The judge and the jury in York were unable to take account of the swirl of passions that would be generated as the lightheartedness of a wedding was changed to desperation around a dying man and then overwhelmed by the grief of bereavement. The court was prevented from considering whether there was in the tumult of human emotions a psychological, rather than occult, explanation for the victimisation of Jennet.

John Webster of Clitheroe in 1677 was to give sound advice in the Preface of his great work, *The Displaying of Supposed Witchcraft*. When accusations arise of Sorcery or charming, he wrote:

> I make bold to mind you of this one thing especially that in things of this nature great heed ought to be taken of the conditions, qualities,

ends and intentions of the Complainants and Informers, who are often more worthy of punishment, than the persons accused.[106]

We shall heed Webster's sober words. As we seek the cause of the accusation against Jennet Preston, our attention will be directed to the 'ends and intentions of the Complainants'.

Consider the predicament of the wedding guests at Bracewell. They have tumbled into a scene of melodrama. Conversation cannot have been relaxed. The matter of inheritance must have been in many minds, yet decency would inhibit comment upon it. Yet it was surely remarkable that within hours, perhaps within minutes, of Heber's daughter sealing a marriage contract with the heir to the Listers, that heir had inherited. In the instant the whole Lister wealth was that of the bridegroom and his new bride; the Heber girl was now the mistress of the Lister estate; her home could be Westby itself. To state this might be to imply that there had been an intention by the Hebers to procure this outcome.

It was safer for guests, as they proffered to each other an explanation for Lister's death, to speculate about witchcraft.

On the subject of death by witchcraft the gentry present had precedents to cite. Many of them will have attended Lord Derby at his seat in Lathom, so could tell of the manner of dying of Lord Ferdinando and of the punishments for witchcraft that ensued. John Starkey would almost certainly have been at the Bracewell wedding; for bewitching him in his childhood Edmund Hartley had been hanged. Roger Nowell's reading of King James' *Daemonologie* would have added authority to their speculations. In the whisperings of the shocked guests trying to account for the tragic accident would be spawned the rumours of witchcraft.

These rumours came to focus upon Jennet Preston, for the dying man repeatedly called out Jennet's name. Both Anne Robinson and the young bridegroom were to testify later to this. They claimed that in shouting Lister had been railing against the person who had bewitched him. Were they correct?

It is striking that the meaning of Lister's dying words, though recorded by hostile witnesses, could be totally different if the emphasis of the words was but slightly realigned. This realignment, at first tentatively, we will attempt.

The stricken Lister was desperate that Jennet should not leave the house. He called her name again and again, crying

> that Jennet Preston was in the house, look where she is, take holde of her; for Gods sake shut the doors, and take her, shee cannot escape away. Look about for her, and lay hold on her.[107]

Did he call thus because he believed Jennet was bewitching him and should be apprehended? Or did Lister in his last moments want Jennet near him? Was Lister calling out against Jennet, or calling for her? Did he wish her away, or did he wish for the comfort of her presence?

The other words which Lister cried contain a very physical image.

> Jennet Preston lays heavie upon me, Preston's wife lays heavie upon me.

We will want to observe more narrowly that long-standing relationship between Jennet and Thomas Lister senior which Thomas Potts referred to as undeniable. Had there been a special fondness between them?

Potts in his introduction reveals that Jennet had access to Westby and was entertained there by Thomas Lister senior with a kindness that was well-known:

> this Jennet Preston was for many yeares well thought of and esteemed by Master Lister who afterwards died for it Had accesse to his house, kind respect and entertainment; nothing denied her she stood in need of. Which you that dwelleth near them in Craven but can and will witnesse it?[108]

Lister senior and Jennet Preston were of same age, we have deduced—thirty-eight at the time of Lister's death, younger together these 'many yeares' before. Jennet lived 'neare Master Lister of Westbie'.[109] It may be that her family, the Balderstons, had long connections with the Lister household for the Thomas Lister who died in 1542 bequeathed to 'Nicholas Balderston 40/-' and to 'Agnes Balderston 1 guye stirke'.[110]

Assume from these hints that Jennet was the mistress of Thomas Lister. A dynamic is then provided which explains the elements of her victimisation. Jane, wife to Thomas Lister senior, would feel humiliated when, in a public scene, her dying husband had on his lips not her own name, but that of Jennet. He called not for his wife, but for another whom he loved. But if, then or later, those who heard the cries and those to whom an account of them was circulated came to presume that Thomas called Jennet's name not because he loved her, but because he believed that Jennet was bewitching him, well enough. This in the widow's discomfiture would preserve her dignity.

It would be easy for the widow to persuade herself that Jennet was a witch. Sexual attraction is beguiling, bewitching. Anne Boleyn was not the only mistress whose allure was attributed by others to witchcraft.

Anne Robinson and Thomas Lister junior testified that

> after he was dead, & layd out to be wound up in his winding-sheet, the said Jennet Preston comming to touch the dead corpes, they bled fresh bloud presently in the presence of all that were then present.[111]

Was Jennet forced to press her finger against the dead body as a test to establish that she had murdered the gentleman? Had Jennet been so compelled, and, albeit impossible, had the corpse bled, Jennet's guilt would have been manifest. It is inconceivable then that her trial for the murder should have been delayed for four years. Absurd too, if Thomas Lister junior knew Jennet had murdered his father, would be Potts' story that Lister junior continued to show kindness to her. For Potts wrote:

> The favour and goodnesse of this Gentleman Master Lister now living, at his first entrance after the death of his Father extended towards her, and the reliefe she had at all times, with many other favours that succeeded from time and time, are so palpable and evident as no man can denie them.[112]

If then Jennet approached the corpse she will have done so as one who came as a dear friend to mourn or as a household retainer to perform the sad offices with the winding-sheet.

The Victimisation of Jennet

A NIMOSITY towards Jennet would accumulate gradually. At Westby Jennet's position would become uncertain. Thomas' body was buried in the family vault in Gisburn Church on 8 February. Amongst mourners a mistress is ignored; attention and sympathy attend the widow. In the weeks that followed Jennet, accustomed at Westby to free access and many favours, soon would sense cold reserve and later find the door closed in her face. Benefaction would end. If she had worked at Westby, her employment would cease. The widow, her sexual resentment unrestrained, Uncle Leonard and the new young master would mutter against her.

Then a year later Jane the widow died. Here was a double tragedy; some of her children were very young. She was buried at Gisburn on 20 February 1608.

Suffering and death are perplexing. They seem to demand explanation. In the twentieth century when misfortunes strike we lack the belief-system which would allow us to search our neighbourhood for the woman who has bewitched us. But even today families of victims of murder or manslaughter are relieved when the perpetrator is convicted; they say they can now resume their normal living. By attributing death to human agency, mourners can transform grief into anger. Their thoughts are given focus and their actions are given an aim. We speculate that such a process operated within Thomas Lister junior. Michael Dalton in his seventeenth-century handbook for magistrates stated that witchcraft may be suspected 'when a healthful body shall be suddenly taken . . . without probable reason or natural cause appearing'.[113]

Court records of witchcraft cases in the sixteenth and seventeenth centuries show that, typically, accused and accuser knew each other and that the accuser was of a higher social class. Accused and accuser were bound in a relationship in which under the old neighbourly

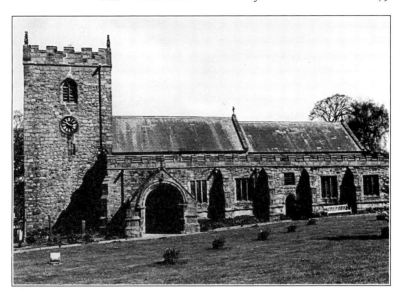

Gisburn Church is little changed since the burial there of
Thomas Lister senior in 1608.

ethic friendship or charity between them might be expected. But
friendship had soured. Often tensions had arisen when one had
been refused some alms or favours. The one who denied the
kindness, uncertain how he should have reacted, then believed that
the other was consumed with resentment. He would assuage his
conscience by convincing himself that the one refused the alms was
a moral monster, undeserving, a wicked witch. Keith Thomas's
analysis of witchcraft prosecutions fits the dilemma of Thomas Lister
junior and Jennet Preston:

> Close examination of those cases where the circumstances can be
> adequately reconstructed reveals that the charge was only levied
> when the accuser felt, not merely that the witch bore a grudge
> against him, but that the grudge was a *justifiable* one. The witch,
> in other words, was not thought to be acting out of mere vindic-
> tiveness; she was avenging a definite injury. It was not just that the
> victim and the witch had quarrelled. The important point is that,
> paradoxically, it tended to be the witch who was morally in the

right and the victim in the wrong. This result corresponds with what anthropologists have found elsewhere.[114]

This is the dynamic which impels the tragedy of Jennet Preston. After the death at the wedding, Jennet would continue to expect some charity, or so the seventeen-year-old Thomas Lister would surmise. But, responding to his mother's resentment, he ceased to provide it, despite knowing his late father's affection for Jennet. Embarrassed and agitated, he would fantasise about Jennet's resentment. Were Jennet thoroughly malign, were she a witch, his churlishness would be vindicated, his anxiety released, his equilibrium regained. Yet more secure would be the new balance of his psyche if other disasters were attributed to the malignity of Jennet. Hence besides the death of his father we find Jennet accused of causing loss to his 'goods and Cattel' and of killing the Dodgson child.

When the Dodgson trial failed, young Lister polished up memories of the traumatic death of his father. Anne Robinson supported his reinterpretation of the crying out of the dying man and his 'evidence' about the bleeding corpse. She was easily persuaded, for she was probably a family retainer. In his own will written just seven years after the trial Thomas Lister refers to a cottage 'in the occupation of Agnes Robinson of Gisburne'.

Roger Nowell, the Lancashire Magistrate, guided the hand of Thomas Lister, and stiffened his purpose. Nowell supplied Lister and Heber with information about Jennet's attendance at Malkin Tower. He would convince Lister that Jennet had planned at Malkin Tower to kill both him and his uncle Leonard and that, if not brought to trial again, she would endanger his life.

The psychic drive within young Lister explains the subterfuges of his prosecution—the hiding of evidence about the true circumstances of the death in Bracewell, the fabrication of the story about the touching of the corpse. It explains why the young Lister was concerned to defame her to whom his father had shown surpassing kindness.

At the prosecution in York no evidence was adduced that Jennet was a wise-woman. No curses are quoted. No one testified that she made 'pictures' or charmed with teeth from human skulls. She was accused neither of blighting ale, nor of curing it, neither of having a familiar, nor of pledging her soul to the devil. Jennet, it seems, was not a wise-woman. In this she was unlike Demdike and Chattox and their families. Jennet was accused of witchcraft because her presence disconcerted Thomas Lister junior. Jennet had been the mistress of his father, but was innocent of the charge of witchcraft.

James: Religious Scruples
and Malign Magic

JENNET's destiny was shaped by Lister, but also by the witch-hunting enthusiasm which had gripped Roger Nowell, the supplier of depositions about her. Her prospects thereby were bound up with those of the Pendle circle. We shall be able to deduce more clearly what were the forces that impelled Nowell's obsession when we look at the further evidence that Nowell gained.

We were led to wonder about the religious beliefs of those whom Jennet met at Malkin Tower when we noted that the Spirit of Alizon was 'christened'. Witches, one might guess, would be satanists who worshipped the devil in abominable ceremonies. But was this true of the Devices? Were they rather secret Catholics attached to the old ways and at odds with the new-fangled simplicity of Protestant worship in the parish churches? Did radical Christianity influence them? Or were they just not religious at all?

It happens that when Roger Nowell interviewed James Device on 27 April much of what the young man said related to religion. Other commentators have held James' evidence to be fanciful foolishness. Edgar Peel and Pat Southern in *The Trials of the Lancashire Witches*, for instance, describe James as 'evidently half-witted' and characterise his evidence as 'inexplicable nonsense and triviality.'[115] Certainly at his trial, having suffered four months in prison and with the gallows looming, James cut a sorry figure:

> . . . being brought forth to the Barre . . . [he] was so insensible, weake, and unable in all thinges, as he could neither speake, heare, or stand, but was holden up when hee was brought to the place of his Arraignement.[116]

Before Nowell four months earlier, however, James had been helpful, just as he had been to Henry Hargreaves the constable. He was a callow country lad, reared in poverty, isolated, unsure of himself, bored and excitable. But this young man was no simpleton. He had religious scruples, was a Christian and, clearly, no demonist.

Consider what James told Nowell, or what Nowell understood, about his 'giving of his soul' to a familiar. About Easter day two years before

> there appeared in [James'] sight, hard by the new Church in Pendle, a thing like unto a browne Dogge, who asked [him] to give him his Soule, and he should be revenged of any whom hee would: wherunto [he] answered, that his Soule was not his to give, but was his Saviour Jesus Christs, but as much as was in him . . . to give, he was contented he should have it.[117]

As with Demdike and Alizon he told a talking-dog story in the family tradition. In his dialogue with the dog we find that James insists that he should make no pledge that would compromise his Christian faith. His soul belonged to 'his Saviour Jesus Christ'.

Had James thereby given his soul to the brown dog? Nowell the magistrate was unsure about this. He later asked Thomas Covell, gaoler and Coroner at Lancaster, to question James more straitly. Covell and two Lancaster magistrates did so at the castle. They reported fairly. James reiterated the subtle, Christian qualification. He said he could only give such affection as was consistent with his soul belonging to Christ Jesus. He said

> That his Spirit Dandie, being very earnest with him to give him his soule, He answered, he would give him that part thereof that was his owne to give: and thereupon the said Spirit said, hee was above CHRIST JESUS, and therefore hee must absolutely give him his Soule: and that done, hee would give him power to revenge himselfe against any whom he disliked.

> And he further saith, that the same Spirit did appeare unto him after sundrie times, in the likenesse of a Dogge, and at every time most earnestly perswaded him to give him his Soule absolutely: who answered as before, that he would give him his owne part and no further. And he saith, that at the last time that the said Spirit was with him, which was the Tuesday next before his apprehension, when he could not prevaile with him to have his Soule granted unto him, as aforesaid; the said Spirit departed from him,

then giving a most fearefull crie and yell, and withall caused a great flash of fire to shew about him.[118]

In the event the Court was in no mood to note that James Device, however odd the mode of his alleged conversation, was telling of his battle to remain true to faith in Christ.

At the end of his statement James may have said that the dog was 'gone in a flash', which the wonder-seeking magistrate understood not as metaphor but as occult pyrotechnics.

James Device had further religious traits. He attended Communion, presumably at Newchurch. His grandmother, Demdike, he said, had asked him on Maundy Thursday two years previously 'not to eat the Bread the Minister gave him, but to bring it and deliver it to such a thing as should meet him on his way homewards'. No doubt in reality Demdike wished for it herself, for consecrated bread was valued as an ingredient in medicines. James at the altar-rail would need to secrete the bread without attracting the attention of the minister. In the event James 'did eate the Bread'. On his return he met, he said, 'A thing in the shape of a Hare' which asked for the bread, was angry that James did not have it, and 'threatned to pull this Examinate in peeces'. James' response to this strange encounter was a religious one, he 'marked himself to God'. The making of the sign of the cross, we may note, was a gesture from old Catholicism frowned upon by new Puritans. It proved effective, he reported; the hare vanished.[119]

In James there is an ambivalence. Pious on the one hand, on the other hand he and his family would make magic 'pictures' to bring harm to others.

James told of two occasions when death had followed his own magic. One concerned Anne Towneley, wife of Henry Towneley of Carr Hall, a prominent person in the neighbourhood. James said that 'two or three days after' the previous episode (which, if we take his dating seriously would mean on Easter Saturday or on Easter Day, 1610) he went 'to the Carre Hall'. There 'Mistress Towneley' accused him and his mother of digging peat without permission—'to have stolne some Turves of hers'. She sent him packing—'badde him packe the doores'—and 'as he went forth of the doore, the said Mistress Towneley gave him a knock betweene the shoulders'. A day or two after 'a thing like a black dog' which

Carr Hall, Barrowford; rear view taken in 1954, shortly before its demolition. Mistress Anne Towneley ejected James Device from the house. Later Jennet Device saw Mistress Anne 'in the kitchen there, nothing well'.

said its name was Dandy, suggested he make 'a Picture of Clay, like unto the said Mistress Towneley.' This he did. He

> dried it the same night by the fire: and within a day after, hee . . . began to crumble the said Picture, every day some, for the space of a weeke: and within two daies after all was crumbled away; the said Mistress Towneley died.

Young Jennet Device, his sister, later confirmed this. She had heard her brother and Dandy plan the murder, she said, and 'about a week after, [she] comming to the Carre-Hall, saw the said Mistris Towneley in the kitchin there, nothing well'.[120]

The second death was that of 'John Duckworth of the Lawnde'. Again it followed physical contact. James said that Duckworth 'in Lent last one' had promised him an old shirt, but when James went to collect it, Duckworth 'denied him thereof.' Dandy appeared, and asked: 'Thou didst touch Duckworth.' 'Yes' replied James. 'Yes (said the Spirit againe) thou didst touch him, and therefore I have power of him'. James 'joyned with the said Spirit' with the intention to kill John Duckworth, 'and within one weeke, then next after, Duckworth died.'[121]

James' sister, Jennet Device, alleged in Court that she had heard James and Dandy also plan to kill John Hargreaves of Goldshaw Booth and, on another occasion, Blaze Hargreaves of Higham, both of whom had died.[122]

His mother, James said, also made magical images. Her dog Ball persuaded Elizabeth to make 'a Picture of clay like unto John Robinson alias Swyer' (James was later to steal a sheep belonging to his family). She had dried it and then crumbled it little by little over three weeks. James himself had seen his mother 'take clay at the West-end of her house' and make this picture. Within two days of it being all 'mulled away', John Robinson was dead.[123]

Later Elizabeth herself confirmed that she had done this. She accounted for her actions by telling that this John Robinson had taunted her with having had a bastard child.[124]

On another occasion, James said, he, when walking near the home of Chattox and her daughter Anne Redferne, had seen

three Pictures of Clay, of halfe a yard long, at the end of Redfernes house, which Redferne had one of the pictures in his hand, Marie his Daughter had another in her hand, and the said Redferne's wife . . . had an other Picture in her hand, which Picture she . . . was then crumbling.[125]

The ends of the houses, whether Malkin Tower or Redferne's house, figure as the places where clay images were made. The significance of this is not clear. As James turned away from Redferne's house 'there appeared unto him a thing like a Hare, which spit fire at him'. One wonders again if Nowell misunderstood. Did James, using the adjective as an expletive, speak of a 'spitting hare'?

James then said that about a year past his mother Elizabeth together with Alice Nutter had killed by witchcraft a certain Henry Mitton of Rough Lee. His grandmother, Demdike, had told him about this. The two had murdered Mitton because Demdike had wanted them to, James said: 'Demdike had asked the said Mitton a penny; and hee denying her thereof, thereupon she procured his death'.[126]

The story seems far-fetched for Alice Nutter was an uncharacteristic friend of Demdike's; she was not short of a penny. Potts wrote of Alice:

> it is certain she was a rich woman; had a great estate, and children of good hope: in the common opinion of the world, of good temper, free from envy or malice.[127]

Harrison Ainsworth, author of *The Lancashire Witches* considered Alice Nutter's 'great estate' to be Roughlee Hall, but Gladys Whittaker has shown that Alice Nutter did not live in that big house but at a more modest farm, probably at Crowtrees near the Hall.[128]

On the grounds of committing this unlikely murder over a penny denied to her friend, and for being present at Malkin Tower, Alice Nutter, a widow of seventy with five children, was condemned to death. Her silence, and that of her family, in the face of the allegations suggest some deeper family mystery. Maybe, as Gladys Whittaker suggests, Alice's son Miles, who would inherit her wealth and was at that time in debt, colluded in her accusation.

Demdike as a wise-woman was called out to heal. James said that Henry Bulcock came to Malkin Tower 'about St Peters day last' to ask Demdike to cure his child who had been bewitched. Demdike went. Bulcock asserted that his child had been bewitched by Demdike's grand-daughter Alizon. Alizon responded exactly as later she was to do both before the accusing pedlar and before the Court; she 'fell downe on her knees, & asked the said Bullocke forgiveness, and confessed to him'.[129]

Amongst James' evidence are irrelevances about strange caterwaulings and other doings of cats and dogs, fair subjects for a conversation but curious in a deposition. Their inclusion is no sign of James' craziness. They point rather to the obsessiveness of Nowell, for it was he who chose to record them. To us they are entertaining. James told that when he was 'ten Roodes distant' from Malkin Tower he heard 'a voyce of a great number of Children screiking and crying pittifully, about day-light gate.' And another day 'he heard a foule yelling like unto a great number of Cattes: but what they were [he] cannot tell'. No doubt Nowell suspected that here was evidence of babies being boiled to make magical potions.

Nowell even thought it worth recording James' tale of a cat jumping on him in bed:

about three nights after that, about midnight of the same, there
came a thing, and lay upon him very heavily about an houre, and
went then from him out of his Chamber window, coloured blacke,
and about the bignesse of a Hare or Catte.[130]

To the obsessed mind ordinary events are laden with significance.
   That ended James' evidence. Religious, he nevertheless engaged
in the malign side of his family's magic. A certain wonder seems
to be in his accounts of deaths that followed his making of pictures,
as though he still puzzled about their cause. Was it chance, or had
they died because he had crumbled the clay?

The Little Wench
and more of Chattox

Nine-year-old Jennet Device provided other information about those who met at Malkin Tower. She was the darling of the court in Lancaster, the 'little Wench' or the 'yong Maide', as Potts called her, who on account of her small stature was stood upon a table to speak. Asked by the judge, the young girl identified those present at Malkin Tower:

> shee looked upon and tooke many by the handes, and accused them to be there.[131]

The sweet child seems to have delighted in damning all her family. It was no wonder that Elizabeth, her mother, expostulated in the Court at her daughter's behaviour. She

> cryed out against the child in such a fearfull manner, as all the Court did not a little wonder at her, and so amazed the child, as with weeping teares she cryed out unto my Lord the Judge, and told him she was not able to speak in the presence of her Mother.

Her mother was removed. The child, unabashed, continued. She said 'her Mother is a Witch, and this shee knoweth to be true'. The girl recounted how Elizabeth, her mother, had on three occasions summoned Ball, 'her Spirit . . . in the likenesse of a browne Dogge', to help her to kill John Robinson alias Swyer of Barley, his brother James Robinson of Barley, and 'one Mitton of the Rough-Lee'. All of them had died. James, she said too, 'hath been a Witch for the space of three yeares'. She had heard him plan with his 'Blacke-Dogge . . . called Dandy' to kill 'John Hargreives, of Gold-shey-booth . . . since which time the said John is dead'.

The only other deposition is one taken by the Lancaster

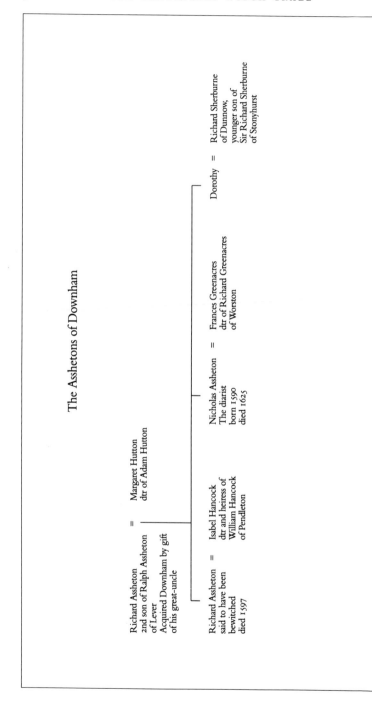

The Asshetons of Downham

Richard Assheton
2nd son of Ralph Assheton
of Lever
Acquired Downham by gift
of his great-uncle

=

Margaret Hutton
dtr of Adam Hutton

Richard Assheton
said to have been
bewitched
died 1597

=

Isabel Hancock
dtr and heiress of
William Hancock
of Pendleton

Nicholas Assheton
The diarist
born 1590
died 1625

=

Frances Greenacres
dtr of Richard Greenacres
of Worston

Dorothy

=

Richard Sherburne
of Dunnow,
younger son of
Sir Richard Sherburne
of Stonyhurst

magistrates from Chattox who then had been in prison seven weeks. In reply to what must have been a question sent by Nowell and put to her by the magistrates, Chattox said that

> Demdike shewed her, that she had bewitched to death, Richard Ashton, Sonne of Richard Ashton of Downeham Esquire.[132]

Richard Assheton was, like Nowell, Lister and Bannister, the head of a leading family in the Pendle area. He had died in 1597 or thereabouts (his widow remarried in 1598), but despite Chattox's allegation, the Assheton's played no part in the prosecutions at Lancaster. Chattox could without inhibition attribute a murder to Demdike, for Demdike was dead; she had not survived incarceration in Lancaster gaol.

Chattox changed her account of the giving of her soul. Now she claimed to have given her soul to the devil at Demdike's persuasion and in Demdike's house. She said, 'The Devill appeared unto her in the liknes of a Man, about midnight'. After first denying him, she had asked the devil

> what part of her body hee would have . . . who said, hee would have a place of her right side neere to her ribbes, for him to sucke upon: whereunto shee assented.[133]

Previously we have not supposed that the witnesses had been tortured. Questioning under torture was not sanctioned by English law. But these 'admissions' by Chattox, gained in the gaol-rooms themselves and by the gaoler, have the marks of coercion. Evidence about the sucking was probably extracted as Chattox's body was brutally examined for witches marks.[134] What she said next is as fantastic as confessions in Austrian, French or Scottish witch cases where those seeking release from the pain of rack or boots or thumbscrew would confirm the bizarre imaginings of those who tortured them.

Chattox told of a magical banquet, supernaturally illumined, spread before Demdike and herself at Malkin Tower:

> There was a thing in the likenes of a spotted Bitch, that came with the sayd Spirit unto Demdike, which then did speake unto her in [her] hearing, and sayd, that she should have Gould, Silver, and worldly Wealth, at her will. And at the same time she saith, there were victuals, viz. Flesh, Butter, Cheese, Bread, and Drinke, and

bidde them eate enough. And after their eating, the Devill called Fancie, and the other Spirit calling himselfe Tibbe, carried the remnant away: And she sayeth, that although they did eate, they were never the fuller, nor better for the same; and that at their said Banquet, the said Spirits gave them light to see what they did, although they neyther had fire nor Candle light; and that they were both shee Spirites, and Divels.[135]

Spells

W E have saved until now consideration of the three charms which Roger Nowell quotes in his text. Through them we can gain insight, uncontaminated by Nowell's mediation, of the practice in which Chattox and the Devices were engaged. We are introduced to a company of like practitioners.

1. *Three Biters hast thou bitten*

Chattox told Roger Nowell of the charm she had used to amend John Moore's drink which had been 'forspoken or bewitched'. Nowell wrote the words like this:

A Charme

Three Biters hast thou bitten,
The Hart, ill Eye, ill Tonge:
Three bitter shall be thy Boote,
Father, Sonne, and Holy Ghost
a Gods name.
Five Pater-nosters, five Avies,
and a Creede,
In worship of five wounds
of our Lord.[136]

Even in the seventeenth century this formula sounded archaic. The words are more apt for healing a person than for righting badly fermented beer. They make better sense if we correct line 2 to read: 'Ill hart . . .' and line 3 to read: 'Three better . . .'

The person bewitched is addressed as if he had been bitten by three snakes: 'You have been bitten by three biters'. Ambiguity is probably intentional in the next line; its sense could be either: 'a malicious heart, a malicious eye and a malicious tongue (of a witch are the biters)' or 'a sick heart, a sick eye and a sick tongue' (you will have because you have been bitten).[137] Our paraphrase continues: 'but to your help shall come three better than that—they are the Father, the Son and the Holy Ghost.' 'Boote' means 'help'; it was a word surviving especially in spells.[138]

Similar was a charm used in 1622 by a London doctor, Richard Booker. Booker believed a patient had been bewitched, so he anointed him pronouncing: 'Three biters have bit him—heart, tongue and eye; three better shall help him presently—God the Father, God the Son, and God the Holy Spirit'.[139]

'A Gods name' signifies that the action is being done 'in Gods name'. The five Lord's Prayers, the five Ave Marias and the Creed would be said in full; what we have here are directions.

Prayers of the church served as spells. Henry Matthew of Guisley in the West Riding admitted to the court of the Archbishop of York in 1590 that sixteen years previously he had washed a woman's sore eyes and said three Paternosters and a Creed. He had now stopped using such methods, he said, because they had caused others to regard him as 'a charmer'.[140] Elizabeth Mortlock in Cambridgeshire in 1566 would cure children troubled by the 'fairy' with:

> Five Paternosters in the worship of the five Wounds of our Lord, five Aves in the worship of the five Joys of our Lady, and one Creed in the worship of the blessed Father, the Son and the Holy Ghost . . . and the Apostles [Creed], in the vulgar tongue.

She then did some curious diagnosis with the patient's girdle or belt.[141] So did Anne Greene of Gargrave, only eight miles distant from Gisburn, but forty-one years after Chattox's time. Like Chattox, Anne Greene used the archaic word 'Boote' in her cure. In 1653 she was charged of witchcraft by a certain John Tatterson—she had given him an ear-ache, (the scribe miswrote it here as heartache) and when asked to put it right she had not cured the ache to Tatterson's satisfaction. Anne Greene explained

> that she sometimes useth a charme for curing the heart each, and used it twice in one night unto John Tatterson of Gargrave, by crossing a garter over his eare, and sayeing these words, 'Boate, a Gods name', 9 times over. Likewise for paines in the head she requires their water and a locke of their heire, the which she boyles together, and afterwards throws them in the fire and burnes them; and meddles not with any other diseases.[142]

In Chattox's charm, the words 'In worship of the five wounds of our Lord' express late medieval piety. Devotion to the wounds of Christ was a popular cult in England until the Reformation. A 'Mass of the Five Wounds' was often requested in pre-Reformation wills. The 'Image of Pity', which showed the wounds of Christ, was, writes Dr Eamon Duffy, 'endlessly reproduced . . . as cheap block-prints to be pinned up in the houses of the poor'. The woodcut took the form of a Pope saying mass, with a Man of Sorrows depicted over the altar, while an inscription to be found below promised vast indulgencies to any who repeated before the image five Paternosters, five Aves and a Creed.[143]

A close parallel to Chattox's charm is to be found in a Lancashire deposition of 1643. A certain Henry Baggilie learnt from his father both the charm and the way to sing it; his father had learnt it from a Dutchman. It was a serious affair to be a charmer, for Baggilie said that he suffered in his body in the same place that he cured on another. He received no money either, but only a bit of food for his pains.

> The examination of Henrie Baggilie
> taken at Chadderton the twentie sixte day
> of May Ano domini 1634

> Who being examined saith that About twentie yeares since this examinats father was taught by A dutcheman certain Englishe wordes and praiers to repeate; whereby to blesse or helpe anie sicke person or cattell in there extremitie; which are Tell the thou forspoken Toothe and Tonge: Hearte and Hearte Aike: Three thinges thee Boote most: the father, Sonne and Holighuoste with the Lordes praier and the Bolcene [?] three tymes over: All which wordes with the manner of a singe them he this examinat learned of his father and hath made use of dyverse tymes though more frequently for these two yeares last paste when people have come to him this examinate to bless there freindes or cattel: And further this examinat confesseth that alwaies when he came to the partie ill affected, if the same needed to his blessinge, then he pronounced the wordes and praiers aforesaid in utteringe of which wordes and during all the tyme of his blessinge, he this examinat for all suche tyme hath alwaies beene suddenlie taken with sickness and lamenesse and that alwaies in the same manner that the man or beaste that hee blessed was troubled withall; And lastly this examinat saith that what he

hath blessed hath recovered and this examinat hath only received
Meale or cheese or comodities of the like nature but never did
take silver or anie other reward but such as before herein is Ac-
knowledged: And further confesseth not.[144]

2. *In hoc signum*

Young Jennet Device told our second charm to the court at
Lancaster. Her mother, Elizabeth, had taught the formula to her.
Its purpose was 'to get drinke'; she said that James,

> hath confessed to her that he by this power hath gotten drinke:
> and that within an houre after the saying the said Prayer, drinke
> hath come into the house after a very strange manner.[145]

The charm is this:

> Crucifixus hoc signum vitam Eternam. Amen.

In late latin 'crucifixus' by itself took the meaning: 'Christ
crucified'; it would be said while making the sign of the cross.
James, we recall, had 'marked himself to God' when he met the
angry hare.

'In this sign is eternal life', relates to the cross. It is a common
pre-Reformation liturgical formula. The word 'In' has been omitted
in the Latin.

3. *Steck, steck hell doore*

The third charm was recited to the court by nine-year-old Jennet
Device, no mean feat for it is thirty-one lines long. Roger Nowell
will have rehearsed his star-witness. James Device, it seems, had
dictated the words to Nowell, for James' name appears below them
and young Jennet said that her brother James had affirmed that this
'Prayer . . . would cure one bewitched'.

Edgar Peel and Pat Southern in *The Trials of the Lancashire Witches*
write about this charm: 'Whatever its origin this pathetic piece
seems so garbled that it is very doubtful if it had any meaning to
its users'.[146] We shall try to elucidate its meaning. Roger Nowell
recorded it like this:

A Charme

Upon Good-Friday, I will fast while I may
Untill I heare them knell
Our Lords owne Bell,
Lord in his messe
With his twelve Apostles good,
What hath he in his hand
Ligh in leath wand:
What hath he in his other hand?
Heavens doore key,
Open, open Heaven doore keyes,
Steck, steck hell doore.
Let Crizum child
Goe to it Mother mild,
What is yonder that casts a light so farrandly,
Mine owne deare Sonne that's naild to the Tree.
He is naild sore by the heart and hand,
And holy barne Panne,
Well is that man
That Fryday spell can
His Childe to learne;
A Crosse of Blew, and another of Red,
As good Lord was to the Roode.
Gabriel laid him downe to sleepe
Upon the ground of holy weepe:
Good Lord came walking by,
Sleep'st thou, wak'st thou *Gabriel*,
No Lord I am sted with sticke and stake,
That I can neither sleepe nor wake:
Rise up *Gabriel* and goe with me,
The stick nor the stake shall never deere thee.
Sweet Jesus our Lord, Amen.

James Device[147]

The Devices used this text as a charm, but its form is that of a religious drama. Fragmentary though it is, its imagery is consistent; it refers to those events which the Church recalls on Maundy Thursday and Good Friday. The Last Supper, the Garden of Gethsemane and the Crucifixion figure, though not in order, and there is a related theme, the Last Judgement, favourite subject of medieval frescoes.

A book published in 1612, the very year of the Pendle Witch-trials, prints part of this same text. Its author, John White, 'Minister of Godsword at Eccles' in Lancashire, entitled his book *The Way to the True Church wherein the Principle Motives persuading to Romanism are familiarly disputed.* White urges the Archbishop of York and the Bishop of Chester to establish a ministry of preachers to expound Protestant principles 'for what man is he whose heart trembles not to see simple people so farre seduced, that they know not how to pronounce or say their daily prayers.' An impatient Calvinist, White was horrified that medieval practices continued amongst people in Lancashire. Disdainfully, he gave examples to show 'the maner how the vulgar sort of people, addicted to Papistry, say their praiers: the which I have observed by living and conversing with them: and set down for no other purpose but to note the pitiful ignoranse and confusion whereinto the Church of Rome plungeth her children.' This prayer, he said, 'they call the white Pater Noster':

> White Pater noster, Saints Peters brother,
> What hast i'th t'one hand? White booke leaves.
> What hast i'th t'other hand? Heaven yate keys.
> Open heaven yates, and steike hell yates:
> And let every crysom child creepe to its owne mother:
> White Pater noster, Amen[148]

The White Pater Noster from Eccles must share a source with lines 6-13 of the Device's charm. In both St Peter holds the keys of heaven in his hand. The versions differ about what else Peter is holding. In Eccles they say, 'the white leaves of a book'; the Devices say, 'Ligh in leath wand'. 'Ligh' is modern 'lie': 'leath' could be 'lithe' and a 'wand' in northern usage was a flexible stick. If so, in Peter's hand 'lies a supple stick' either as a rod of office or as a bar with which to bolt hell's gate. An intriguing alternative would derive the last two words from Anglo-Saxon roots where Lið-won (or lith-won) means 'a little'. This would give a music-hall progression of question and answer:

> What's he got in the one hand?
> Not a lot.
> What's he got in the other hand?
> The key of Heaven's door.

St Peter was always represented as holding the keys of heaven. But iconography differed about what should be shown in his other hand. When the text was used in a church where there was a particular representation of Peter it would be sensible to adapt the words.

The vocabulary of the 'spell' is ancient, but exact; James learnt well and dictated with care. Roger Nowell recorded it scrupulously. 'Steck' from the early middle-english 'steken' means 'thrust' or 'stab', hence 'shut and fasten' a door with a pin or bolt. A 'steckle' was a 'bar of a door'.[149]

'Crizum' is 'chrisom', a white cloth given at baptism; so 'crizum child' came to mean a young child. In bills of mortality 'chrisom child' designated

A deathbed scene from *The Art of Dying*, a late mediaeval devotional work, shows images also included in James' 'Charm': St Peter holds the key of heaven, Christ hangs on the cross, an angel attends whilst demons flee.

young babes who could still be enwrapped in their baptism clothes. The use of chrisoms at baptism, though instructed in the *First Prayer Book* of Edward VI ('The Minister was to put upon [the child] his white vestment, commonly called the chrisome, and to say: Take this white vesture as a token of innocency . . .') was discontinued from 1552.

Some words of the charm were archaic by 1612; others remained in regional dialect. 'Farrandly' meant 'pleasantly' (it was used, by the dialect poet Tim Bobbin [J. Collier] as late as 1750: 'Yo cooms farrantly off'); 'Panne' is the skull or head; 'Barne' is obscure, unless cognate to Scottish 'bairn', a child; 'Learne' is 'teach', as in present Lancashire dialect; 'sted' is 'beset with [dangers]'; 'deere' means 'harm', and was used by Edmund Spenser. 'Messe' is the 'Mass', a word which in the English Church ceased to be the designation of

A Regnault primer shows the Seven Sorrows of Mary. James' 'Charm' similarly describes the crucifixion from Mary's perspective: 'Mine owne deare Sonne that's naild to the Tree'.

the Communion Service from the accession of Elizabeth. 'Roode' is the 'cross'.

The fragments of an ancient meaning seems then to be these. I will fast on Good Friday until I hear a bell tolling. This may be the consecration-bell at Mass on Easter Day, or it may be a bell that would be rung on Good Friday itself.[150] Jesus is at the Last Supper (called here a mass) with his twelve apostles, amongst whom is Peter holding the keys of heaven and the bar of the gate of hell. The crucifixion is then experienced from the perspective of Mary, the mother of Jesus.[151] This is consonant with late medieval devotion focused on the Sorrows of Mary evident in the thirteenth-century 'Stabat Mater' and many fifteenth-century Books of Hours. The 'light so farrandly' may, in a Marian sequence, have once referred to the light of angels at Jesus' birth, but here it is a stranger light that Mary sees, that which seems to shine from the crucified Jesus. Mary looks at his pierced heart and hand and at her son's head, probably because pierced with the crown of thorn. A person does well to spell out the meaning of that Good Friday to his son or daughter.

The next two lines seem fragmentary. The first suggests that above the rood-screen in church the crosses of the two malefactors were painted blue and red; the second, that Jesus was being taken to the Cross.

The name 'Gabriel' appears three times. Here James Device has faltered. If one substitutes the name 'Peter' these lines fit the events of the evening of Maundy Thursday when Christ and his disciples had left the supper-table (the 'messe' of line 4), for, while Jesus prayed in the Garden of Gethsemane, Peter, James and John slept until awakened by Jesus when soldiers with 'swords and staves' (compare: sticke and stake) came to arrest him.[152] The words have a double meaning, a metaphorical level of interpretation: a Christian sleeping in death will not be harmed by the stabbing of hell but will be awakened by Christ to the life of the resurrection. This conclusion happens to be appropriate for a charm—'the stick or the stabbing implement shall never harm you'.

Probably the name Gabriel had occurred in a preceding couplet, now lost, which spoke of the angel which appeared to Jesus as he agonised in prayer.[153]

'Sweet Jesus our Lord' was a common devotional ending; it ends another of the 'ignorant' Romish prayers which John White of Eccles deplored.

James Device may have considered the text to be but a venerable religious formula useful for his purpose. But what he dictated was no mumbo-jumbo. It made sense and antique words were faithfully remembered. Did he, or did one of his family, act in this religious drama in Newchurch on some more happy Good Friday? The chapel at Newchurch was part of a parish which long clung to medieval ways.

It turns out that the three 'charms' of these supposed witches are texts of unimpeachable Catholic orthodoxy. Had they been uttered by priests or within a church of the late medieval period, they would be unexceptional. The Devices' and Chattox's use of them was unusual only in that they were lay-people, they were outside a church setting, the reformation had occurred two generations past, and they were using these formulae to cure the bewitched, to get drink or to amend ale which had fermented badly.

We may be confident of the broad Christianity of those who uttered these formulae. Words impose an allegiance; these words are infused with Christian faith. No satanist would utter such charms.

Catholicism in Whalley Parish

WHEN Archbishop Grindal entered his Northern Province of York in 1570, he had been dismayed at the continuance of popular Catholicism. To Lord Cecil in London he wrote that 'this seemeth to be, as it were, another church, rather than a member of the rest'. He lamented that holy days and feasts were still celebrated, beads were told and 'they offer money, eggs etc at the burial of their dead.'[154]

In 1612 when the Puritan John White of Eccles characterised those who used the White Pater Noster as 'the vulgar sort of people, addicted to Papistry' he was not mistaken. 'And it cannot be answered,' he continued 'that these are the customs of a few simple people: for this I say is general throughout the country [i.e: Lancashire], the whole body of the common people popishly addicted, practically nothing else, untill it please God by the ministrie of his Gospel, to convert them.'[155]

Seventy years later John Webster of Clitheroe referred to the Catholic sympathies, the Popery, of those who resorted to witches

in the North of England, where ignorance, Popery, and superstition doth much abound, and where for the most part the common people, if they chance to have any sort of the Epilepsy, Palsie, Convulsions or the like, do presently perswade themselves that they are bewitched, fore-spoken, blasted, fairy-taken, or haunted with some evil spirit.[156]

The contemporaries of the Devices or Chattoxes understood that wise-men, wise-women and those that resorted to them had their milieu in conservative religion.

Those who lived on the slopes of Pendle Hill had reason for holding to the traditional faith. Newchurch was one of fifteen chapels-of-ease in the unwieldy parish of Whalley, which covered 180 square miles and had a population of about 10,000.[157] In Whalley parish in Elizabeth's reign religious conservatism had reached scandalous proportions.

The Vicar of Whalley, George Dobson was a covert Papist. He was denounced in 1561 by Bishop Pilkington of Durham who called him 'as evil a vicar as the worst'. Ten years later Dobson was 'detected for a naughty papist and that he keepeth and proclaimeth holy days abrogated and harboureth papists'. Dobson made no defence and, as punishment, had to read in his church a declaration about holy days. Peter Carter, the schoolmaster of Whalley, shared Dobson's persuasion, for in the same year Carter was 'privy with the roving priests'.[158]

In 1573 Dobson had to deny a charge that he had buried a recusant priest in the church late at night and two years later, in a case which was referred to the High Commission in York, the Vicar was accused of teaching that the 'Church of England is a defiled and spotted church'. At Easter he was said to have given to certain of his parishioners special 'consecrated hosts' saying that in them was salvation', but to have claimed that 'in the other there was nothing worthy of acceptance'. Dobson was in a paradoxical position: the vicar of his parish, he taught about Anglican worship:

> no man may come to it lawfully in time of divine service except he at his coming in heart exempt himself from this service and all that is partaker of it, and make his prayer by himself according to the doctrine of the Pope of Rome.[159]

Through legal confusion the prosecution at York failed, but parishioners at Whalley, amongst whom would be Nowell, were incensed. At the visitation of 1578 they complained again 'that their vicar hath lately been suspected of Popery,'[160] and that he had been lax in the provision of sermons for the dependent chapelries of the parish. That was not his only laxity; it was also alleged of this thinly disguised Catholic that he was

> a common drunkard, and such an ale-knight as the like is not in our parish, and in the night when most men be in their bed at their rest then he is in the ale-house with a company like to himself, but not one of them can match him in his ale house tricks, for he will, when he cannot discern black from blue, dance with a full cup on his head, far passing all the rest.[161]

What a fellow!

George Dobson finally 'resigned' in 1580, soon after Bishop Chadderton visited Whalley. Christopher Haigh pays an ironic tribute to George Dobson's service to Catholicism: 'Though he had served the Church of England for more than twenty years, Dobson's contribution to the survival of traditional religion was probably as great as that of any recusant priest.'

Priests serving at Newchurch would be under Dobson's direction. So it happened that the parish where Chattox and Demdike lived remained virtually Catholic until those two were almost fifty years old.

In the years that followed Dobson's removal recusancy and Catholic sympathy continued strongly in the area. Priests of the English Mission frequented Lancashire. Two members of the Nutter family from Pendle were Catholic priests secretly in England in the 1580s. John Nutter, born at Reedley Hollow, an Oxford graduate, was quickly apprehended; on 12 February 1583 at Tyburn he was hanged, disembowelled and quartered. His brother Robert, who assumed the surname Rowley, was at times committed to the Tower and to Wisbeach Castle. In the spring of 1600 he escaped to Lancashire, but was recaptured and executed at Lancaster on 26 July, 1600. A nephew of theirs, Ellis Nutter, despite his uncles' fates, was ordained priest in 1601 and by 1603 was in the English College in Rome training for the English Mission.[162] It is not known how closely related these Catholic priests were to the husband of Alice Nutter, the 'rich woman' with a 'great estate' who made no defence when charged with witchcraft.

Whalley Church. The box pew on the right belonged to Roger Nowell.

Demdike and the Devices were at home in Catholic

culture. When Demdike's child had been in danger she cried 'Jesus save my child'. James, feeling threatened, 'marked himself to God'. James attended Communion. He held fervently that 'his Soule was not his to give, but was his Saviour Jesus Christs'. Of the charms they used, one offered the protection of the Trinity; one that of the sign of the cross; the third was a recitation about the Passion of Christ.

The evidence, however, falls short of proving that the Malkin Tower meeting was called to celebrate a Catholic liturgy on Good Friday, intriguing though that notion is because, fortuitously, an exactly appropriate text for worship is contained in the long 'Charm'.

Grindletonianism

THE 'Christening of the Spirit of Alizon' planned for Good Friday at Malkin Tower, if correctly given a religious interpretation, does not echo the practice of Catholics, but rather that of Seeker religious radicals. We have established the traditional Catholicism of the Devices and Chattox. Is it conceivable that they may also have been influenced by the Seekers?

A centre of radical Christian enthusiasm lay no further away than the slopes beyond the Ribble at the northern side of Pendle. There lay Grindleton, a village whose name was reviled by both Calvinists and Anglicans as a by-word for dangerous indiscipline and anti-nomianism.[163] Neither presbyterian order, nor the hierarchical order of episcopacy would satisfy the free spirit of Grindleton.

Three years after Jennet's trial Roger Brearley was to become Curate of Grindleton, but the Grindletonianism of which he became the exemplar 'probably antedates him', writes Christopher Hill. 'Familism probably got hold here [in the extreme north-west of Yorkshire] in Elizabeth's reign and interest in it extended over most of the area'.[164] This Familism was a species of Seeker belief which emphasised the friendship and economic sharing of those filled with the Spirit.

In Grindleton we find ourselves within the thought-world of a 'Christening of the Spirit'.

We may gain a flavour of Grindletonian beliefs from some of the fifty charges brought against Brearley 'and his congregation' in 1617. For Brearley, as for Quakers a generation later, spiritual enlightenment given by the Spirit within had more authority even than the word of the Bible: 'A motion rising from the spirit is more to be rested in than the Word itself' . . . 'It is a sin to believe the Word . . . without a motion of the spirit'.

For Grindletonians, a person imbued with the Spirit needed

no ordination; his words were self-authenticating: 'A man having the spirit may read, pray or preach without any other calling whatsoever'.

Roger Brearley taught, it was said, that those who were spirit-inspired, could do no evil; they had achieved prelapsarian perfection: 'The child of God in the power of grace doth perform every duty so well, that to ask pardon for failing in matter or manner is a sin' . . . 'The Christian assured can never commit a gross sin'. For those in the Spirit, heaven seemed to have come to earth: 'They cannot have more joy in heaven than they have in this life by the spirit'.

Brearley sermons collected in *A Bundle of Soul-convincing, Directing and Comforting Truths* have passages of tender beauty. Religion for him was not something intellectual, mere 'heady opinions', but involved the heart and the life. 'No one,' he says 'ever knows Christ without walking on foot with Him in His death and miserie'. A 'forensic Christianity', one of 'the conceit of knowledge', he says in a lovely image, is as though we should 'know' a country by reading books and studying maps about it 'without ever going there'. He had shaken himself free from creeds and rituals: 'Bread and wine are silly things where the heart is not led further'. Tender-hearted towards the poor, he was happy himself to embrace voluntary simplicity: 'Brown bread and the gospel is good fare'.[165]

John Webster of Clitheroe, whose *The Displaying of Supposed Witchcraft* we have quoted, knew Grindleton. Its liberating theology he shared when in London with his friends John Everard and William Erbery and through them and others the influence of this vibrant congregation spread far beyond the valley of the Ribble. Governor Winthrop in Massachusetts in the 1630s attributed the heresies of Mistress Anne Hutchinson to Grindletonianism. Christopher Hill writes: 'Grindleton, lying at the foot of Pendle Hill, George Fox's Mount of Vision, should perhaps have a more prominent place on maps of seventeenth-century England than is usually accorded to it'.[166]

Further study is needed of the Grindletonian and Seeker influences in Pendle and Craven before the coming of Brearley in 1615. The breakdown of the ecclesiastical discipline of the parish churches made those parts a fertile seedbed for Seeker ideas. Amongst the Devices and their friends it seems not unlikely that some radical

Seeker ideas could co-exist with elements of religious conservatism. Congenial to the Devices would be the teaching that they as lay people, if inspired by the Spirit, could exercise leadership in spiritual matters.

We can speak only in probabilities, but it seems not unlikely that the intended 'Christening of the Spirit' at Malkin Tower was to have been an initiation of Alizon into a lay group of Christians influenced by the familism of Grindleton, but still holding to many of the pieties of Catholicism.

Charmers and William Perkins

THE analysis of their charms helped us to see the Pendle witches in the context of others who provided useful spells for villagers in need. There were many wise-men and wise-women.

> Let a mans childe, friend, or cattell be taken with some sore sicknes, or strangely tormented with some rare and unknown disease, the first thing he doth, is to bethink himselfe and inquire after some wise-man or wise-woman, & thither he sends and goes for help.

These were the words of a hostile commentator, the theologian, William Perkins, published in 1608. Charmers he tells us, were by no means unusual:

> Alas! . . . Charming is in as great request as Physicke, and Charmers more sought unto than Physicians in time of need. There be charmes for all conditions and ages of men, for divers kinds of creatures, yea for every disease; as for head-ach, tooth-ach, stitches, and such like.[167]

Those who consulted wise-men and -women were not only the poor. In 1580 Margaret, the separated wife of Henry, Earl of Derby, the grand-niece of King Henry VIII, sought relief from rheumatic pains in the cures of 'wizards and cunning men'. She wrote to Sir Francis Walsingham to complain that the charges against her of meddling in black magic 'doth more vex my heart and spirit than any infirmityes have done my body.[168]

In the seventy-three years between 1567 and 1640 some 117 presentments for charming, witchcraft and sorcery came before the church courts in York. Serious cases of witchcraft would have been dealt with by the assizes. In the church court, eighteen of the presentments involved the lifting of spells from or the casting of spells upon animals, and nineteen from or upon humans; thirteen involved trying to find lost or stolen goods by witchcraft, and eighteen involved the telling of fortunes by divination.[169] For instance, Thomas Horrocks, Vicar of Broughton in Craven, in the 1570s was alleged to be a wizard; he was presented for unlicensed preaching, for immorality, for exorcism and for claiming to recover stolen goods through witchcraft.

Reginald Scot in 1584 wrote that every parish had its miracle-worker, and some had seventeen or eighteen. Robert Burton concurred; there was a cunning man in every village, he said. In England, it seems there were as many wise-men and -women as there were parochial clergy, and perhaps many more.[170]

Chattox, Demdike and their families were village wizards of this sort. They offered to the community about them the healing of people and animals. Their medicine was probably based on genuine herb lore, and perhaps no less effective than the purgings and blood-lettings of official medicine. Their service would include the finding of lost goods and fortune-telling and the making of love-potions. They would also seek to harm people by means of their picture-magic and curses. The consecrated host and teeth from human skulls were employed by them as amulets or ingredients.

Other Lancashire cases reveal similar practitioners. In 1582 Alexander Atherton, a yeoman, claimed before the Star Chamber that magic had been used to make him fall in love with Elizabeth Winstanley. In 1634 in Ormskirk it was alleged that a wizard John Garnet had divined that the body of a missing man would be found in certain marl-pits in Up-Holland.[171]

Parliamentary statutes imposed severe penalties on practitioners of magic. Despite this there had been wide tolerance for the activities of the charmers. Bishop Latimer in 1552 stated in a sermon:

> A great many of us, when we be in trouble, or sickness, or lose anything, we run hither and thither to witches, or sorcerers, whom we call wise-men . . . seeking aid and comfort at their hands.[172]

In the early seventeenth century, however, local tolerance was challenged by an aggressive Protestantism.

Amongst the gentry of the Blackburn Hundred, Roger Nowell was a leader of such Protestantism. On his study desk at Read would be William Perkins' book *A Discourse of the Damned Art of Witchcraft*. Perkins, whose works presented a systematic Calvinism in clear and persuasive language, was the most eloquent of the

Cambridge Puritans. His teaching at the University produced a school of ardent followers which made him 'the dominant influence in Puritan thought for the forty years after his death'. In the 1590s William Perkins lectured on Witchcraft in Emmanuel College. Published posthumously in 1608, this *Discourse . . .*, deceptively urbane in style, expressed within the cool idiom of Calvinism the witchcraft ideas which had a century earlier been engendered by Catholic Inquisitors in the Holy Roman Empire. Perkins undermined English tolerance of village witchcraft.[173]

To understand Roger Nowell and the tragedy he caused we must take note of William Perkins.

'Witchcraft is a rife and common sinne in these our daies',[174] preached the Cambridge theologian. Witchcraft phenomena to Perkins was no illusion. The devil could appear in 'the likeness of man or some other creature' and is able to 'utter a voyce in plaine words and speach, answerable to man's understanding'. Roger Nowell, having read this, was to produce examples. Similarly, when Nowell wrote of the giving of the soul to an imp and of the devil's promise of assistance, he was following exactly in the pattern that Perkins had led him to expect:

> The ground of all Witchcraft is a league or covenant made betweene the Witch and the Devill; wherein they doe mutually bind themselves each to other . . . The devill . . . for his part promiseth to be ready to his vassals command, to appeare at any time in the likeness of any creature, to consult with him, to aide and helpe him in any thing he shall take in hand, for the procuring of pleasures, honour, wealth or preferment, to goe for him, to carry him whether he will, in a word, to do for him whatsoever he shall command.[175]

Perkins distinguishes between two sorts of witches, the 'bad witch' and the 'good witch'. For the activities of the good witch we may think of the healings that Demdike was called out to perform (though she and her family engaged also in malign magic; they crossed Perkins' categories). Perkins describes first the harm, deaths and diseases caused by the 'bad witch', and then he writes of the 'good witch' in these terms:

> The Good witch is he or shee that by consent in a league with the devill, doth use his help, for the doing of good onely. This cannot hurt, torment, curse or kill, but onely heal and cure the

A DISCOVRSE

OF THE DAM-

NED ART OF WITCH-CRAFT; SO FARRE FORTH

as it is reuealed in the Scriptures, and *manifest by true expe-rience.*

FRAMED AND DELIVERED *by* M. WILLIAM PERKINS, *in his* ordi-narie course of Preaching, and now published *by* THO. PICKERING *Batchelour of* Diuinitie, and Minister of Fin-*shingfield in Essex.*

WHEREVNTO IS ADIOYNED a twofold Table; one of the order and Heades *of the Treatise;* another of the texts of Scripture explaned, or vindicated from the cor-*rupt interpretation of the* Aduersarie.

PRINTED BY CANTREL LEGGE, Printer to the Vniuersitie of *Cambridge.*

1 6 0 8.

William Perkins was the leader of Cambridge Puritan theologians. In his *Discourse,* published posthumously, he argued that witches who do good, even more than those who do bad, deserve to be hanged.

hurts inflicted upon men and cattell, by badde Witches. For as they [the bad witches] can doe no good, but onely hurt; so this can doe no hurt, but good onely . . . And the good witch is commonly tearmed the *unbinding witch*.[176]

Perkins' argument now produces its awful surprise. The good witch, the village charmer, is not to be treated more leniently than the bad witch, he asserts. The very reverse. 'Of the two, the more horrible and detestable Monster is the Good Witch'. This is because good witches, 'being commonly called Wisemen or Wise-women' are more popular than bad witches. The favour that good witches win is due to the greater subtlety of their devilish activities. For instance, Perkins writes, a person resorting to a good witch to beg a cure for a friend who has been forespoken by a bad witch,

first tells him the state of the sicke man: the witch being then certified of the disease, prescribeth either Charmes of words to be used over him, or other such counterfeit means, . . . The means are received, applied and used, the sick partie accordingly recovereth, and the conclusion of it all is, the usual acclamation: oh happie is the day, that ever I met with such a man or woman to helpe me! Here observe, that both have a stroke in this action: the bad witch hurt him, the good healed him; but the truth is, the latter hath done him a thousand fold more harm than the former. For the one did onely hurt the bodie, but the devill by means of the other, though he hath left the bodie in good plight, yet he hath laid fast hold on the soul, and by curing the body, hath killed that.[177]

The last words of Perkins' *Discourse* emphasise that all wise-men or -women, good or bad, merit the death sentence. Charmers, and others who 'doe any thing (knowing what they doe) which cannot be effected by nature or art', must be put to death, because of the covenant they have made with Satan:

Men doe commonly hate and spit at the damnifying Sorcerer, as unworthie to live among them, whereas the other is so deare unto them that they hold themselves and their countrey blessed that have him among them, they flie unto him in necessitie, they depend upon him as their god, and by this meanes, thousands are carried away to their final confusion. Death therefore is the just and deserved portion of the good witch.[178]

We have noted the abundance of charmers in England; William

Perkins, a theologian admired for his wisdom and goodness, was advocating a massive bloodbath. Roger Nowell, from a family which made an outstanding contribution to Elizabethan protestantism, found in Perkins' writings a guide. Here was authoritative advice which he could give to his fellow gentry, to Thomas Lister, to Thomas Heber and to Robert Holden. If 'good witches' ought to die, how much more ought Jennet Preston and Demdike, Chattox and their families.

Roger Nowell's
Protestant Heritage

R OGER NOWELL was about sixty years old in 1612. He had married Katherine, daughter of John Murton Esq, and in 1591 had succeeded his father to the Read estate. In 1610 he was High Sheriff of Lancashire. He died in 1623.

Roger Nowell's grandfather, yet another Roger, had been 'a very irreligious man, and never attended any public worship', yet this grandfather's two half-brothers, great-uncles to our Roger Nowell, were amongst the most eminent divines of their day. Both had been born at Read. These great-uncles brought the Nowell household into contact with the universities, with London and with Protestant thinking.

Uncle Alexander Nowell, born in 1507, had been the Dean of St Paul's Cathedral in London nearly throughout the reign of Elizabeth.

At Brasenose in his youth, Alexander Nowell had shared accommodation with John Foxe, the martyrologist. Both were fired by the theology of Calvin. During Mary's reign Alexander sought the safety of exile first in Strasbourg and then in Frankfurt, where he engaged in the religious disputes of the exiled communities. Queen Elizabeth on her accession shrewdly appointed Nowell to the Deanery of St Paul's, from whence he helped to shape the Elizabethan Settlement and to reconcile Protestants to it. Alexander's lasting memorial is the catechism, memorised by generations of children. 'The good old man', Izaak Walton calls Alexander, who made 'the good, plain, unperplexed catechism printed in our good old service-book'. Childless himself, Alexander held dear the home and county of his birth. In 1578 he became a fellow of the College at Manchester, he endowed Middleton School, and he received

Alexander Nowell, 1507–1602, Dean of St Pauls and kinsman of
Roger Nowell of Read.

from Elizabeth licence of absence from his deanery in 1580 so that
he might inquire into the state of religion in Lancashire. The
conservatism of Lancashire religion concerned the government;
Nowell's sane protestantism, high standing and family connections

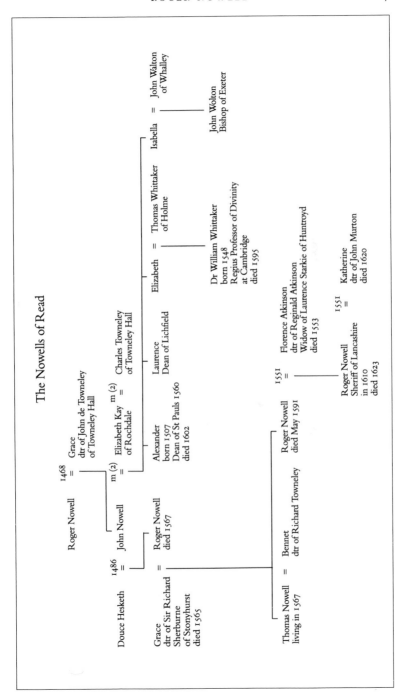

The Nowells of Read

Roger Nowell $=$ 1468 Grace
dtr of John de Towneley
of Towneley Hall

m (2) $=$ Elizabeth Kay m (2) $=$ Charles Towneley
of Rochdale of Towneley Hall

Douce Hesketh $=$ 1486 John Nowell

Grace $=$ Roger Nowell
dtr of Sir Richard died 1567
Sherburne
of Stonyhurst
died 1565

Alexander
born 1507
Dean of St Pauls 1560
died 1602

Laurence
Dean of Lichfield

Elizabeth $=$ Thomas Whittaker
of Holme

Isabella $=$ John Walton
of Whalley

Dr William Whittaker
born 1548
Regius Professor of Divinity
at Cambridge
died 1595

John Wolton
Bishop of Exeter

Thomas Nowell $=$ Bennet
living in 1567 dtr of Richard Towneley

Roger Nowell
died May 1591

1551 $=$ Florence Atkinson
dtr of Reginald Atkinson
Widow of Laurence Starkie of Huntroyd
died 1553

Roger Nowell
Sheriff of Lancashire
in 1610
died 1623

1551 $=$ Katherine
dtr of John Murton
died 1620

would make him a good ambassador. In fact Alexander's half-brother John Towneley was one of the county's leading recusants, frequently imprisoned; in 1584 Nowell interceded for him. Alexander Nowell, eloquent and judicious, retained his faculties and energy into old age; in his eighty-ninth year was elected President of Brasenose College, Oxford. He died in 1602.[179]

Laurence, Alexander's younger brother, similarly sought exile during Mary's reign. As a young man he had been an even more zealous Calvinist. Appointed Dean of Lichfield in 1559, he devoted himself to antiquarianism, became an authority on the Anglo-Saxon language, and compiled the first lexicon of that tongue.[180]

The careers of two nephews of Alexander and Laurence, second cousins of Roger, will also have been watched with sympathetic interest in Read Hall. Dr William Whittaker, having been a protégé of Alexander, had been Master of St John's College, Cambridge and had held the office of Regius Professor of Divinity from 1580 until his death in 1595. A divine of inflexible Calvinism, Whittaker was a strong anti-Romanist and, together with his colleague William Perkins, held that the Pope was anti-Christ. The other nephew in this remarkable ecclesiastical family was John Wolton, also a former exile and then from 1579 to 1594 Bishop of Exeter.

Thus it was that Protestant influence was strong in the Nowell household. As Roger Nowell sat in the family box-pew in Whalley Church and mused on his family's sacrifices for the reformed faith, he must often have seethed at the antics of the Vicar, George Dobson.

The Marian exiles in Geneva, Basle, Strasbourg and Frankfurt imbibed the developed witchcraft doctrines which Calvinism had assimilated from Catholicism. When the exiles returned on the accession of Elizabeth, they helped to disseminate these ideas within England, and influenced the newly assembled Convocation in 1563 to plead that 'there be some penal yea capital pains for witches and sorcerers.' Strasbourg, the former home of Erasmus, had been an island of sanity within the witch-crazed district of Alsace, but even so Alexander and Laurence, when visiting Read, may have conveyed to their young grand-nephew something of the fervour with which the church on the continent persecuted witchcraft.

The 7. in Lancashire

ROGER NOWELL'S paternal relations disposed him towards Puritanism. His late mother's Starkie relations skewed this interest particularly towards witchcraft. Roger Nowell's mother had been the widow of Laurence Starkie when she married Roger's father in 1551. More recently her Starkie grandson had been involved in a cause celèbre.[181]

Nicholas Starkie was half-nephew to Roger Nowell; he was son and heir of Roger's half-brother Edmond Starkie. In 1578 Nicholas Starkie had married Anne, the daughter of John Parr of Cleworth near Leigh in Lancashire. It happened that Anne inherited Cleworth before Nicholas Starkie came into the Starkie inheritance of Huntroyd, so at Cleworth they lived for a while with their young family.[182] The turmoils of that Starkie household became known even in London; the King discussed them; playwrights wrote of them.

The year was 1595, just a dozen years before the death of Thomas Lister; sixteen years before the trials of the Lancashire witches. Roger Nowell would be forty-four-years old. In that year Nicholas Starkie's two children, John and Ann, aged about twelve and ten, began to have convulsions. Their father, alarmed, spent £200, a vast sum, on the fees of doctors, but the children were not cured. He consulted a Catholic priest; that priest however claimed not to have his book of exorcisms. Starkie, convinced that the youngsters were bewitched, then engaged a wise-man, Edmund Hartley, to join the household at an annual salary of £2. Hartley's task was to calm the two devil-possessed children, and he had some success for about a year and a half, using 'certayne popish charmes and herbes'.

But then things fell awry. Hartley believed he was underpaid, the fits became more furious, and three other girls being brought up in the Starkie's house also became possessed. So did Jane Ashton,

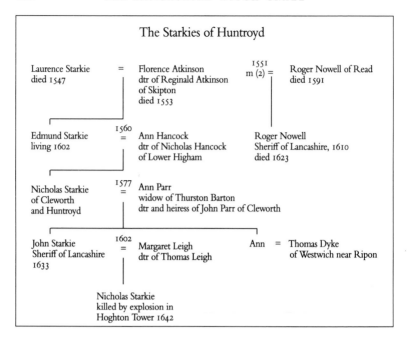

a maid aged thirty and Margret Byrom, a thirty-three-year old spinster, a relation of the family. The house became bedlam. The children and the older two romped, screamed, howled, and held their breath until they were blue in the face. One discerns method in their madness. They delighted in 'filthy and unsavourie speeches', especially during sermons in church, so that they scarce were taken there for two years. When Scripture was read or anyone prayed they fell into fits, though at other times they might be quite well. John Starkie, approaching fourteen years old now, would deliver pious discourses for hours, denouncing 'strange sinnes' and warning of the fearful judgements of God.

The Starkies believed that the seven were possessed by demons; we can see indications of sexual hysteria. Hartley, it was claimed, had bewitched them. His method of bewitching, the girls told, was by kissing them. He had also kissed the maid and the thirty-three-year old, and had lain upon her bed. Mistress Starkie, on one occasion, asked them 'how they were handled'. They all replied, 'that an angell like a dove was come from God, and that they must follow him to heaven, which way so ever he would lead them,

CLEWORTH HALL, TILDESLEY.

LANCASHIRE

destroyed 1805.

Cleworth Hall, Tyldesley, near Leigh.
Between 1594 and 1597 this was the scene of 'the strange and grievous vexation
by the devil of 7 persons in Lancashire'.

though it were never so little a hole'. One of the girls made a hole
in the wall under her bed through which her 'lad', as she called
her demon, might enter.

In the Assizes in March 1597 Edmund Hartley was tried for
witchcraft. Despite all the Starkie's stories the court could 'find no
lawe to hange him'. Nicholas Starkie then recalled before the Court
that once, whilst visiting his father in Whalley, Hartley, who was
with him, had entered a little wood, had invited him to tread out
on the ground a magic circle 'the compass of a yard and a half with
many crosses and partitions', and had uttered words of a short spell.
The jury were convinced. Hartley was condemned to death. The
rope broke at the execution and Hartley, unexpectedly alive, 'peni-
tentlie confessed'. He was then hanged successfully.

Meanwhile Nicholas Starkie, his children still beset by fits, had
consulted the famed master of the occult arts, Dr John Dee, then

Above: From *Newes from Scotland*, 1591, the account of witchcraft of Dr Fian and his accomplices. Left: From the frontispiece of Christopher Marlowe's *Dr Faustus*, 1604, edition of 1636.

The drawing of circles, for which Edmund Hartley was convicted, was a technique of astrology and necromancy.

Warden of Manchester College. Dee advised him to seek out godly preachers who might treat the children with fasting and prayer. Two Puritan ministers, John Darrel from Ashby-de-la-Zouche and George More from Caulk in Derbyshire, having heard about the need during a Calvinist 'exercise', travelled to Cleworth. Darrel and More each later wrote accounts of the whole Starkie affair and told how the country-house drama was brought by them to a strange climax.[183] After a night in prayer, Darrel assembled the whole household. Armed with the word of Scripture, he and More confronted the demons. The seven possessed bellowed, blasphemed and convulsed, while the godly ministers disputed for hours with the powers of darkness. Eventually all lay unconscious, then one after another arose freed from their possession; they convulsed no more and continued thereafter in good health, except for the maid, Jane Ashton, who relapsed and went to live with a Catholic uncle.

A TRVE NARRATION

OF THE STRANGE AND GREVOVS VEXATION

BY THE DEVIL, OF 7. PERSONS IN LANCA-
SHIRE, AND VVILLIAM SOMERS
OF NOTTINGHAM.

*WHEREIN THE DOCTRINE OF POSSESSION AND
DISPOSSESSION OF DEMONIAKES OVT*
of the word of God is particularly applyed
vnto *Somers,* and the reſt of the
perſons controuerted: togea-
ther with the vſe we are to
make of theſe workes
of God.

BY IOHN DARRELL, MINISTER,
of the word of God.

*He that is not with me, is againſt me: and he that ga-
thereth not with me, ſcattereth. Math.12.30.*

PRINTED 1600.

John Darrel's account of his 'exorcism' of the Starkie household. In 1598 Darrel
was imprisoned by the High Commission and 'condemned for a counterfeyte'.

This family history alone would have stirred Roger Nowell's interest. But the Cleworth story became embroiled in wider controversies, for in 1598 John Darrel, the exorcist, was accused of a series of fraudulent exorcisms. In a show trial he was brought before the High Commission itself charged with being an imposter who had trained his patients to simulate possession so that he might pretend to cure them. Those sitting in judgement included the Archbishop of Canterbury, the Bishop of London, and the two Lord Chief Justices. Darrel was condemned; he 'was, by the full agreement of the whole court, condemned for a counterfeyte'. He and George More, his companion, 'who took upon him to justifie the said Darrell, and had otherwise greatlie misbehaved himself', were 'deposed from the Ministery, and committed to close prison'.

Within a year Darrel, More and several others of the Puritan persuasion had published at least ten books and pamphlets on the various charges against Darrel. Amongst them George More published in 1600 *A True Discourse concerning the Certaine Possession and Dispossession of 7 Persons in one familie in Lancashire*. On the other side, Samuel Harsnett, the chaplain to Bancroft, Bishop of London, published in 1599 the damning evidence before the court; his book was entitled *A Discovery of the Fraudulent Practises of John Darrel*.

Because of the influence of these controversies on the Lancashire and Yorkshire trials, we should consider Darrel's curious career in more detail.

23

Little Darrel's Tricks

DARREL was in his mid thirties, a Cambridge graduate and a preaching minister whom even his detractors agreed was otherwise morally exemplary. He had been involved in two supposed exorcisms before going to Cleworth. In 1586 he had purported to dispossess a certain Katherine Wright who lived near Blackwell in Derbyshire. When Darrel brought before the magistrates a woman whom he accused of bewitching Katherine, the justices, unimpressed, acquitted the one charged and threatened Darrel himself with imprisonment. Before the High Commission in 1598 Katherine Wright was to admit that Darrel had instructed her to simulate trances, to answer in a strange voice, and to say that the devil within her bore the name of Middlecub.[184]

About Darrel's 'exorcism' of Thomas Darling, 'The Boy of Burton', we have much information, for a supporter of Darrel, Jesse Bee of Burton-on-Trent, wrote his account too.[185] Darling had been thirteen in 1596. A clever lad who later went to Oxford, he was when young deeply pious and was impressed by a national leader of Puritan extremism, Arthur Hildersham, incumbent of Ashby-de-la-Zouche. Thomas Darling convulsed, vomited strangely, and purported to see visions of green angels and of a green cat. Hildersham visited him, as did Darrel. Darling accused a sixty-year-old woman, Alice Gooderidge, of bewitching him; she was imprisoned and died in custody. Most extraordinary were the conversations between angels and devils, or devil with devil, that, like a ventriloquist, Darling uttered while in his trances. They were dramatic *tours de force*, and rich in theological content. Opinions differed as to whether he was inspired by the devil or by God. Darling was later to testify before the High Commission that Darrel had coached him in his feigned possession, and then had pretended to dispossess him. Shortly after, Darling retracted this testimony.

After creating a stir by this 'exorcism' in Burton-on-Trent, Darrel went to the Starkies. No allegations were made at the time that the healing at the Starkie home had been feigned by Darrel, though in 1677 John Webster of Clitheroe remarked that Darrel's account of it was 'full of untruths, impossibilities, absurdities and contradiction.'[186]

From Lancashire Darrel had gone to Nottingham where he was engaged as a preacher in the parish church. There lived William Sommers, a musician's apprentice aged about twenty.

Sommers suffered from contortions during which, it was said, a lump about the size of an egg ran about his body. Crowds would gather in Nottingham and before them, possessed, Sommers would at times vomit extraordinarily and act with gross obscenity.[187] In front of these audiences Darrel dispossessed Sommers, an act several times renewed as Sommers would relapse. The interest in Nottingham was enormous. People flocked to hear Darrel preach, though the Vicar complained 'they could hear of nothing in his sermons, but of the Devil'. Sommers then was used by Darrel to identify witches; Darrel thereby procured the imprisonment of several women. However one lady so accused happened to be the relative of an Alderman of the city, who with his friends retaliated. William Sommers was placed in an institution. The Mayor and Aldermen went to interrogate him there and to them Sommers confessed to collusion with Darrel in a complex imposture. Sommers showed how he had simulated his convulsions, and, to order, frothed at the mouth. Later Sommers was to retract and then again to renew this confession. Nottingham meanwhile was polarised in controversy. John Darrel, accused of masterminding all these deceits, was, as we have seen, tried by the High Commission. Before that court Sommers testified that Darrel had begun to coach him as early as 1592, had sent him to Burton-on-Trent to learn from the dissembling of Thomas Darling, and had continued to rehearse his performances in Nottingham.

Darrel's imprisonment by no means ended the controversies. Arthur Hildersham and several other notable Puritan clergy had assisted Darrel in his dispossessions. Here was an issue of faith. Contemporaries were quick to see the trial as an important struggle for ascendency between the Calvinists and the liberal 'Lutheran' party that rejected predestination. Bishop Bancroft of London, shortly to be Archbishop, and his chaplain, Samuel Harsnett (later to be Archbishop of York) represented the rational, very Anglican, position of the latter.

Samuel Harsnett, this bishop's chaplain, engaged in controversy about witchcraft on two fronts, with the Catholics and with the Puritans.[188] In the one direction he exposed the deceptions of the Jesuit William Weston and eleven other Catholic priests who had purported in 1585 to exorcise six demoniacs in Denham, Buckinghamshire. In the other direction he refuted the claims of Darrel and his Puritan supporters. In his view, just as Catholics were using feigned exorcisms to give spurious authority to the mass, to relics, or to the old liturgy, so the Puritans by their pretended exorcisms aimed to display the power of the word of Scripture truly preached by themselves alone. Harsnett was right in this assessment. George More in his account of the Starkie case reveals his awareness of the political dimension:

> If the Church of England have this power to cast out devils, then the Church of Rome is a false church; for there can be but one true church, the principal mark wherof (as they say) is to work miracles, and of them this is the greatest, namely to cast out devils.

Harsnett, the future Archbishop, cool and intelligent, just did not believe in magical or devilish agencies. The 'learneder and sounder sort' denied, he said, that possession could be caused by witchcraft; he warned against accepting witches confessions; and he gave 'melancholia' as a psychological explanation of witchcraft phenomena. For their part the Puritans believed that the Bishops of Canterbury and London hated those who 'desire reform of the church, among whom they accompt M. Dor. [Darrel] and M. Moore'.[189] This was true enough; the bishops did not wish to promote the Puritan agenda.

So it was that to believe in witchcraft, to believe in the reality of possession and of exorcism, had become a shibboleth for Calvinism and the emergent Puritanism. The liberal 'Lutheran' party, later to be designated as Arminians, could contrariwise be identified by scepticism about witchcraft. The issue had become political, and would not subside. It gained momentum from the ideological struggle between Puritans and Arminians in the early seventeenth-century church and state. While views were polarising, the Puritans chose to publish posthumously in 1608 William Perkins' lectures on witchcraft.

For the Starkie family the publicity of the debate must have been unwelcome. In Ben Jonson's play *The Divell is an Asse* performed in 1616, twenty years after the Starkie drama began, the main character in the burlesque is persuaded to simulate possession and to accuse his wife of having bewitched him; his friends advise him to copy the impostures taught by Darrel:

> Did you ne'er read, Sir, little Darrels tricks,
> With the boy o' Burton, and the 7. in Lancashire
> Sommers at Nottingham? All these do teach it,
> And wee'll give out, Sir, that your wife has bewitched you.[190]

By 1612 the Starkie family were living at Huntroyd as near neighbours of their kinsman, Roger Nowell. Nowell, by discovering witches in 1612 aligned himself with the Starkies amidst the still current debates. Just as Nicholas Starkie had contrived the execution of Hartley, so Nowell procured the deaths of the witches of Pendle and, through influence on Lister, of Jennet Preston. Just as Hartley had used 'certayne popish charmes and herbes', so Nowell's victims had recited charms from old Catholic liturgies. Just as Puritan leaders had exorcised the Starkie children, so Nowell coordinated the Puritan gentry to rid his area of witchcraft. Anti-Catholicism was a sub-text at the trial in 1597; so it was too in 1612. Above all Nowell was clearly asserting, as had Darrel, More, and Hildersham and those of Puritan temper, that he believed that witchcraft was for real.

John Darrel was a role-model to inspire Roger Nowell's pursuit of witches.

Thomas Lister
and the Guilt of Schism

I N Craven and Pendle, and down the Valley of the Ribble many of the gentry remained Catholic. Towneleys, Southworths, Sherburns, Tempests paid heavy fines, built priest-holes, sent their sons to Douai, and entertained priests of the illegal Catholic Missions. Thomas Lister junior however was a Protestant, as were the Hebers, the Nowells, the Asshetons of Whalley, and those of Downham.

The will Lister junior was constrained to make in 1619 is prefaced in Protestant fashion:

> In the name of God amen: I Thomas Lister of Arnolesbiginge in the Countie of York Esquire sick in bodie but whole in mind Praised be Almightie God doe make my last will and testament in manner and form followinge First I give and bequeath my Soul to almighty god my maker trustinge by the meritt of his Sonne Jesus Christ to be partaker of his heavenlie kingdome . . .[191]

But the Protestantism of Thomas Lister junior cannot have been without anguish, for his grandmother was, or had been, a Catholic recusant.

The grandmother of Thomas Lister junior, mother of Thomas Lister senior, was Alice, daughter of Sir Richard Hoghton. She was still alive at the time of Jennet Preston's trial and was living at Newsholme with her second husband, William Pratt. Thirty five years before, in 1577, she, 'Alice Lyster, wief of Thomas Lyster, gent, of Gisburne in Craven', had been reported with a few score others by Archbishop Sandys of York to the Privy Council as a Catholic. Alice's fine for her recusancy was then being paid by 'her husband, 20£ per annum in lands.'[192]

To be a Catholic involved commitment to sacrifice. If political alliances shifted or if there was some alarm in London, extreme

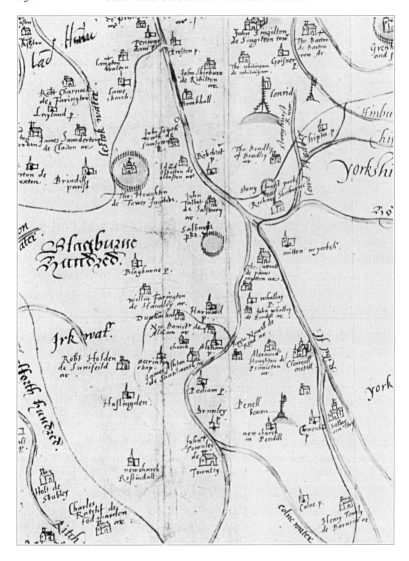

The sketch map drawn for Elizabeth I's minister William Cecil, Lord Burghley,
especially locates the homes of those gentry whose Catholic sympathies might
constitute a threat. Those who enter our story are John Townley de Townley,
Henry Townly de Barnside, Nic Banister de Altham, Robt Holden de Sunifeild,
Richard Shirburne of Stony hurst park, Tho: Houghton de Tower and John
Southworth de Samsbury. West is to the top of the map, with the River Ribble
(*Ribil fl:*) flowing towards it. Pendle Hill (*Penell*) with its beacon can be seen
near to the bottom right.

horror might erupt, tearing apart the securities of the life of pro-
vincial gentry. In the letter of Archbishop Sandys, one sees near
the name of Alice Lister the name of Margaret Clitheroe, wife of
a butcher in York. In 1586 Margaret Clitheroe refused to plead to
the charge of harbouring priests. She was about thirty years old and
pregnant. Her torture, known as *peine forte et dure*, was designed to
extract a plea from recalcitrant prisoners so that their trials might
proceed. She was crushed beneath a door upon which heavy weights
were progressively piled 'to the quantitie of seven or eight hundred
weight at the least, which breaking her ribs caused them to burst
forth of her skin.' So she died. Likewise for harbouring priests a
layman from the family of Horrock Hall near Parbold, Lancashire
suffered martyrdom. Probably he was known to the Listers. Oxford
educated, he described himself:

> My name is John Rigby, a poor gentleman of the house of Harrock
> in Lancashire; my age is about thirty years.

In Southwark on 12 June 1600 he was hanged, then cut down
so that he stood 'like a man a little amazed' before the executioner
lopped off his genitals and extracted his bowels. When the executioner reached up inside to grasp his heart, the crowd observed that
Rigby was 'yet so strong he thrust the men from him who held
his arms.'[193]

Between 1585 and 1603 a hundred priests and fifty-three lay
people were executed for their Catholic faith. Each martyrdom
must have opened again in the Listers the wounds of the guilt
of schism.

A further Catholic kinsman of the Listers had been the arch-traitor
of Elizabethan England. Cardinal William Allen was the grandson
of the Thomas Lister of Arnoldsbigging (Westby) who in 1492 had
married Isabel de Clideroe. Their daughter Jane, the Cardinal's
mother, born at Westby, was a lady of notable holiness. William
was born in 1532 at the Allen home in Rossall on the Fylde coast.
When eight years old the future Cardinal had been bequeathed 'one
Royal of gold' in the will of 1540 of his uncle, Thomas Lister of
Westby.[194]

This Catholic great-uncle of our Thomas Lister senior was Principal of St Mary's Hall, Oxford during Mary's reign. On the queen's

Cardinal William Allen. His mother was Jane Lister of Westby.
Allen, exiled in Douai, trained the priests of the English Mission and urged
rebellion against Queen Elizabeth in support of the Spanish Armada.

death, while Alexander Nowell and other Protestant exiles returned
to England, William Allen fled to Louvaine before returning in
secret to Lancashire to promote the Catholic Mission amongst the
gentry. By 1570 he was back in France where he established the
English College at Douai, the seminary of the Catholic Mission,
and intrigued with Popes and with Philip of Spain to promote

rebellion in England and the invasion of the country. Infamously, while the Spanish Armada was assembling, William Allen, created Cardinal in 1587, called on English Catholics to co-operate with the invading Spanish. Allen intrigued with William Stanley, a Catholic privateer, who in the summer of 1588 had command of the 'English Legion', a trained body of English and Irish Catholics, waiting at Nieuport to join the Armada. He supported the Bull of Pope Pius V which pronounced that Elizabeth was excommunicate, that it was no sin for Catholics to kill her, and that it was a duty to overthrow her monarchy.[195]

For the Listers one can scarce imagine a more embarrassing kinsman. They would seek to distance themselves from him. They knew that Allen's politicising of the Catholic faith caused many Catholics to suffer imprisonment and death as traitors. Fr John Nutter from Pendle, for instance, when committed to Marshalsea in 1582 was asked: 'What would you do in case the Pope shall invade the kingdom?' His reply was evasive: 'I will do as a good Catholic ought to do.' His execution followed.

Cardinal Allen's personal charm is well attested. He seemed humble and kind. He was a scholar of eminence, responsible in part for the Douai translation of the Bible, and was an able apologist for the Roman church. But ideologically he was inflexible. Insensitive to the true temper of the English, he did disservice both to his own confession and to the stability of England. The Cardinal placed upon Catholics in England and upon those priests whom he educated a burden of martyrdom largely of his making.

Thomas Lister junior conformed to the established church, but this must have caused him the pain of guilt for betraying a Catholic family tradition. One surmises that Thomas Lister junior had the Puritan passion of an anxious convert.

Margaret Pearson of Padiham

ROGER NOWELL enlisted other magistrates to further the hunt for witches. On 27 April, when Nowell questioned the Devices, his near-neighbour from the hall at Altham, the old man Nicholas Bannister, sat with him. Those two met again on 5 May to take a statement from Henry Hargreaves, the Constable. They were joined then by a third magistrate, Robert Holden, who, being husband of Alice Bannister, was Nicholas Bannister's son-in-law.[196] It seems that Nowell encouraged the other two to prosecute witches in their localities. Both Bannister and Holden were to arraign witches at the Lancaster Assizes in cases unconnected with the Pendle circle. Both prosecutions, it happened, were ill-conceived.

Nicholas Bannister will have told Nowell about Margaret Pearson of Padiham who had twice been acquitted of witchcraft. She should be charged again. So she was, but the depositions which Potts published show that Nicholas Bannister's prosecution of her was an ill-prepared, last-minute job. Margaret Pearson was charged with killing by witchcraft a 'Mare of the goods and Chattels of one Dodgeson'. Bannister produced only two written depositions; neither date from before Margaret had been committed to Lancaster gaol. One imagines Bannister's panicky haste to justify his imprisoning of the woman. A certain Jennet Booth testified on 9 August about a toad. When she had been in Margaret Pearson's house to card wool she had, she said, seen in the hearth 'a Toade, or a thing very like a Toade' which Margaret had removed with tongs.[197] The second deposition was supplied by Old Chattox, fellow-prisoner of Margaret's in Lancaster. Chattox, probably tortured to utter these absurdities, claimed that Margaret Pearson had confided that she, Margaret, and her 'Spirit . . . in the likeness of a Man, and cloven footed . . . came in at a loop-hole into the Dodgeson's stable', and 'together did sit upon his Horse or Mare untill the said Horse or

Margaret Pearson was sentenced to be pilloried on market days at Clitheroe, Padiham, Whalley and Lancaster.

Mare died'. Chattox added that Margaret and her Spirit had 'bewitched unto death one Childer's wife, and her daughter'.[198]

Potts says that 'divers witnesses' testified in open court 'to prove the death of the Mare and divers other vild and odious practices by her committed'.[199] The Court found Margaret Pearson guilty, a shameful verdict when one considers the fatuity of the evidence. She was spared the sentence of death. Imprisoned for a year she was ordered:

> You shall stand upon the Pillarie in open Market, at Clitheroe, Paddiham, Whalley and Lancaster, four Market dayes, with a Paper upon your head, in great Letters, declaring your offence.[200]

Roger Nowell had pushed Nicholas Bannister beyond his abilities. The poor man was clearly distressed at his botched effort; he made his will on 15 August 1612, two days before the hearing,[201] and died before the year was out.

The Witches of Samlesbury

B ANNISTER'S son-in-law's prosecution was a yet more spectacular failure. Disaster was evident from the outset. Robert Holden, the son-in-law, was a Catholic; Nowell had been unwise to excite his interest.

The Holden's lived at Holden Hall, Haslingden. Robert is marked as a Papist in the freeholders list of 1600. His son Ralph was a recusant in 1629. It may be that Robert practiced such outward conformity in religion as was consistent with his being a magistrate, but his Catholic sympathy is clear.

The Puritan Nowell prosecuted as witches religious dissidents, representatives of lingering peasant Catholicism, the Devices and Chattox. In a mirror image of this, the Catholic Robert Holden prosecuted those who were religious dissidents in the Catholic sub-culture of Samlesbury.

Samlesbury, westward down the Ribble from Clitheroe and Whalley, was a Catholic village set around the hall of the South-worths, one of the county's two leading recusant families. A South-worth, Jane, was one of the three accused. Jane Southworth had been shunned by the former Lord of the Manor, Sir John South-worth, even though she was the wife of his own grandson. So had testified a certain William Alker, and he said that he had heard Sir John say 'that he liked her not, and that he doubted she would bewitch him' (The negative is understood).[202] Sir John had died seventeen years before, but the influence of this inflexible knight, 'very illiterate' according to Strype's *Annals*, overlay the trial of the Samlesbury Witches in 1612.

Sir John Southworth had been Sheriff of Lancashire in 1562, 1568 and 1569. Samlesbury Hall, a magnificent black and white timber structure, became a focus for Catholicism. Probably Robert Holden resorted to it for secret masses. In 1592 a search was made

Samlesbury Hall. The hall, the seat of Sir John Southworth, was a refuge for
Catholics. One of Sir John's sons, the priest Christopher Southworth,
encouraged a girl to accuse his nephew's widow of being a witch.

of the Hall. There were found twenty-four 'books of papistrie'
including a *Treatise of Schism* showing that 'all Catholicks must absent
themselves from hereticall conventicles, to wit, prayer and sermons.'
Arrested in Bath in 1569, Sir John appeared before the Council. In
1581 he was a prisoner in the New Fleet prison in Manchester. For
a time he was confined in rooms in Manchester College, before
being taken to London in 1584. Probably he spent much of his
time in prison until his death in 1595.[203]

Sir John, Alker had said, liked not Jane. Jane was the natural
daughter by Isabel Wood of another notable Catholic, Sir Richard
Sherburne of Stonyhurst; she had married John, grandson of Sir
John and eldest son of Thomas.[204] The reason for Sir John's dislike
those years before was revealed when the witch accusation collapsed
in 1612. It was because Jane, like the Bierley women accused with
her, had forsaken the Catholic faith, or, as Potts puts it: 'they were
once obstinate Papists, and now came to Church.'

This was not the first occurance of religious disharmony within
the Southworth family. We know from a letter sent by Sir Francis
Walsingham in 1584 that Sir John Southworth had similarly been

The Southworths of Samlesbury Hall

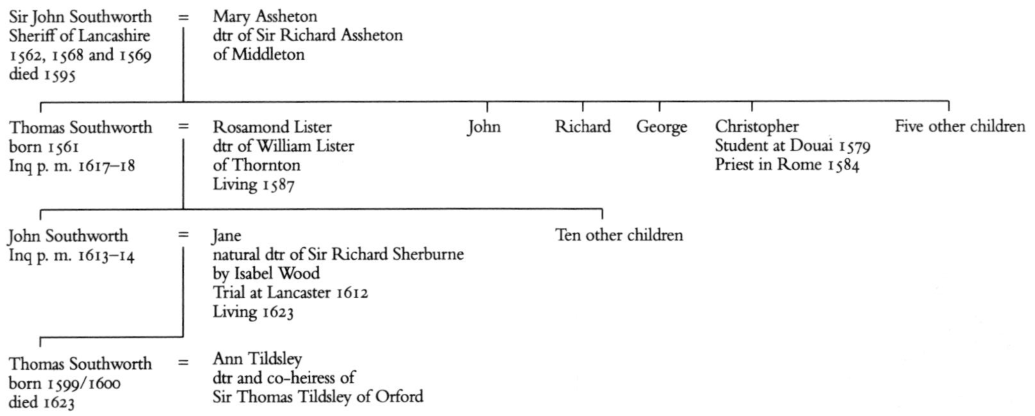

Sir John Southworth
Sheriff of Lancashire
1562, 1568 and 1569
died 1595

= Mary Assheton
dtr of Sir Richard Assheton
of Middleton

Thomas Southworth
born 1561
Inq p. m. 1617–18

= Rosamond Lister
dtr of William Lister
of Thornton
Living 1587

John   Richard   George

Christopher
Student at Douai 1579
Priest in Rome 1584

Five other children

John Southworth
Inq p. m. 1613–14

= Jane
natural dtr of Sir Richard Sherburne
by Isabel Wood
Trial at Lancaster 1612
Living 1623

Ten other children

Thomas Southworth
born 1599/1600
died 1623

= Ann Tildsley
dtr and co-heiress of
Sir Thomas Tildsley of Orford

Lower Hall, Samlesbury, the jointure house of Jane Southworth.

grievously disappointed in his son Thomas, Jane's father-in-law, for Thomas too had conformed to the established church, perhaps because he had married Rosamund Lister of Thornton, a protestant kinswoman of the Listers of Westby. 'Sir John Southworth', according to Walsingham, 'hath a purpose to disinherit his eldest son, only because the young gentleman, as is said, is not ill-affected (like the father) but well given in religion; and to dispose his lands upon some other of his children.' Walsingham sought to prevent this, and seemingly was successful.[205]

In 1612 Jane was newly widowed. She lived at Lower Hall, Samlesbury. Her father-in-law, Thomas, was still alive; he died in 1617 but is not mentioned in the records of the trial. One of Thomas' brothers does figure. He was Christopher Southworth, a Catholic priest.

Robert Holden's main witness was a fourteen-year-old girl, Grace Sowerbutts, who told odious tales about two of her family, her grandmother Jennet Bierley and her aunt Ellen Bierley.[206] She testified to Holden that her grandmother 'in the likenesse of a black Dogge, with two legges' had persuaded her to try to drown herself in the Ribble. Another night, she said, her aunt and her grandmother had taken a baby from the side of its sleeping parents, Thomas Walshman and his wife, had thrust a nail through its navel and had sucked from the hole. When the baby died the two had disinterred

Witches exhuming and feasting upon corpses. From the *Compendium Maleficarum*, Milan, 1626. Grace Sowerbutts of Samlesbury claimed to have witnessed similar sights.

the body from Samlesbury Church, had cooked it, eaten it and had seethed the bones in a pot

> and with the Fat that came out of the said bones they said they would anoint themselves that thereby they might change themselves into other shapes.

Grace claimed to be an eye-witness. She claimed too that they, with Jane Southworth, had crossed the Ribble, taking Grace with them, and had danced at night with 'black things' on the river bank

> and after the dancing the said black things did pull downe the said three Women and did abuse their bodies, as this Examinate thinketh, for shee saith, that the black thing that was with her, did abuse her bodie.

Evidence about Jane Southworth seems to have been added by Grace to her original fantasy of family spite. Grace alleged that Jane Southworth had battered her in lofts and on hay-stacks and had thrown her in a ditch, each time leaving her in a bewitched, cataleptic condition. She said too that Jane had danced on the river bank.

In court Holden's case relied upon Grace's evidence. Under questioning the girl's tissue of deception was revealed. The case collapsed; Grace retracted all. Two magistrates were deputed to question her more privately and to them she confessed that a

Catholic priest, 'Master Thompson', an alias of Fr. Christopher Southworth, had rehearsed her in the whole fabric of untruth. Grace was a Catholic; she had been sent to the priest 'to learne her prayers.' Potts tells us that the priests' motive was to get revenge on the three ladies each of whom had renounced the Roman faith.[207]

Fr. Christopher Southworth, fourth son of the late Sir John, had studied in the English College in Rome. Arrested in 1587, he had been incarcerated for a time at Wisbeach Castle. Christopher would find secret accommodation in his family Hall at Samlesbury; in 1624 he was still at large.[208] Probably the priest had lent an unwisely sympathetic ear to the hysterical outpourings of the teenager, and then, seeing the possibilities, had coached Grace to present her case well. Like his father before him, Christopher may have been motivated by chagrin that Jane Southworth had renounced the family faith, by the chance to disinherit Jane's Protestant offspring, and by the wish to discredit the three converts in the eyes of the Catholic community at Samlesbury. Fr Christopher may have intended in due course to 'exorcise' Grace Sowerbutts, just as Fr Weston and other priests had pretended to dispossess demoniacs to induce admiration for their faith. Robert Holden, the Catholic magistrate, will have been driven by those same motives.

Catholic and Protestant animosities run like a sub-text throughout our history. Hugh Trevor-Roper argued that the crazes of witch-persecution in Europe occurred according to a geographical pattern. Persecution flared at the fault-lines between confessional traditions. Near the interface between Catholics and Calvinists or that between Catholics and Lutherans, where those who promoted the one conformity met with resistance, there dissidents were created. On them obloquy would be piled. Scape-goated, marginalised, they were charged with the same crimes as had been the deviants of the medieval era, the Jews and the Cathars. It was said that they boiled babies and met in unspeakable 'sabbaths' of sexual depravity.

The Samlesbury accusations enact this thesis. Holden, the covert Catholic magistrate, pursued dissident Protestant members of the Catholic community of Samlesbury. The obverse confessional prejudice had been displayed fifteen years earlier in the Starkie case: then Hartley who used 'Popish charmes' was hanged, and Darrel and More had exorcised the children after triumphant Calvinist prayers.

John Webster of Clitheroe, himself a man of mystical depth, was taught by his Lancashire experiences that the deceptions of supposed witchcraft or exorcism were usually engendered by religion:

> We may note, that when such strange Impostures or false Miracles are pretended, there is commonly some sinister and corrupt end aimed at, under the cloak of Religion, and that those that are most ready to publish such things as true Miracles and Divine Revelations, are generally those that did complot and devise them.[209]

The Unease of Henry Towneley

ONE Catholic, Henry Towneley of Carr, was called to give evidence in the trial of the Pendle witches. James Device stood accused of having bewitched to death Towneley's wife, Anne. Potts notes that

> Master Nowell humbly prayed Master Townley might be called, who attended to prosecute and to give evidence.

But then Potts, excusing himself on the grounds of length, declines to record Towneley's evidence.[210] Why was this?

Henry Towneley of Carr was a kinsman of Sir John Towneley of Towneley Hall, half-brother to Alexander Nowell. Sir John Towneley, like Sir John Southworth, at great personal cost had held to the Catholic faith during Elizabeth's reign. Sir John Towneley's wealth and influence within Lancashire were such that the Council was much worried by 'his great power in the county' and dared not leave him in peace. The cost of his Catholicism was listed on a portrait of Sir John which formerly hung in Towneley Hall:

> . . . for professing the apostolical catholick Romaine Faith, was imprisoned first at Chester castell, then sent to marishalsea, then to yorke castell, then to the blockhouses in hull, then to the Gatehouse in Westminster, then to manchester, then to broughton in Oxe-forthshire, then twice to Elie in Cambrigesh^r, and so now of 73 years old and blinde, is bound to kepe with in five myles of towneley his house, who hath since the statute of 23° paid in to the exchequer 20 £ every month and doth still, that there is paid allready above five m£ [£5,000]. 1601.[211]

Henry Towneley of Carr was a grandson too of that other Catholic magnate, Sir Richard Sherburn of Stoneyhurst; his mother happened to be half-sister of Jane Southworth, one of the accused.

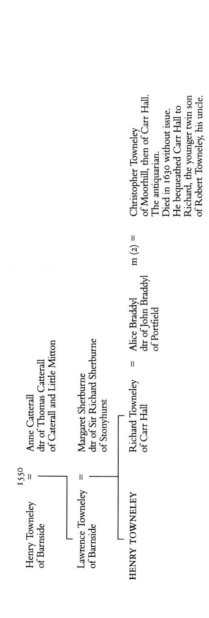

The Towneleys of Carr Hall

Henry Towneley
of Barnside

1550
=

Anne Catterall
dtr of Thomas Catterall
of Caterall and Little Mitton

Lawrence Towneley
of Barnside

=

Margaret Sherburne
dtr of Sir Richard Sherburne
of Stonyhurst

Richard Towneley
of Carr Hall

=

Alice Braddyl
dtr of John Braddyl
of Portfield

HENRY TOWNELEY

m (2) =

Christopher Towneley
of Moorhill, then of Carr Hall.
The antiquarian.
Died in 1650 without issue.
He bequeathed Carr Hall to
Richard, the younger twin son
of Robert Towneley, his uncle.

Information from *The County Families of England – Lancashire*, Vol. I, 1873.

Genealogies of this branch of the Towneleys are not consistent. Thomas Potts' record shows that in 1612, and for two years before, a Henry Towneley was master of Carr Hall. If this was the same Henry Towneley who married in 1550, he would be very aged by then. The *County Families of England* write of the younger Henry Towneley that he 'died young', and Dr Whittaker (*History of Whalley*, p. 127) believed that Richard Towneley was the eldest son of Laurence. Nevertheless the younger Henry Towneley (whose name is in capitals), is probably he who is mentioned in the indictment that James by witchcraft had killed 'one Anne Towneley, wife of Henrie Towneley of the Carre, in the Countie of Lancaster Gentleman'.

Sir John Towneley and his family, 1601. Towneley, one of the richest men in Lancashire, endured repeated imprisonment for his Catholic allegiance.

It seems likely that in court Henry Towneley, having given his evidence about James Device, became disgruntled that the Samlesbury case on the one hand laid charges against his aunt and on the other hand, following the debacle, was being used for anti-Catholic propaganda. Towneley became unwilling for Potts to quote his evidence for what he now discerned were religiously partisan purposes.

In the Court-house Towneley would see gathered other Protestant gentry. This will have reinforced his unease. The twenty-five-year old Richard Shuttleworth from Gawthorpe was in court;

Towneley Hall, near Burnley, the home of Sir John Towneley.

his family accounts show that.[212] He was the nephew of that Sir Richard Shuttleworth, Chief Justice of Chester, whom Robert Nutter had accompanied to Wales and Chester nineteen years before. This young Sir Richard was to be a heroic Colonel on the Parliamentary side in the civil war, and in 1646 was one of the laymen of the Third Lancashire Presbyterian Classis.

Furthermore, one of the magistrates deputed to question Grace Sowerbutts was a distinguished spokesman for the Puritan party, the clergymen and magistrate William Leigh. Leigh, Rector of Standish since 1586, was a preacher of distinction 'esteemed for his learning and godliness' far beyond the county. A preacher admired by Ferdinando, Earl of Derby, Leigh had attended the nobleman in his last moments in 1594 when it was held that the Earl had been either consumed by witches or poisoned by Papists. King James, having heard William Leigh preach, appointed him to be one of the tutors of his accomplished eldest son, Prince Henry, 'the darling of the Puritans'. Leigh's writings include a beautiful funeral tribute to a young much-loved and pious Puritan lady, *The Soule's Solace against Sorrow*, published in 1612, and a famed sermon delivered on the discovery of the Gunpowder Plot entitled *Great Britaines Great Deliverance from the Great Danger of Popish Powder*.[213] The diary of Nicholas Assheton for the years 1617 and 1618 shows that William

The Shuttleworths of Gawthorpe

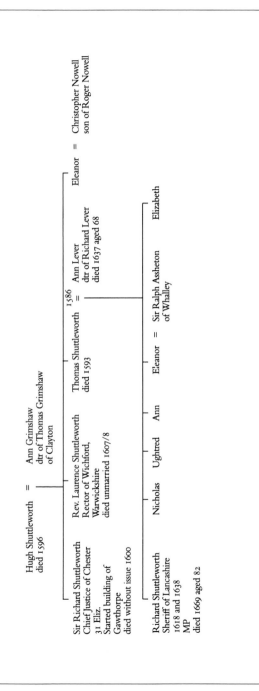

Hugh Shuttleworth = Ann Grimshaw
died 1596   dtr of Thomas Grimshaw
of Clayton

Sir Richard Shuttleworth   Rev. Laurence Shuttleworth   Thomas Shuttleworth = Ann Lever   Eleanor = Christopher Nowell
Chief Justice of Chester   Rector of Wichford,   died 1593   1586   dtr of Richard Lever   son of Roger Nowell
31 Eliz.   Warwickshire   died 1637 aged 68
Started building of   died unmarried 1607/8
Gawthorpe
died without issue 1600

Richard Shuttleworth   Ughtred   Ann   Nicholas   Eleanor = Sir Ralph Assheton   Elizabeth
Sheriff of Lancashire   of Whalley
1618 and 1638
MP
died 1669 aged 82

Source: *Lancashire Pedigrees*, by Parker

Leigh was on familiar terms with the gentry of Pendle and Craven. Frequently he preached at Slaidburn.

In such anti-Catholic company one can see that Henry Towneley would be ill at ease, though the Catholic sympathies of Sir Thomas Gerrard and of Sir Richard Hoghton, also present, will have afforded him some support.

Confessional animosity, repressed under the veneer of gentlemanly propriety, was so powerful a motive for the witch persecution that, from the perspective of history, the Lancashire witch trials of 1612 seem like a phoney-war presaging the wider and more direct blood-letting of the 1640s. In the Civil War Towneleys, Sherburns, Southworths, Hoghtons and Tempests were to opt for the King, whilst Shuttleworths, Asshetons, Starkies, Nowells, Hebers and Listers strove for Parliament and the Commonwealth.

Verdicts

A T Lancaster on Wednesday 19 August Sir Edward Bromley pronounced judgement on the following, as Potts records:

> Anne Whittle, alias Chattox; Elizabeth Device, James Device, Anne Redferne, Alice Nutter, Katherine Hewet, John Bulcock, Jane Bulcock, Alizon Device, and Isabel Roby.

The last named, from Windle, had been arraigned on a quite separate charge of witchcraft. The sentence on them all was:

> You shall all go from hence to the Castle, from whence you came; and from thence you shall all be carried to the place of execution for this Countie; where your bodies shall bee hanged untill you be dead; and GOD HAVE MERCIE UPON YOUR SOULES.

Twenty-three days earlier a similar death sentence had been passed in York on Jennet Preston. Judge Altham 'pronounced Judgement against her to be hanged for her offence'.

About Jennet Preston's execution on Wednesday 29 July we know only this; that 'even at the gallowes' she 'died impenitent' and 'would confesse nothing'.

What Jennet did say is not recorded. In her last moments did she recollect the affection with which Thomas Lister senior had cherished her? Did she grieve about the wedding four years since at which the good man had died? Did she catalogue the ordeal with which she had been visited—how they first accused her of beguiling their father, then of bewitching him, of causing that death which was sorrow to her, and then that of his widow, of any cow in the herd, and of a baby? Was she vexed that Thomas Lister junior should have sworn that the dear corpse of his father had bled at her touch? Wryly did she note that her kindness in going to Malkin Tower had, through the machinations of Roger Nowell, been ill-rewarded? Did she smile that any should believe that the

The hanging of witches—from *Englands Grievance Discovered*
by R. Gardiner, 1655.

ordinary meeting at Malkin Tower had been a sabbath of witches?
In spirit was she one with those awaiting trial in Lancaster? As she
neared the scaffold was she vouchsafed some searing insight in which
the Puritan ethic of Lister, Heber, and Nowell crumbled—that ethic
which had scorned the sensuality of her nature, had condemned
her for its imaginary witchcraft, and was unrelenting in pious
savagery? Ignoring those urging her to confess, did Jennet trust to
some truer, more mysterious God, a God of compassion and infinite
understanding, a God whose generosity was for her well symbolised
by the very hospitality with which Thomas Lister senior had always

welcomed her? Or did Jennet despair? Were her last thoughts for
her husband William who had stood by her, for her friends and
relations who had supported her, for the land between Pendle and
Ribble which had been her only home for thirty-seven summers?
In the imposing City of York, amidst a taunting crowd, while the
executioner, who had a job to do, tested his knot, did not the
world to her feel cold and strange, and she as desolate as a discarded doll?

We have chronicled the circumstances that had disposed Pendle
and Craven, an area of uncommon Catholicism, to be the arena
for witch persecution in 1612. The gentry had split socially into
Catholic and Protestant groupings foreshadowing allegiance in the
Civil War; Catholic practices continued amongst the common
people, exciting the anxiety of godly Puritans; belief in witchcraft
had become a touchstone of Calvinist allegiance through the Starkie
case and Darrel controversies; and literature on witchcraft, available
to Roger Nowell, had persuaded him that witches would compact
with the devil and would meet in unspeakable sabbaths. This was
the dry tinder which the persecution of Jennet Preston, accompanied
by one major mishap, ignited. The mishap was that Alizon was
present when a pedlar fell lamed by a stroke. So were revealed to
Nowell some of the activities of the Pendle wise-men and -women.
From these elements the fate of the Pendle witches proceeded with
the inevitability of a tragic play. Jennet Preston's death in York was
succeeded by the hanging in Lancaster of the nine from Pendleside.

Jennet's tale is no happy one. However her 'friends and kinsmen'
from Gisburn stood by her; they continued to lambast the magistrates
and judiciary. To do this in the face of the Lord of the Manor
showed rare spirit. Thomas Potts would not have written and
published his attempted defence of the judges had the people of
Gisburn not voiced their indignation.

Coda:
John Webster and
Sir John Assheton

SIXTY-THREE years after the terrible events of 1612, John Webster of Clitheroe completed *The Displaying of Supposed Witchcraft*, the most effective of all the seventeenth-century critiques of witchcraft. We have quoted it frequently. Webster presented the book in manuscript form to the Royal Society on 4 March 1674/5, and a group of three, which included William Petty and John Pell, was appointed 'to peruse it, and report their opinion'. Sir Jonas Moore, vice-president of the Royal Society, gave *The Displaying . . .* the imprimatur of that scientific body. He wrote an introduction. The book was published in London in 1677.

Webster chose to dedicate his book to the magistrates of the West-Riding of Yorkshire, to the successors of that very bench of magistrates that had prosecuted Jennet Preston in 1612. On the title page are listed the magistrates from Gisburn and its surrounds: . . .

> Dedicated to his Worshipful and honoured friends, Thomas Parker of Braisholme, John Asheton of the Lower Hall, William Drake of Barnoldswick-coat, William Johnson of the Grange, Henry Marsden of Gisborne, Esquires and his majesties Justices of Peace and Quorum in the West Riding of Yorkshire.

The five magistrates John Webster honoured with his dedication because

> you have all been Gentlemen, not only well known unto me for many years, as being my near Neighbours, but also with whom I have been freely admitted to a Noble and Generous converse, and have been trusted and honoured by you in your Domestick concerns, wherein by my Medical Profession, I might be serviceable to you.

Browsholme, in John Webster's parish of Mitton, the home then, as now, of
the Parker family with whom Webster enjoyed 'generous converse'.

In 'generous converse', two generations after Jennet's death, the
local magistrates had continued to brood over her story. Henry
Marsden lived in Gisburn Hall, sited where the Vicarage now stands.
He served as M.P. for Clitheroe from 1680-1685. William Drake,
born in 1608, built Coates Hall in 1667, and died in the year that
The Displaying . . . was published. Thomas Parker's family live in
Browsholme still; wisely they had played no part in the witchcraft
prosecutions.

'John Asheton of the Lower Hall', the tenth son of the family
of Whalley Abbey was, one might say, a Lister by marriage, so we
might consider the life of this friend of John Webster in more detail.
Childless himself, he had married a young Lister widow and lived
in the jointure house of the Listers, Lower Hall (subsequently to
be main Lister house and to be known as Gisburne Park). There
he cared for his infant step-children and step-grand-children. Like
John Webster, John Assheton practised as a doctor.

To John Assheton, with the hind-sight of history, Thomas Lister
senior's death at Bracewell in 1607 at the age of thirty-eight would

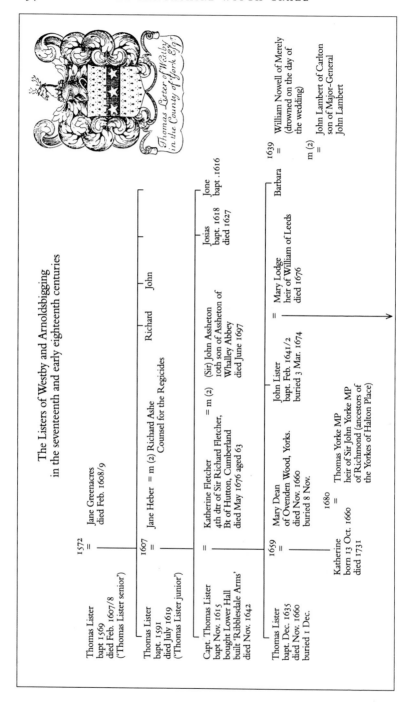

The Listers of Westby and Arnoldsbigging
in the seventeenth and early eighteenth centuries

Thomas Lister of Westby in the County of York Esq[r]

Thomas Lister
bapt 1569
died Feb. 1607/8
('Thomas Lister senior')

1572
=

Jane Greenacres
died Feb. 1608/9

Thomas Lister
bapt. 1591
died July 1619
('Thomas Lister junior')

1607
=

Jane Heber = m (2) Richard Ashe
                    Counsel for the Regicides

Richard   John

Capt. Thomas Lister
bapt Nov. 1615
bought Lower Hall
built 'Ribblesdale Arms'
died Nov. 1642

=

Katherine Fletcher
4th dtr of Sir Richard Fletcher,
Bt of Hutton, Cumberland
died May 1676 aged 63

= m (2) (Sir) John Assheton
            10th son of Assheton of
            Whalley Abbey
            died June 1697

Josias
bapt. 1618
died 1627

Jone
bapt. 1616

Thomas Lister
bapt. Dec. 1635
died Nov. 1660
buried 1 Dec.

1659
=

Mary Dean
of Ovenden Wood, Yorks.
died Nov. 1660
buried 8 Nov.

John Lister
bapt. Feb. 1641/2
buried 3 Mar. 1674

=

Mary Lodge
heir of William of Leeds
died 1676

Barbara

1639
=

William Nowell of Merely
(drowned on the day of
the wedding)

m (2)
=

John Lambert of Carlton
son of Major-General
John Lambert

Katherine
born 13 Oct. 1660
died 1731

1680
=

Thomas Yorke MP
heir of Sir John Yorke MP
of Richmond (ancestors of
the Yorkes of Halton Place)

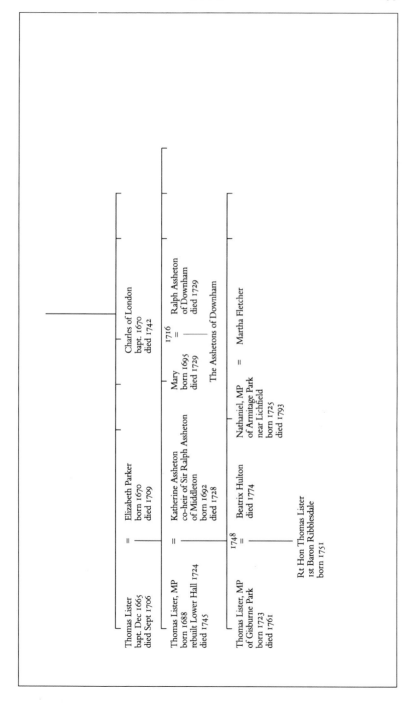

Thomas Lister
bapt. Dec 1665
died Sept 1706

= Elizabeth Parker
born 1670
died 1709

Charles of London
bapt. 1670
died 1742

Thomas Lister, MP
born 1688
rebuilt Lower Hall 1724
died 1745

= Katherine Assheton
co-heir of Sir Ralph Assheton
of Middleton
born 1692
died 1728

Mary
born 1695
died 1729

1716
=

Ralph Assheton
of Downham
died 1729

The Asshetons of Downham

Thomas Lister, MP
of Gisburne Park
born 1723
died 1761

1748
=

Beatrix Hulton
died 1774

Nathaniel, MP
of Armitage Park
near Lichfield
born 1725
died 1793

= Martha Fletcher

Rt Hon Thomas Lister
1st Baron Ribblesdale
born 1751

be revealed as part of a pattern which needed no occult explanation. Some genetic defect must have caused successive generations of Listers, child, grandchild and great-grand-child, to die each in his twenties.

Briefly we can chronicle this work of the grim reaper.

Thomas Lister junior, Jennet's persecutor, died aged twenty-eight in 1619; his wife Jane (Heber) then married Richard Ashe, who was to act as Counsel for the Prosecution at the trial of Charles I. Thomas and Jane's son Thomas was but three when he succeeded. A talented young man, he attended Oxford and Grays Inn, purchased the Lower Hall, built what is now the Ribblesdale Arms in Gisburn, and, aged twenty-seven, as 'Captain Thomas Lister' rode to join the Parliamentary troops in 1642. Suddenly he collapsed and died. The eldest of his three children, Thomas again, was seven years old. The children's widowed mother, Kathrine, remarried John Assheton, three years her junior; it was John Assheton and Kathrine who welcomed Oliver Cromwell and Major General John Lambert to Lower Hall in 1648. Young Thomas, having attended Grays Inn, married Mary Deane in 1659. He was aged twenty-four but within a year both bride and groom were dead, their babe in arms Katherine orphaned. Thomas' brother John inherited. He had seven sons, but died at the age of 33 when his eldest, Thomas, was nine years old. Upon this Thomas, his step-grandchild, John Assheton was to settle estates in Malham and elsewhere, for John Assheton, though a tenth son, had, beyond all expectation, inherited the Whalley estates in 1692 as last of his direct line.

Kindly Sir John Assheton did not move to Whalley. He distributed clothes to the poor, was their surgeon and physician and gave to Gisburn Church the silver chalice and paten still in use. His wife's grandson erected the monument in his memory that graces Gisburn church's north wall.

John Assheton's friend John Webster possessed profound erudition and a penetrating mind. *The Displaying of Supposed Witchcraft* shows a robust scholar who could engage an entrenched belief-system with the weapons of theology, philosophy, and the new experimental sciences. A fine story-teller, he delights with anecdotes about chicaneries and impostures he had seen perpetrated in the fairs and homesteads of Craven.

John Webster had been a clergyman. After Cambridge and medical studies, he was ordained by the Bishop of Durham and served in 1634 as curate of Kildwick-in-Craven. While there a transforming experience, probably inspired by Roger Brearley, turned him to Grindletonian radicalism. The post became untenable, for Webster came to attack both prelacy and presbyterianism, convinced that true religion was founded on an inner spring of life which the imposition of human order could only distort.

In 1543 Webster was Master of Clitheroe Grammar School, but during the Civil War practised as a field surgeon with the Parliamentary troops of Colonel Shuttleworth's regiment and was, he writes, 'a chaplain in the Army'. Under the Commonwealth provisions he was appointed Vicar of Mitton, near Clitheroe, where Brearley's old chapel at Grindleton was within his parish; there he often preached in accord with its traditions. John Webster remained at Mitton only four years, 1648 to 1652, then moved to London 'engaged in some employment in the Lord's work in this great city.' Books flowed from his pen: *The Saints Guide*, *The Saints Perfect Freedom* and a scheme for the reorganisation of university education to take account of the new scientific learning, *Academiarum Examen* (London, 1654). With his friend William Erbery he engaged in religious debate at All Hallows, Lombard Street, where their radical rejection of ministers, liturgy and ordinances in the church provoked what some considered a tumult.

John Webster returned to Clitheroe, discarded the epithet 'clericus', and enjoyed the powers of Chief Magistrate of the town from October 1657 until October 1659. He practiced as doctor and surgeon, studied the hermetic arts and investigated the properties of ores and metals. His *Metalographia* was published in 1671. *The Displaying of Supposed Witchcraft* was his last book, no less radical than his former publications.[214]

Webster's title-page proclaims his courageous scepticism—'Supposed Witchcraft' is no more than the deceits of imposters or the delusions of those afflicted in mind. The Faustian compact with the devil, the enormities of the witches sabbath and the transmutation of witches—the whole paraphernalia of the Catholic and Calvinist witch-myth—are 'utterly disproved'. Opposition was provoked. This Webster expected: 'Those crossing the vogue of the common

A: 780

THE
DISPLAYING

OF SUPPOSED

WITCHCRAFT.

Wherein is affirmed that there are many sorts of

Deceivers and Impostors,

AND

Divers persons under a passive *Delusion* of

MELANCHOLY and *FANCY.*

But that there is a *Corporeal League* made betwixt the
DEVIL and the WITCH,

Or that he sucks on the *Witches Body*, has *Carnal Copulation*, or
that *Witches* are turned into *Cats*, *Dogs*, raise Tempests, or
the like, is utterly denied and disproved.

Wherein also is handled,

The Existence of Angels and Spirits, the truth of Apparitions, the Nature of
Astral and Sydereal Spirits, the force of Charms, and Philters;
with other abstruse matters.

By *John Webster*, Practitioner in Physick.

False etenim opiniones Hominum praeoccupantes, non solùm surdos, sed & caecos faciunt, ita ut
videre nequeant, quae aliis perspicua apparent. Galen. lib. 8. de Comp. Med. .

LONDON,

Printed by *J. M.* and are to be sold by the Booksellers in *London*. *A 677.*

The *Displaying of Supposed Witchcraft* by John Webster of Clitheroe,
published in 1677, attacked the fantasies that sustained witch-hunts.

opinion, have not wanted their loads of unworthy and unchristian scandals cast upon them.[215]

But at Lower Hall and Gisburn Hall, at Browsholme, and Sawley Grange and Barnoldswick Cote, Webster found intellectual stimulus and understanding, the more welcome in that age of political reaction when the doors of academia, of the church, and even of membership of the Royal Society, were closed to radicalism such as his.

With touching gratitude Webster writes to his five friends in the Dedication of his book:

> It is not unknown to you, that I have had a large portion of Trouble and Persecution in this outward world, wherein you did not like many others stand aloof off, as though you had not known me, but like persons of Justice, and true Magnanimity, durst look upon and assist wronged innocency, though besmeered over with the envious dirt of malicious scandals, and even in that very conjuncture of time, when the whole giddy Troop of barking dogs, and ravenous wolves, did labour to devour me. But then, even then did put to your helping hands, and were free to declare what you knew of mine innocency.[216]

Having tasted persecution of one sort, Webster used his intellectual power to counter the persecution of defenceless supposed witches.

In *The Displaying of Supposed Witchcraft*, Webster refers several times to Chattox, to Demdike and to the Devices, but not, it so happens, to Jennet Preston—this, one imagines, out of deference to his host.

When Sir Jonas Moore gave *The Displaying* . . . the authority of the Royal Society he provoked dissention even within that enlightened body for Joseph Glanville, though an able apologist for the Society's scientific method, believed in witchcraft. In 1681, in intellectual retaliation, Glanville published *Saducisimus Triumphatus* in which he sought to expose what he called 'the marvellous weakness and gullerie of Mr Webster's *Display*'. Dr Henry More FRS in a contribution to that book abused 'the profane impudence of J. Webster' and mocked 'his beloved Hags.'[217]

In his foreword to *The Displaying* . . . Sir Jonas Moore, writing on behalf of the Royal Society, does not refer to his own connection with events to which John Webster had alluded. Yet Sir Jonas, great astronomer and mathematician, inventive military engineer and

EFFIGIES JONÆ MOORE
Aº Ætat: 35. 1649

H. Stone Pinxit.   T. Cross Sculpsit

Sir Jonas Moore, 1618–79, arithmetician, civil engineer and astronomer,
wrote a preface on behalf of the Royal Society to John Webster's book.
Sir Jonas had been born in Pendle Forest to a family which Chattox was
said to have bewitched.

drainer of the Fens, had been born on the slopes of Pendle Hill in White Lee in Higham Booth.[218] That was in 1618. His father would be that 'John Moore of Higham Gentleman' who had accused Chattox of bewitching his ale. His elder brother, had he lived, would have been the boy John who died in 1610 because, so it was alleged, Chattox had made 'pictures' to cast a spell upon him. Chattox had confessed that her brown dog had bitten the Moore's family brown cow, had driven it to frenzy and had caused its death.

That generation of men, whose forebears had persecuted the witches in 1612, struggled to come to terms with the guilt of their families and neighbours. They attempted to redeem the wastes of history and to prevent the recurrence of such injustice. Employing the scepticism of the scientific method, they dared to think anew.

O beata culpa! Had Jennet not suffered and been unjustly killed, and had her friends at Lancaster not similarly suffered, it is unlikely that within the society of Craven and Bowland would have been written *The Displaying of Supposed Witchcraft*. That visionary, indignant, humane book by John Webster tore asunder myths which in her day had choked Jennet and had for too long ensnared the minds of the west. Webster's was a dominant influence in bringing an end within two decades to all English witch-hangings.[219] The names of wise John Webster, of his generous friends, Thomas Parker, Sir John Assheton, William Drake, William Johnson, Henry Marsden and of Sir Jonas Moore, deserve to be cherished by those who live around their ancient homes and upon whom, had they not wrought to redeem the past, the memory of Jennet Preston would indeed 'lay heavy'.

APPENDIX I

THE
ARRAIGNEMENT
AND TRIALL OF
JENNET PRESTON, OF
GISBORNE IN CRAVEN,

In the County of Yorke.

At the Assizes and General Goale

·Delivery holden in the Castle of Yorke.

In the Countie of Yorke, the xxvii, day of

July last past, *Anno Regni Regis* JACOBI

Angliae, &c., Decimo, and Scotiae

quadragessimo quinto

BEFORE

Sir JAMES ALTHAM *Knight*, one

Of the Barons of his Magesties Court of Exchequer;

And SIR EDWARD BROMLEY Knight another of

The Barons of his Majesties Court of Exchequer;

His Majesties Justices of Assize, Oyer and Terminer

And General Goale Deliverie, in the Circuit

of the North Parts

LONDON:

PRINTED BY W. STANSBY FOR JOHN BARNES and

are to be sold at his Shoppe neere Holborne Conduit

1612.

ARRAIGNMENT

AND TRIALL OF JENNET PRESTON,

Of Gisborne, in Craven, in the Countie of Yorke, at

the Assizes and General Gaole Delivery, holden at the

Castle of Yorke, in the Countie of Yorke,

the seven and

twentieth day of July last past, Anno Regni Regis Jacobi,

Angliae &c. Decimo & Scotiae xlvj.

Jennet Preston

Many have undertaken to write great discourses of Witches and many more dispute and speake of them. And it were not much if as many wrote of them as could write at al, to set forth to the world the particular Rites and Secrets of their unlawful Artes, with their infinite and wonderfull practises which many men little feare till they seaze upon them. As by this late wonderfull discoverie of Witches in the Countie of Lancaster may appeare, wherein I find such apparant matter to satisfie the world, how dangerous and malitious a Witch this *Jennet Preston* was, How unfit to live, having once so great mercie extended to her: And againe to revive her practises and returne to her former course of life; that I thinke it necessary not to let the memorie of her life and death die with her; But to place her next to her fellowes and to set forth the Arraignement Triall and Conviction of her, with her offences for which she was condemned and executed.

And although shee died for her offence before the rest, I yet can afford her no better place than in the end of this Booke in respect the proceedings was in another Countie:

You that were husband to this *Jennet Preston*; her friends and kinsfolkes, who have not beene sparing to devise so scandalous a slander out of the malice of your hearts, as that she was maliciously prosecuted by Master Lister and others; Her life unjustly taken away by practise; and that (even at the Gallowes where she died impenitent and void of all feare or grace) she died an innocent woman, because she would confesse nothing: You I say may not hold it strange, though at this time, being not only moved in conscience, but directed, for example sake, with that which I have to report of her, I suffer you not to wander any further; but with this short discourse oppose your idle conceipts able to seduce others: And by charmes of imputations and slander, laid upon the Justice of the Land, to clear her that was justly condemned and executed for her offence; That this Jennet Preston was for many yeares well thought of and esteemed by *Master Lister* who afterwards died for it Had accesse to his house, kind respect and entertainment; nothing denied her she stood in need of. Which of you that dwelleth near them in Craven but can and will witnesse it? which might have encouraged a woman of any good condition to have run a better course.

The favour and goodnesse of this Gentleman Master *Lister* now living, at his first entrance after the death of his Father extended towards her, and the reliefe she had at all times, with many other favours that succeeded from time to time, are so palpable and evident to all men as no man can denie them. These were sufficient motives to have perswaded her from the murder of so good a friend.

But such was her execrable Ingratitude, as even this grace and goodnesse was the cause of his miserable and untimely death. And even in the beginning of his greatest favours extended to her, began shee to work this mischiefe, according to the course of all Witches.

This *Jennet Preston*, whose arraignement and Triall, with the particular evidence against her I am now to set forth unto you, one that lived at Gisborne in Craven, in the Countie of Yorke, neare Master *Lister* of Westbie, against whom she practised such mischiefe; for having cut off *Thomas Lister* Esquire, father to this Gentleman now living, she revenged herself upon his sonne; who in short time received great losse in his goods and Cattel by her meanes.

These things in time did beget suspition, and at the Assizes and Generall Gaole delivery holden at the Castle of Yorke in Lent last past, before my Lord *Bromley*, shee was indicted and arraigned for the murder of a child of one *Dodg-sonnes*, but by the favour and mercifull consideration of the Jurie thereof acquited.

But the favour and mercie was no sooner extended towardes her, and shee set at libertie, But shee began to practise the utter ruine and overthrow of the name and blood of this Gentleman.

And the better to execute her mischiefe and wicked intent, within foure dayes after her deliverance out of the Castle at Yorke, went to the great Assembly of Witches at *Malking Tower* upon Good-Friday last: to pray aide and helpe, for the murder of Master *Lister*, in respect he had prosecuted against her at the same assizes.

Which it pleased God in his mercie to discover, and in the end, howsoever he had blinded her, as he did the King of AEgypt and his instruments, for the brighter evidence of his own powerfull glory; Yet by a Judicial course and triall of the Law, cut her off, and so delivered his people from the danger of her Devilish and wicked practises: which you shall heare against her, at her, arraigne-ment and Triall, which I shall now set forth to you in order as it was performed, with the wonderfull signes and tokens of GOD, to satisfie the Jurie to find her guiltie of this bloudie murther, com-mitted foure yeares since.

Indictment

This *Jennet Preston* being prisoner in the Castle at Yorke, and indicted, for that shee felloniously had practised, used, and exercised divers wicked and devilish arts, called Witchcrafts, Inchantments, Charmes, and Sorceries, in and upon one *Thomas Lister* of Westby in Craven, in the Countie of Yorke Esquire, And by force of the same witchcraft felloniously the said *Thomas* Lister had killed, *Contra Pacem &c*, being at the Barre, was arraigned.

To this Indictment upon her Arraignment, shee pleaded not guiltie, and for the triall of her life put herselfe upon God and her Country.

Whereupon my Lord *Altham* commanded Master Sherriffe of the Countie of Yorke, in open Court to return a Jurie of sufficient Gentlemen of understanding, to passe betweene our Sovereigne Lord the Kings Majestie and her, and others the prisoners, upon their lives and deaths; who were afterwards sworne, according to the forme and order of the Court, the prisoner being admitted to her lawfull challenge.

Which being done, and the Prisoner at the Barre to receive her Triall, Master *Heyber*, one of his Majesties Justices of the Peace in the same Countie, having taken great paines in the proceedings against her; and being best instructed of any man of all the particular points of evidence against her, humbly prayed, the witnesses hereafter following might be examined against her, and the several Examinations, taken before Master *Nowel*, and certified, might openly be published against her; which hereafter follow in order, viz.

The Evidence for the Kings Majestie
Against Jennet Preston, Prisoner at the Barre

Hereupon were diverse Examinations taken and read openly against her, to induce and satisfie the Gentlemen of the Jurie of Life and Death, to find she was a Witch; and many other circumstances for the death of M *Lister*. In the end *Anne Robinson* and others were both examined, who upon their Oaths declared against her, That M *Lister* lying in great extremitie, upon his death-bedde, cried out unto them that stood about him; that *Jennet Preston* was in the House, look where she is, take holde of her; for Gods sake shut the doors, and take her, shee cannot escape away. Look about for her, and lay hold of her, for she is in the house: and so cried very often in his great paines, to them that came to visit him during his sicknesse.

Anne Robinson, and Thomas Lister

Being examined further, they both gave this in evidence against her, that when Master *Lister* lay upon his death-bedde, hee cried out in great extremitie; *Jennet Preston* lays heavy upon me, *Preston's* wife lays heavy upon me; helpe me, helpe me: and so departed, crying out against her.

These, with many other witnesses, were further examined, and deposed, That *Jennet Preston*, the Prisoner at the Barre, being brought to M. *Lister* after he was dead, and layed out to be wound up in his winding-sheet, the said *Jennet Preston* comming to touch the dead corpse, they bled fresh bloud presently, in the presence of all that were then present: which hath ever been held a great argument to induce a Jurie to hold him guiltie that shall be accused of murther, and hath seldome or never, fayled in the Tryall.

But these were not alone; for this wicked and bloud-thirstie Witch was no sooner delivered at the Assizes holden at Yorke in Lent last past, being indicted, arraigned and by the favour and mercie of the Jurie found not guiltie, for the Murther of a Child by Witchcraft; but upon the Friday following, being Good-Friday, shee rode in hast to the great meeting at *Malking-Tower*, and there prayed aide for the murther of M. *Thomas Lister: as at large shall appeare, by the severall Examinations hereafter following; sent to these assizes from Master Nowel* and others his Majesties Justices of the Peace in the Countie of Lancaster, to be given in Evidence against her, upon her Triall, viz.

The Examination and Evidence of JAMES DEVICE, *of the Forrest of Pendle, in the Countie of Lancaster, Labourer, taken at the House of* JAMES WILSEY, *of the Forrest of Pendle in the Countie of Lancaster, the seven and twentieth day of Aprill, Anno. Reg. Regis* JACOBI *Angliae, &c* Decimo ac Scotiae quadragessimo quinto.

Before

ROGER NOWEL *and* NICHOLAS BANESTER, *Esquires, two of his Majesties Justices of the Peace within the Countie of Lancaster, viz.*

This Examinate saith, That upon Good-Friday last about twelve of the clock in the day time, there dined in this Examinates said mothers house a number of persons, whereof three were men, with this Examinate, and the rest women; and that they met there for these three causes following (as this Examinates said Mother told this Examinate): First was for the naming of the Spirit, which *Alizon Device*, now Prisoner at Lancaster, had, but did not name him, because shee was not there. The second cause was for the deliverie of his said Grand-mother, this Examinates said sister *Alizon*, the said *Anne Chattox*, and her daughter *Redferne*, killing the Gaoler at Lancaster; and before the next Assizes to blow up the Castle there; to that end the aforesaid Prisoners might by that means make an escape and get away. All which this Examinate then heard them conferre of. And the third cause was, for that there was a woman dwelling in Gisborne Parish, who came into this Examinates said Grand-mothers house, who there came, and craved assistance of the rest of them that were then there, for the killing of Master

Lister of Westby; because, as she then said, he had borne malice unto her, and had thought to have her put away at the late Assizes at Yorke; but could not. And then this Examinat heard the woman say, that her power was not strong enough to doe it her selfe, being now lesse than before-time it had beene.

And he also further saith, That the said *Prestons* wife had a Spirit with her like unto a white Foale, with a blacke-spot on the forehead. And further, this Examinat saith, that since the said meeting, as aforesaid, this Examinat hath beene brought to the wife of one *Preston* in Gisburne Parish aforesaid, by *Henry Hargreives* of Goldshey, to see whether shee was the woman that came among the said Witches, on the saide last Good-Friday, to crave their aide and assistance for killing the saide Master *Lister*: and having had full view of her; hee this Examinate confesseth, That shee was the selfe-same woman which came among the said Witches on the said last Good-Friday, for their aide for the killing of the said Master Lister; and that brought the Spirit with her, in the shape of a white Foale, as aforesaid.

And this Examinate further saith, That all the said Witches went out of the said house in their own shapes and likenesses, and they all, by that they were forth of the doores, were gotten on horse-backe like unto Foales, some of one colour, some of another, and *Prestons* wife was the last; and when she got on horse-backe, they all presently vanished out of this Examinates sight: and before their said parting away, they all appointed to meete at the said *Prestons* wifes house that day twelve-month; at which time the said *Prestons* wife promised to make them a great feast; and if they had occasion to meete in the meane time, then should warning be given that they all should meete upon Romles-moore. And this Examinate further saith, That at the said feast at Malking Tower, this Examinate heard all give their consents to put the said Master *Thomas Lister* of Westby to death: and after Master *Lister* should be made away by witch-craft, then all the said Witches gave their consents to joyne altogether to hancke Master *Leonard Lister*, when he should come to dwell at the Sowgill, and so put him to death.

The Examination of HENRIE HARGREIVES *of Goldshey-booth, in the Forrest of Pendle, in the Countie of Lancaster Yeoman, taken the fifth day of*

May, Anno Reg. Regis Jacobi Angliae, &c, Decimo, ac Scociae quadragessimo quinto.

Before

ROGER NOWEL, NICHOLAS BANNESTER and ROBERT HOLDEN, *Esquires; three of his Majesties Justices of the Peace within the said Countie.*

This Examinat upon his Oath saith, That *Anne Whittle,* alias *Chattox,* confessed unto him, that she knoweth one *Preston's* wife neere Gisburne, and that the said *Prestons* wife should have beene at the said feast, upon the said Good-Friday, and that she was an ill woman, and had done Master *Lister* of Westby, great hurt.

The Examination of ELIZABETH DEVICE *mother of* JAMES DEVICE, *taken before* ROGER NOWEL *and* NICHOLAS BANESTER, *Esquires, the day and yeere aforesaid, viz.*

The said *Elizabeth Device* upon her Examination confesseth, That upon Good-Friday last, there dined at this Examinates house, which shee hath said are Witches, and doth verily thinke them to be Witches; and their names are those whom *James Device* hath formerly spoken of to be there.

She also confesseth in all things touching the killing of Master Lister of Westby, as the said *James Device* hath before confessed.

And the said *Elizabeth Device* also further saith, That at the said meeting at Malking-Tower, as aforesaid, the said *Katharine Hewyt* and *John Bulcock,* with all the rest then there, gave their consents, with the said *Prestons* wife, for the killing of the said Master *Lister.* And for the killing of the said Master *Leonard Lister,* she this Examinate saith in all things, as the said *James Device* hath before confessed in his Examination.

The Examination of JENNET DEVICE, *daughter of* ELIZABETH *late wife of* JOHN DEVICE, *of the Forrest of Pendle, in the Countie of Lancaster, about the age of nine yeares or thereabouts, taken the day and yeare above said:*

Before

ROGER NOWEL AND NICHOLAS BANESTER, *Esquires, two of his Majesties Justices of the Peace in the Countie of Lancaster.*

The said Examinate upon her examination saith, that upon Good-Friday last there were about twenty persons, whereof only two were men, to this Examinates remembrance, at her said Grand-mothers house, called Malking-Tower aforesaid, about twelve of the clocke: all which persons, this Examinats said Mother told her were Witches, and that she knoweth the names of divers of the said Witches.

After all these Examinations, Confessions, and Evidence, delivered in open Court against her, his Lordship commanded the Jurie to observe the particular circumstances, first, Master *Lister* in his extremitie, to complaine hee saw her, and requested them that were by him to lay hold on her.

After he cried out, shee lay heavie upon him even at the time of his death.

But the conclusion is of more consequence than all the rest, that *Jennet Preston* being brought to the dead corps, they bled freshly, And after her deliverence in Lent, it was proved she rode upon a white Foal, and was present in the great assembly at Malkin-Tower with the Witches, to intreate and pray for aide of them, to kill Master *Lister*, now living, for that he had prosequuted against her.

And against these people you may not expect such direct evidence, since all their workes are the workes of darknesse, no witnesses are present to accuse them, therefore I pray God direct your consciences.

After the Gentlemen of the Jurie of Life and Death had spent the most part of the day, in consideration of the evidence against her, they returned into Court and delivered up their Verdict of Life and Death.

The Verdict of Life and Death

Who found *Jennet Preston* guiltie of the fellonie and murder by Witch-craft of *Thomas Lister*, Esquire; contayned in the Indictment against her, &c.

Afterwards, according to the course and order of the Lawes, his Lordship pronounced Judgement against her to bee hanged for her offence.

And so the Court arose.

Here the wonderful discoverie of this *Jennet Preston*, who for so many yeares had lived at Gisburn in Craven, neare Master *Lister*. one thing more I shall add to all these Examinations, and Evidence of witnesses, which I saw, and was present in the Court at Lancaster, when it was done at the Assizes holden in August following.

My *Lord Bromley* being very suspicious of the accusation of *Jennet Device*, the little wench, commanded her to look upon the prisoners, that were present, and declare which of them were present at *Malkin-Tower*, at the great assembly of Witches on Good-Friday last: shee looked upon and tooke many by the handes, and accused them to be there, and when shee had accused all that were there present, shee told his Lordship there was a woman that came out of Craven that was amongst the Witches at that feast, but shee saw her not among the Prisoners at the Barre.

What a singular note was this of a Child, amongst many to misse her, that before that time was hanged for her offence, which shee would never confesse or declare at her death? here was present old *Preston* her husband, who then cried out and went away: being fully satisfied his wife had Justice, and was worthie of death.

To conclude then this present discourse, I heartilie desire you, my loving friends and Countrie-men, for whose particular instructions this is added to the former of the wonderfull discoverie of Witches in the Countie of Lancaster: And for whose particular satisfaction this is published; Awake in time, and suffer not yourselves to be thus assaulted.

Consider how barbarously this Gentleman hath been dealth withal; and especially you that hereafter shall passe upon any Juries of Life and Death; let not your connivence, or rather foolish pittie, spare such as these, to exequute farther mischiefe.

Remember that shee was no sooner set at libertie, but shee plotted the ruine and overthrow of this Gentleman, and his whole Familie.

Expect not, as this reverend and learned Judge saith, such apparent proofe against them, as against others, since all their workes, are the workes of darknesse: and unlesse it please Almightie God to raise witnesses to accuse them, who is able to condemne them?

Forget not the bloud that cries out unto God for revenge, bring it not upon your own heads.

Neither do I urge this any further, then with this, that I would alwaies entreat you to remember, that it is as great a crime (as *Soloman* sayth, *Prov.* 17.) to condemne the innocent, as to let the guiltie escape free.

Looke not upon things strangely alledged, but judiciously consider what is proved against them.

And that as well all you that were witnesses, present at the Arraignment and Triall of her, as all other strangers, to whom this discourse shall come, may take example by this Gentleman to prosecute these Hellish Furies to their end: labor to root them out of the Commonwealth, for the Common good of your Countrey. The greatest mercie extended to them is soone forgotten.

GOD graunt us the long and prosperous continuance of these Honourable and Reverend Judges, under whose government we live in these North parts: for we may say, that GOD Almightie hath singled them out, and set them on his seat, for the Defence of Justice.

And for this great deliverance, let us pray to GOD Almightie, that the memorie of these worthie Judges may bee blessed to all posterities.

Rental of Pendle Forest 1608/9

A LIST of the tenants of the Forest of Pendle was compiled three years before the trials of the Lancashire witches. As we should expect, the list includes names of many who figure in the account of the trial. In the rental, the names are those of the heads of households, the subdivisions those of the booths of the Forest, and the rent ascribed is an indication to us of the wealth of each household.

Below is printed the rental. An asterisk (★) shows that in the notes which follow we comment, directly or indirectly, upon the name beside it.

A true and perfect Rentall of all his Majesties Tenants within the forest or chase of Pendle

		£	s.	d.
Filliclose				
★ Richard Townley Esq.		10	13	4
Huntersholme And Westclose				
★ Richard Shuttleworth Esq.		3	13	7
John Cronkshay		2	3	10¾
John Crook		2	2	4½
	Sum	7	19	10¼
Rough Lee vaccary.				
Chr: Nuttall, Clerk			3	3¾
★ Henry Robinson			7	7
★ John Bulcock			3	0
Chr: Bawden		1	13	4
Richard Bawden			16	8
Robert Smith			16	1½
James Sclator and his wife			3	8½
Chr: Blakey and Simon			13	10

	£.	s.	d.
James Redehough		5	6½
★ Roger Mitton	1	2	2½
★ Miles Nutter		11	7
★ William Robinson		5	4
John Crook		12	6
John Varley		11	4
★ Henry Mitton		2	4½
Hugh Hartley		16	0
Ellen Hartley		15	7
★ John Robinson		10	10
John Cunliffe	1	18	1
William Hartley *alias* Trock		6	0¼
William Hartley, John Hartley and Robert, infants and heirs of Henry Hartley, deceased		6	
Lawrence Stephenson			8
John Bawden		16	8
Sum	13	12	3

Bareley Booth

	£.	s.	d.
Richard Woodroof, Gent.	1	0	0
James Hartley	1	0	0
★ Chr: Robinson	1	0	0
James Bollard	1	0	0
★ John Robinson	1	0	0
★ Hugh Hargraves		15	0
Tho: Varley		15	0
Ingram Bollard		13	4
James Manknowles		10	0
John Higgin		6	8
Sum	8	0	0

Whitley Booth

	£.	s.	d.
★ Chr. Bulcock	1	0	10
Robert Baley		13	3½
Nicholas Robinson		13	3½
Henry Hartley		8	11
Jeoffrey Hargraves		8	11
Eliz: Robinson			4
★ Henry Bulcock		13	3½
Roger Bawden		6	4½
Eliz: Bannister		6	4¾

	£.	s.	d.
★ Ellen Robinson		6	4¾
William Emot		5	8
Chr: Hartley		19	9
Edmund Barley		13	4
William Hartley		1	8
Lawrence Hargraves		7	3
Sum	7	5	9½

Goldshaw Booth

	£.	s.	d.
John Cromback and John Moor for Nutters land	1	18	8
William Stephenson	1	0	5½
★ James Hargraves	1	14	7
Nicholas Duxberry	1	14	7
Thomas Robinson	2	0	2½
Nicholas Stephenson	1	5	0
William Bayley		6	2
Lawrence Stephenson		11	0
★ William Nutter and others	1	7	2
★ John Nutter		8	4
★ John Nutter of Bullhole		8	2
William Stephenson		4	6
★ Anthony Nutter		8	0½
Lawrence Stephenson		2	0
Ed[mund] Starky		2	0
Sum	13	14	0½

Barrowford and Rushton Thorns

	£.	s.	d.
★ Lawrence Townley of Carr, Esq.	1	5	0
Carr Milns	1	0	0
Roughlee Milns		2	0
Charles Bannister, Gent.		5	8
Simon Blackow, Gent.		3	0
John Hartley of Admergill	1	9	6
Bernard Blako		2	0
Edward Robinson		16	1
John Hargreaves	1	10	10½
Lawrence Hartley	1	9	6
Robert Hargraves		10	8
James Foulds		5	5
Humphrey Hartley		6	4
John Sutcliffe		6	8

	£.	s.	d.
John Smith and Nicholas		19	9
★ James Robinson		16	1½
James Hartley		10	1¾
Henry Shaw			7¾
Robert Shaw		6	6½
James Bulcock		5	5
Chr: Blackow of Blackall		10	6
Simon and Chr: Blacow		3	1
John Parker		1	8
Edward Marsden		4	8
John Halsey and others for Wilsons		2	6½
Richard Hanson			2
Sum	15	19	4½

Wheatley Carr

	£.	s.	d.
★ Nicholas Townley Esq.	6	6	8

Old Laund

	£.	s.	d.
Ed[mund] Robinson	3	4	11
★ Tho: Crook		1	50
★ Richard Crook		15	6
Sum	4	15	5

New Laund

	£.	s.	d.
★ John Nutter	2	4	5½
★ John Cromacke, John Moor and			
Margaret Nutter	4	8	11
Sum	6	13	6½

Riddihallows

	£.	s.	d.
Robert Barcroft	6	10	0
Chr: Jackson	1	15	0
★ Henry Nutter	1	15	0
Sum	10	0	0

Nether Higham

	£.	s.	d.
William Anderton, Gent.	6	0	6

Higham Booth

	£.	s.	d.
Henry Parker	1	0	0
★ John Hargraves		9	0
★ Hugh Moor		15	2
★ John Moor of Height		10	0
★ The same for Hugh Moors lands	1	14	6½
Richard Grimshaw	2	0	1

	£.	s.	d.
Chr: Stephenson		2	0
★ Nicholas Hargraves	1	0	0
William Hartley		5	0
★ Ellen Hargraves		5	6
★ Hugh Hargraves		6	8
William Birtwisle		4	0
Roger Hindle		4	6
★ John Moor of Higham	1	3	4
John Robinson son of William			
Robinson, deceased		2	0
Sum	8	16	2½
Sum of the whole	119	16	10½

(from *The Court Rolls of the Honor of Clitheroe*, William Farrar, 1912)

Notes

Numbers in brackets indicate the page number in G. B. Harrison, *The Trial of the Lancashire Witches*.

Filliclose

Richard Townley Esq. was the eldest son of Sir John Towneley, the recusant. He had inherited the Towneley estate in 1608.

Huntersholme and Westclose

Richard Shuttleworth Esq. of Gawthorpe was the nephew and heir of Sir Richard Shuttleworth, the Chief Justice of Chester whom Robert Nutter had accompanied on his fatal journey. It was Richard who attended the trial at Lancaster.

Rough Lee vaccary

Miles Nutter Alice Nutter, who was hanged at Lancaster, was 'a rich woman; had a great estate, and children of good hope' (116). She was 'the wife of Richard Nutter of the Rough Lee (117, 188) and 'Alice Nutter, mother of Myles Nutter' (119). She was also called 'Dick Myles wife of the Rough Lee' (120), from which it appears that her husband answered to the names of both Dick and Miles.

Henry Mitton It was claimed that 'about a year agon' Henry Mitton of the Rough-Lee had been bewitched to death by Elizabeth Device and Alice Nutter for denying Demdike a penny (54, 56).

Bareley Booth

Chr: Robinson   The Robinson family of Barley were 'alias Swyer'. The mutton eaten at Malkin Tower was 'a Wether of Christopher Swyers of Barley' which James had stolen (60).

John Robinson   Elizabeth Device confessed to having made 'a picture of Clay, after the said John Robinson', and to have 'crumbled all the same picture away within a weeke or thereabouts, and about a weeke after the Picture was crumbled or mulled away; the said Robinson dyed.' She did this because John Robinson had taunted her with having a bastard child. The death occurred 'about foure yeares agoe' (53, 54).

Hugh Hargraves   Amongst those at the Malkin Tower meeting was, said Jennet Device, 'the wife of Hugh Hargreives, under Pendle' (77). James Device similarly reported the presence of 'the wife of Hugh Hargreives of Burley' (62). Under Pendle is a farmhouse on the slopes of the hill above Barley. Despite the Devices' evidence, the wife of Hugh Hargraves was not brought to trial. Was this because the Constable, 'Henry Hargreives of Goldshey-Booth' was a brother or cousin to her husband?

Whitley Booth

Chr: Bulcock   Jane Bulcock, wife of Christopher Bulcock of the Mosse End, and John her son, were hanged at Lancaster. James Device and Jennet Device gave evidence that they had attended the Malkin Tower assembly, and that John had turned the spit before the fire. Potts maintains that the Bulcocks had confessed, but does not record their confession. At their trial however 'impudently now they forsweare, swearing they were never at the great assembly at Malking Tower . . .: Crying out in very violent and outragious manner, even to the gallowes, where they died impenitent' (131). Moss End is the name of a farm near Bulhole in Goldshaw Booth, though this Rental suggests that we might look for another Moss End in Wheatley Booth to the north of Barley, perhaps on Black Moss Road.

Henry Bulcock   Henry Bulcock asked Demdike to cure a child of his whom, he said, Alizon had bewitched. Hearing this allegation: 'Alizon fell downe on her knees, and asked the said Bulcock forgivenesse; and confessed to him, that she had bewitched the said Child.' That was 'about St Peters Day last one'(146).

Goldshaw Booth

James Hargraves   The Constable was 'Henrie Hargreives of Goldshey-booth . . . Yeoman'(182). He took James Device to Gisburn to identify Jennet Preston. Also he dug up at Malkin Tower a 'picture' and four human teeth (44). Perhaps he was the son of James.

Jennet Device overheard her brother James and Dandy plan to kill 'John Hargreives of Gold-shey-booth . . . since which time the said John is dead.' That was about three years before 1612 (72).

John Nutter of Bullhole Elizabeth, daughter of Chattox, had been to 'the house of John Nutter of the Bull-hole, to begge or get a dish full of milke.' Chattox had churned it in 'a Kan', which John Nutter's son misliked. He spilt Chattox's milk, after which a Cow belonging to John Nutter died. So Alizon Device told(47). She also said that Demdike had once been called out 'about ten of the the clocke in the night' at the request of John Nutter to amend a cow of his that was sick. Nevertheless next morning the cow was dead (23, 24).

Anthony Nutter Anne, the daughter of 'Anthony Nutter of Pendle' died three weeks after laughing in a way that Chattox thought insolent. That was 'about two yeares agone'(46).

Barrowford and Rushton Thorns

Lawrence Townley of Carr, Esq. Laurence Towneley was the father of Henry Towneley whose wife Anne had died after an altercation with James Device. James had made and crumbled a picture of Anne (68).

James Robinson James Robinson, who had lodged at Greenhead eighteen years before, gave evidence that Robert Nutter believed himself bewitched by Chattox and Anne Redferne. He also said that about six years ago his ale had been spoilt after being tasted by Chattox, who had been hired by his wife to card wool in his house (40).

Wheatley Carr

Nicholas Townley Esq. was the seventh son of Sir John of Towneley Hall.

Old Laund

Tho: Crook and *Richard Crook* Margaret Crooke gave evidence against Chattox and Anne Redferne. She was the daughter of Christopher Nutter of Greenhead, and sister to the dead Robert and to John (111). Born in New Laund, Margaret seems to have married a tenant of Old Laund, unless her husband was the more wealthy John Crook of Huntersholme and Westclose or, if he is a different man, the John Crook of Rough Lee.

New Laund

John Nutter This will be the son of the late Christopher Nutter of Greenhead, although at the trial when he gave evidence about the death of his brother Robert, he was designated 'John Nutter of Higham Booth' (112).

John Cromacke, John Moor and Margaret Nutter Margaret Nutter is Margaret

Crooke's maiden name. The property, with its large rental of £4-8-11, must be Greenhead. That these three together inherited gives substance to Chattox's assertion that old Robert Nutter's wife had wished the death of her grandson, young Robert, so that 'the Women their Coosens might have the land' (37).

Riddihallows

Henry Nutter   The Catholic priests John and Robert Nutter had been born in Reedly Hollow. John was executed at Tyburn in 1583, Robert at Lancaster in 1600. Ellis Nutter, their nephew, was ordained priest in 1601. We do not know how closely this family was related to the husband of Alice Nutter, convicted of witchcraft.

Higham Booth

John Moor of Height   was the father of Sir Jonas Moore, born in 1618. He was also probably the 'John Moore of Higham Gentleman' who had accused Chattox of bewitching his ale and whose son had subsequently died (46). Chattox admitted that her dog had bitten John Moore's cow and caused its death (43). Later in the rental is 'John Moore of Higham' who, if he is a different person, also had a substantial property.

John Hargraves; Nicholas Hargraves; Ellen Hargraves; Hugh Hargraves   Jennet Device said that her brother James procured the death by witchcraft of 'Blaze Hargreves of Higham', who would seem to have belonged to one of these families (72).

Hugh Moor   Chattox was said by Alizon to have bewitched to death 'Hugh Moore of Pendle'. That was 'sixe or seven yeares agoe' which, if accurate, was before the date of the rental (47).

TRAWDEN

A similar Rental of Trawden shows that of the sixteen tenants, two are named *Foulds* and eleven are named *Hartley*. James Device testified that Katherine Hewitt and Alice Gray 'confessed' at Malkin Tower that 'they had killed Foulds wifes child, called Anne Foulds, of Colne' and that they 'had then in hanck a child of Michael Hartleys of Colne'. Trawden adjoins Colne.

Notes

TJP denotes *The Arraignment and Triall of Jennet Preston*; the page-numbers are those in the Appendix of this book.
TLW denotes G.B. Harrison, *The Trial of the Lancashire Witches* which reprints Potts' *Discoverie* . . .

Chapter 1. The Investigation

1. *TJP* 168.
2. *TJP* 165.
3. At Lancaster on 17 and 13 August, beside the Pendle witches were tried on separate charges of Witchcraft: Margaret Pearson of Padiham, Isabel Robey of Windle and eight from Samlesbury. Those from Samlesbury were acquitted; Margaret Pearson was imprisoned and displayed in the stocks; and Isabel Robey was hanged. Elizabeth Southerns, alias Old Demdike, the head of the Malkin Tower family, died before the trial.

Chapter 2. The Silencing of Dissention

4. *TJP* 172.
5. *TJP* 165.
6. *TJP* 166.
7. *TLW* 11.
8. *TJP* 174.

Chapter 3. Gisburn: Jennet's Homeland

9. *TJP* 173.
10. Westby and Arnoldsbigging were initially two adjacent family seats, the latter belonging to the Listers. However about 1520 Thomas Lister of Arnoldsbigging married 'Effamia de Westbye', co-heir of the adjoining estate. Arnoldsbigging, a fortified manor, fell into disrepair, but for two more centuries tended to be given as the name of the residence of the Listers.
11. Rimington appears within Lancashire in Christopher Saxton's map of

Lancashire of 1577 and in Johan Blaeu's map, derived from that of Saxton, of 1648. When one compares Saxton's map of Lancashire with his map of Yorkshire one sees that in the Lancashire map 'Rimington' had been written in error for 'Twiston'. Documentary evidence does not suggest that Rimington, within the ecclesiastical parish of Gisburn, was ever part of Lancashire.

Chapter 4. Thomas Potts' Chronology

12. *TJP* 166–7.
13. G.B. Harrison, *The Trial of the Lancashire Witches*, London, 1929. xliv.
14. *TJP* 167.
15. *TJP* 163, *TLW* 1, 171. The wording of *The Arraignement* . . . has been adapted in places to suit its position as an appendix. The title page shows the intention to publish it as a separate booklet. It may be, however, that publication was later delayed to await the combined printing.

Chapter 5. The Child of One Dodg-sonnes

16. *TJP* 166.
17. *TJP* 169–70.
18. *TLW* 149.
19. *The Parish Register of Bolton-by-Bolland in the County of York 1558–1724* ed. W. J. Stavert, Yorkshire Parish Registers Soc., 1904. The Parish Registers of Gisburn are held in the Parish Church of St Mary, Gisburn. Avril Williams of Crawley, a descendent of the Dodgsons, kindly alerted me to the babe of Bolton-by-Bowland.

Chapter 6. Over the Moors to Malkin Tower

20. *TJP* 169.
21. *TJP* 169.

Chapter 7. Questioning Alizon

22. I believe that James Device was not at this meeting. Potts dated one short piece of James' testimony '30th March', but in part it duplicates word for word his testimony of 27 April. Potts made a mistake in his copying. I deduce that there are two other errors in dating: One of Alizon's depositions is dated xiii not xxx March; and one of Elizabeth Device's is dated 30 March, but fits more sensibly with her other testimony of 27 April. *TLW* 146, 23, 26.
23. *TLW* 140–144.

24. *TLW* 142.
25. *TLW* 140–142.
26. W. Perkins, *A Discourse* . . ., p. 211. But John Webster of Clitheroe in *The Displaying of Supposed Witchcraft*, 1677, had a modern scepticism about the reliability of confessions: 'And though you should find some confidently confessing that they have made a visible and corporeal league with the Devil, and that he hath carnal copulation with them, and that he doth suck upon some parts of their Bodies, and that they are Transubstantiated into Dogs, Cats and the like, or that they fly in the air, and raise Tempests; yet (I hope) I have sufficiently proved by the word of God, the true grounds of Theologie and sound reason, that there never hath been any such Witch existent *in rerum natura*, and so you may know what credit may be given to such Fables and impossibilities.' Epistle Dedicatory.
27. *TLW* 24, 25.
28. *TLW* 45, 46.
29. *TLW* 46, 47.
30. *TLW* 47. Chattox put the milk 'into a Kan, and did charne the same with two stickes acrosse in the same field'. I understand the word 'charne' as 'churn'; Edgar Peel reads it as 'charm', certainly a possibility. E. Peel and P. Southern, *The Trials of the Lancashire Witches*, 1969, p. 23.
31. *TLW* 140. John Webster of Clitheroe in *The Displaying* . . ., 1677, quotes this passage about Demdike's persuading Alizon to show that those who believe themselves to be witches have been taught that delusion by others similarly deluded. Witchcraft is not innate, but learnt: "and we shall find none of these deluded Witches (if they must be so called) but they have been taught by others, that thought themselves to be such also." p. 35.

Chapter 8. Death in Chester and Old Chattox

32. We cannot be sure of this identification. Nutter was a common surname in the Pendle area. Several of the family appear in our story.
33. *TLW* 112, 113. Sir Richard Shuttleworth of Gawthorne was appointed Chief Justice of Chester in 1589. He commenced the building of Gawthorpe Hall and died in 1600.
34. *TLW* 111, 112. Whitsun usually falls in May; Candlemas is 2 February; Maudlintide is the season around St. Mary Magdalene's Day, 22 July; Michaelmas is 29 September.
35. The fine house of Greenhead, in the Parish of Fence, still stands.
36. *TLW* 41.
37. *TLW* 40.
38. *TLW* 33.
39. The Laund. Pendle Forest in medieval times was divided into 'booths' and 'launds'. Booths were originally cow-keepers dwellings and the surrounding area in the upland vaccaries and 'launds' were deer-enclosures. 'Old Laund' and 'New Laund' are nto far far from Greenhead, close to Pendle Water.

40. The other women were 'Loomeshaws wife of Burley, and one Jane Boothman of the same.' 'Burley' here is an erroneous printing of 'Burnley'.

41. *TLW* 36, 37. At the trial Anne Redferne was arraigned first for the murder
of Robert Nutter, but found Not guilty "the Evidence being not very
pregnant against her". She was later tried for the murder of Christopher
Nutter and found Guilty.

42. *TLW* 42, 43. For the charm see page 93.

43. *TLW* 35f.

44. *TLW* 43f.

Chapter 9. Old Demdike and the Making of Pictures

45. *TLW* 16.

46. *TLW* 18, 19. Elizabeth Device had testified, it was claimed, that her mother,
Demdike 'hath a place on her left side by the space of fourty yeares, in such
sort as was to be seene at this Examinates Examination taking, at this present
time.' (*TLW* 26) How long had Demdike been a witch? Potts writes
'Foure-score yeares'; Elizabeth Device implies forty years. Demdike herself
say about 'twenty years past' she met Tibb, but he did not suck her until
six years later. When did Elizabeth give this evidence? The heading says 30
March, but Demdike could only have been examined on 2 April, and
Elizabeth herself appears only otherwise to have been questioned by Nowell
on 27 April. It was then, I believe, that this evidence was given.
John Webster of Clitheroe in *The Displaying . . .*, 1677, says of confessions
of sucking that they 'have no truth-likeliness in them' because of their very
obscenity: 'For the most of them are not credible, by reason of their obscenity
and filthiness; for chast ears would tingle to hear such bawd and immodest
lies; and what pure and sober minds would not nauseate and startle to
understand such unclean stories, as of the carnal Copulation of the Devil
with a Witch, or his sucking the Teat or Wart of an old stinking and rotten
Carkass?'

47. *TLW* 18, 19.

48. *TLW* 19. 'A little before Christmas last' whereas Alizon had dated the incident
'about 2. yeeres agoe'.

49. *TLW* 33.

50. *TLW* 39, 40.

51. C. L'Estrange Ewen, *Witchcraft & Demonianism*, p. 449. *The History of the
House of Stanley*, 1793, p. 165.

52. *TLW* 44.

53. *TLW* 20.

54. William Perkins, *A Discourse . . .*, Cambridge, 1608, p. 149.

55. *TLW* 26.

Chapter 10. The Meeting at Malkin Tower

56. *TJP* 169.

57. *TLW* 55.

58. *TLW* 54. E. Peel and P. Southern, *The Trials of the Lancashire Witches*, 1969, p. 187. They cite the research of Gladys Whittaker into the registers of Colne Parish Church for the information that a family called Sellar lived at White Moor.

59. *TLW* 180, 181, 44.

60. *TLW* 27.

61. J. Brand, *Popular Antiquities of Great Britain*, ed. H. C. Hazlitt, 1870. Cited by Eamon Duffy, *The Stripping of the Altars*, 1992, p. 29.

62. *TLW* 60.

63. *TLW* 74. We see from other references that the Robinson family of Barley were also known as Swyer. *TLW* 74, 76, 60, 53, 57.
    In 1633 a certain Margret Johnson was induced to confess to witchcraft. She had been charged by the inventive imposter, young Edmund Robinson of Wheatley Lane, Pendle. Margret testified 'that Good Friday is one constant day for a yearely generall meeting of witches; and that on Good Friday last they had a meeting near Pendle water-syde'. This 'confession' was probably itself shaped by the famed story of Malkin Tower twenty-one years before, so is not proof that Good Friday had earlier been held to be the day on which witches would meet.

64. *TLW* 60, 75, 59, 136, 126, 118, 134.

65. *TLW* 74, 59, *TJP* 169–70.

66. *TLW* 140–142.

67. *TLW* 18, 35f, 68, 78, 79, 72, 73, 53.

68. *TLW* 59; Edward Fairfax, *Daemonologia*, ed. W. Grainge, 1882, p. 32–34; C. L'Estrange Ewen, *Witchcraft and Demonianism*, 1933, p. 272; K. Thomas, *Religion and the Decline of Magic*, 1971, p. 626.

69. *Newes from Scotland*, 1591 ed. G. B. Harrison, p. 16, printed as an appendix to G. B. Harrison, *King James I, Daemonologie*, 1924.

70. *TJP* 169.

71. *Dictionary of National Biography*. King James confided his daughter Mary to Knyvet to be educated. From the terms of Potts' Epistle Dedicatory in *The Wonderfull Discovery* it seems not unlikely that Potts too was educated by him. *TLW* 3.

72. Christopher Haigh, *Reformation and Resistance in Tudor Lancashire*, CUP, 1975, p. 52.

73. *TJP* 169–70.

74. *TJP* 170.

75. H.L.L. Denny, *Memorials of an Ancient House*, 1913, p. 123; Gisburn Parish Records.

76. *TJP* 170.

77. *TLW* 135, 133.

78. *TLW* 124.

79. *TJP* 170.

80. King James I, *Daemonologie*, 1597, ed. G. B. Harrison, 1924, p. 38. The use of the word 'foal' by both King James and by Nowell helps to confirm that Nowell use *Daemonologie* as his stereotype.

81. *Reginonis abbatis Promiensis libris duo de synodalibus causis*, ed. F. W. H. Wasserschleben, Lipsiae, 1840, p. 355. Cited in C. Ginzburg, *Ecstasies*, 1989, tr. 1990, p. 90.

82. J. Sprenger and H. Kramer, *Malleus Maleficarum*, 1486, tr. M. Summers, 1928. Arrow Edition 1971, pp. 239, 240. This book was supported by the Papal Bull, *Summis Desiderantes Affectibus* issued by Pope Innocent VIII in 1484. The Bull deplored the spread of witchcraft in Germany and authorised his 'beloved sons', the Dominican Inquisitors Henrich Institor (Kramer) and Jakob Sprenger to extirpate it.

83. C. L'Estrange Ewen, *Witchcraft and Demonianism*, 1933, p. 84, 92, 314; John Webster of Clitheroe in *The Displaying* . . ., 1677, p. 68, has this to say about night-flying: 'That a Devil should carry an old Witch in the Air into foraign Regions, that can hardly crawl with a staff, to dancing and banqueting, and yet to return with an empty belly, and the next day be forced, like old Dembdike or Elizabeth Sothernes, and Alizon Denice (sic), to go a begging with a sowr-milk can: is this either probable or likely?'

84. *TLW* 27, 51, 121, 81. *TJP* 167, 173.

85. Sebastien Michaelis, *Pneumalogie*, 1587, Tr. E.A. Ashwin. Cited in C. L'Estrange Ewen, *Witchcraft and Demonianism*, 1933, p. 43.

86. G. Scarre, *Witchcraft and Magic in 16th- and 17th-Century Europe*, 1987, p. 20 ff..

87. *TJP* 170, *TLW* 76.

Chapter 11. Judge Bromley and Judge Altham

88. *Dictionary of National Biography*.

89. Champlin Burrage, *The Early English Dissenters 1550–1641*, Vol. II, 1912, p. 216 ff; Dictionary of National Biography.

90. C. L'Estrange Ewen, *Witchcraft and Demoniaism*, 1933, p. 408.

91. F. R. Raines (ed.), *The Journal of Nicholas Assheton of Downham . . . for Part of the Year 1617, and Part of the Year Following*, 1848.

Chapter 12. The Dying Man's Railing and the Bleeding Corpse

92. *TJP* 168.

93. *TJP* 168.

94. *TJP* 172.

95. William Perkins, *A Discourse* . . ., 1608, p. 210.

96. *TJP* 172, 168. Potts' use of a plural pronoun with 'corpse' is a curiosity. Corpse is derived from the Latin 'corpus', a body, so the modern usage,

rather than that which treats the 's' as a plural ending, better respects the etymon.

97. *TJP* 168–9.
98. King James I, *Daemonologie*, ed. G.B. Harrison, 1924, p. 80.
99. *TLW* 153.
100. Reginald Scot, *Discoverie* XIII, ix; Francis Bacon's *Works*, ii, p. 660.
101. J. Webster, *The Displaying of Supposed Witchcraft*, p. 305-6.
102. Lancashire R.O. QSB 1/170/55–60; *The Autobiography and Correspondence of Sir Simonds D'Ewes*, ed. J.O. Halliwell (1845) i, p. 59. Cited in K. Thomas *Religion and the Decline of Magic*, p. 262.
103. *Op. cit.*, p. 339. Cited in J.A. Sharpe *Witchcraft in Seventeenth Century Yorkshire*. Borthwick Paper, No. 81, 1992, p. 27.

Chapter 13. Wedding Traumas

104. *TJP 168*.
105. Bracewell Parish Registers, Lancashire R.O.
106. J. Webster, *The Displaying of Supposed Witchcraft*, 1677, Epistle Dedicatory.
107. *TJP* 168.
108. *TJP* 166.
109. *TJP* 166.
110. H.L.L. Denny, *Memorials of an Ancient House*, 1913, p. 12. The will is dated 14 March, 1540.
111. *TJP* 168.
112. *TJP* 166.

Chapter 14. The Victimisation of Jennet

113. C. L'Estrange Ewen, *Witch Hunting and Witch Trials*, 1929, p. 269; Cited in K. Thomas, *Religion and the Decline of Magic*, 1971, p. 641.
114. K. Thomas, *Religion and the Decline of Magic*, 1971, p. 659.

Chapter 15. James—Religious Scruples and Malign Magic

115. E. Peel and P. Southern, *The Trials of the Lancashire Witches*, 1969, p. 43.
116. *TLW* 65.
117. *TLW* 68.
118. *TLW* 79. James' conversation with this 'Dogge' bears comparison with the disputes of St Anthony with the devils that beset him in the desert.
119. *TLW* 67.
120. *TLW* 68, 70.
121. *TLW* 69.
122. *TLW* 72, 73.

123. *TLW* 57.
124. *TLW* 54.
125. *TLW* 114.
126. *TLW* 117.
127. *TLW* 116.
128. Gladys Whittaker, *Roughlee Hall – Fact and Fiction*, Marsden Antiquarians, 1980; W. Harrison Ainsworth, *The Lancashire Witches – a Romance of Pendle Forest*, 1884.
129. *TLW* 25.
130. *TLW* 25.

Chapter 16. The Little Wench and more of Chattox

131. *TJP* 173, *TLW* 121.
132. *TLW* 22. The diarist Nicholas Assheton was seven years old when his elder brother Richard died. His diary for the years 1617 and 1618 makes little reference to the Nowells. It may be that there was a frostiness between these two Protestant families.
133. *TLW* 21, 22.
134. John Webster in *The Displaying of Supposed Witchcraft*, describes 'barbarous and cruel acts' inflicted on those accused of witchcraft during their examinations: 'And the like in my time and remembrance happened here in Lancashire, where divers both men and women were accused of supposed Witchcraft, and were so unchristianly, unwomanly, and inhumanely handled, as to be stript stark naked, and to be laid upon Tables and Beds to be searched (nay even in their most privy parts) for these their supposed Witch-marks'. He adds, 'That there are divers Nodes, Knots, Protuberances, Warts and Excrescenses that grow upon the bodies of men and women, is sufficiently known to learned Physicians and experienced Chirurgions . . . If all these were Witchmarks, then few would go free, especially those that are of the poorer sort, that have the worst diet, and are but nastily kept.' p. 82.
135. *TLW* 22.

Chapter 17. Spells

136. *TLW* 42.
137. In Henry Baggilie's version, as we shall see, the words are in the second sense only.
138. 1557 Primer *Praier bef. Sacrament*: 'I come as a wretch to thee my Lord . . . to thee my boote.'
139. K. Thomas, *Religion and the Decline of Magic*, p. 220. Thomas cites seven examples of versions of this formula.
140. Borthwick Institute, R. VI. A 10, f. 61. Cited in K. Thomas, p. 211.

141. Ely Diocesan Records. Cambridge University Library, B 2/5, f. 273. Cited in K. Thomas, p. 217.

142. James Raine (ed.), *Depositions from the Castle of York*, Surtees Society, Vol. XL, 1861.

143. Eamon Duffy, *The Stripping of the Altars*, Yale University Press, 1992, p. 239.

144. Lancashire Record Office, QSB. 1.139.81.

145. *TLW* 79, 80.

146. E. Peel and P. Southern, *The Trials of the Lancashire Witches*, 1969, p. 127.

147. *TLW* 80.

148. John White, *The Way to the True Church . . .*, London, 1612, 4th edn., 1616. Preface.

149. *Peblis to the Play*, 1500 xxiii 'And our doure hes na stekill'.

150. W. Henderson, *Notes on the Folk-Lore of the Northern Counties*, 1879, p. 81. (Cited in *British Calender Customs*, Folk-Lore Society XCVII, 1936): 'The incumbent of Fishlake tells me that, in that village, at 8.00 am on Good Friday, the great bell was solemnly tolled, as for a death or a funeral.'

151. Matthew 26:26, John 20:25.

152. Luke 22:45, 46. Matthew 26:47. John 18:3.

153. Luke 22:43.

Chapter 18. Catholicism in Whalley Parish

154. Quoted in P. Tyler, 'The Church Courts at York . . .', *Northern History*, Vol IV, 1969, p. 90.

155. John White, *The Way to the True Church*, 1612, 1616. Preface.

156. John Webster, *The Displaying of Supposed Witchcraft*, 1677, p. 323.

157. J.K. Walton, *Lancashire, A Social History*, Manchester University Press, 1990, p. 37.

158. C. Haigh, *Reformation and Resistance in Tudor Lancashire*, 1975, p. 259.

159. Haigh, *ibid.*, p. 218.

160. Haigh, *ibid.*, p. 218.

161. Haigh, *ibid.*, p. 240.

162. Joseph Gillow, *Bibliographical Dictionary of the English Catholics*, Vol IV, no date.

Chapter 19. Grindletonianism

163. The vilification to which the antinomianism of Grindleton was exposed is plain in Sir Walter Scott's footnote to *Woodstock*, a Waverley Novel set in the Commonwealth years. Sir Walter's character, the preacher Tomkins, espoused 'peculiar doctrines, which were entertained by a sect sometimes termed the Family of Love, but more commonly Ranters.' Scott explained: 'The Familists were originally founded by David George of Delft, an enthusiast, who believed himself the Messiah. They branched off into various

sects of Grindletonians, Familists of the Mountains, of the Valleys, Familists of Cape Order, &c. &., of the Scattered Flock &c. &c. Among doctrines too wild and foul to be quoted, they held the lawfulness of occasional conformity with any predominant sect when it suited their convenience, of complying with the order of any magistrate, or superior power, however sinful. They disowned the principal doctrines of Christianity, as a law which had been superseded by the advent of David George – nay, obeyed the wildest and loosest dictates of evil passions, and are said to have practised among themselves the grossest libertinism. See Edward's *Gangraena*, Pagitt's *Heresiographia*, and a very curious work written by Ludovic Claxton, one of the leaders of the sect, called the *Lost Sheep Found* – small quarto, London, 1660.' Scott's abuse is culled from his seventeenth-century sources. We should wish to discriminate between the Ranters, the sects of the Familists and the Grindletonians. Sir Walter correctly places Grindletonianism within the context of the radical and ecstatic sects which flourished in those unshackled days.

164. Christopher Hill, *The World Turned Upside Down*, 1972, 1975, p. 81 ff. Brearley's name is also spelt Brierly.
165. R.M. Jones, *Mysticism and Democracy in the English Commonwealth*, 1932, pp. 79–84.
166. C. Hill, *The World Turned Upside Down*, p. 84. R.M. Jones, ibid., pp. 85–90.

Chapter 20. Charmers and William Perkins

167. William Perkins, *A Discourse of the Damned Art of Witchcraft*, p. 174, 153.
168. Margaret's son, Ferdinando, Earl of Derby, allegedly died through the malice of witches, see page 38.
169. J. A. Sharpe, *Witchcraft in Seventeenth-Century Yorkshire*, Borthwick Paper No. 81, p. 3. Citing P. Tyler, 'The Church Courts at York and Witchcraft Prosecutions, 1567–1640', *Northern History* 4, pp. 84–109.
170. R. Scot, *The Discoverie of Witchcraft*, 1584, I ii; R. Burton, *The Anatomy of Melancholy*, 1621, ii, p. 6; Cited in K. Thomas, *Religion and the Decline of Magic*, pp. 291–2.
171. Lancashire Record Office, QSB 1.138 (59); K. Thomas, *op. cit.*, p. 277.
172. Sermons by Hugh Latimer, ed. G.E. Corrie, Cambridge, 1844, p. 534.
173. Perkins died in 1602 at the age of 44. In view of the Device's occupation of begging we may note Perkins' rigorous 'capitalist' ethic which led him to deplore the giving of charity. Beggars are 'for the most part a cursed generation'. 'Rogues, beggars and vagabonds . . . are as the rotten legges, and armes, that droppe from the body . . . To wander up and downe from yeare to yeare to this ende, to seeke and procure bodily maintenance, is no calling, but the life of a beast.' W. Perkins, *Works* III, p. 191; I, p. 755 cited in *William Perkins and the Poor*, in Christopher Hill, *Puritanism and Revolution*, 1958, Penguin, 1990, p. 223.
   In attitude to the poor, the contrast between Perkins and Roger Brearley of Grindleton is marked. Brearley might have had Perkins in mind when

he wrote: 'These (word-notion) Christians are still hard-hearted men, had rather the poor perish in the streets than they want to satisfie their appetites: For if a man would spare the tenth penny that he spends idelie, only to please his lusts would it not relieve a Town? Nay, if that vain waste was spared, which man spends on his lusts (i.e. pleasures), it would keep the poor of a Paroch (parish). And if our garish women would but spare one Lace and garde of five, it would clothe them (the poor) from the cold.' R. Brearley, *A Bundle of Soul-convincing, Directing and Comforting Truths*, 1670, p. 9. Quoted in R. M. Jones, *Mysticism and Democracy*, p. 83.

174. W. Perkins, *A Discourse of the Damned Art of Witchcraft*, 1608, p. 1.

175. W. Perkins, *idem.*, pp. 31, 41, 48.

176. W. Perkins, *idem.*, p. 174.

177. W. Perkins, *idem.*, p. 174.

178. W. Perkins, *idem.*, p. 256. This doctrine was exemplified in Court at Lancaster. Alizon was asked by the Court whether she could help John Law, the stricken pedlar, to his strength and health. 'She answered she could not, and so did many of the rest of the Witches: but shee, with others, affirmed, That if old Dembdike had lived, she could and would have helped him out of that great miserie.' Yet that same Demdike, renowned for healings, could be called by Potts 'a general agent for the Devill in all these parts.' *TLW* 144, 17.

Chapter 21. Roger Nowell's Protestant Heritage

179. *Dictionary of National Biography*; T. D. Whittaker, *A History of the Original Parish of Whalley*, 1800, p. 535 ff; R. Halley, *Lancashire: its Puritanism and Nonconformity*, 1869, Vol. I, pp. 107–18, 142–3.

180. As above.

Chapter 22. The 7. in Lancashire

181. Sources for Starkie and Darrel episodes: George More, *A True Discourse . . .*, 1600; Samuel Harsnett, *A Discovery of the Fraudulent Practices of John Darrel*, London, 1599; John Darrel, *A True Narration . . .*, 1600; Corinne H. Rickert, *The Case of John Darrel*, University of Florida Monographs. Humanities No. 9, Winter, 1962; D. P. Walker, *Unclean Spirits*, Scolar Press, 1981; C. L'Estrange Ewen, *Witchcraft and Demonianism*, 1933, p. 181 ff.

182. Baines in his *History of Lancashire* writes of Cleweth Hall in Tyldesley, Leigh: 'The old mansion was a respectable timber building, with bay windows and gables.' The estate in the nineteenth century was still held by the Starkies and comprised 163 acres.

183. John Darrel, *A True Narration of the Strange and grevous vexation by the devil, of 7. persons in Lancashire; and William Somers of Nottingham. Wherein the doctrine of possession, and dispossession of demonikes out of the word of God is particularly*

applyed unto Somers, and the rest of the persons controverted . . ., 1600. George More, *A True Discourse concerning the certaine possession and dispossession of 7 persons in one familie in Lancashire, which may also serve as part of an Answere to a fayned and false Discoverie which speaketh very much evill . . ., By George More, Minister and Preacher of the Worde of God, and now (for bearing Witnesse unto this, and for justifying the rest) a prisoner in the Clinke, where he hath continued almost for the space of two yeares*, 1600.

Chapter 23. Little Darrel's Tricks

184. C L'Estrange Ewen, *Witchcraft and Demonianism*, p. 182.

185. Jesse Bee (and John Denison), *The most wonderful and true storie, of a certain Witch named Alse Gooderige of Stapenhill, who was arraigned and convicted at Darbie at the Assises there. As also a true report of the strange torments of Thomas Darling, a boy of thirteene yeres of age, that was possessed by the Devill, with his horrible fittes and terrible Apparitions by him uttered at Burton upon Trent in the Countie of Stafford, and of his marvellous deliverance*, London, 1597.

186. J. Webster, *The Displaying . . .*, 1677, p. 274.

187. John Webster of Clitheroe in *The Displaying . . .* 1677, comments about curious spewings: 'Many of these vomitings of strange stuff, and the like have been meer counterfeit juglings and Impostures, as was manifest in the Boy of Bilson Sommers of Nottingham and diverse others: besides, I that have practiced Physick about forty years could never find any such thing in truth and reality, but have known many that have counterfeited these strange vomitings, and the like, which we and others have plainly laid open and detected.' p. 252.

188. Samuel Harsnett, *A Discovery of the Fraudulent Practices of John Darrel*, London, 1599; Samuel Harsnett, *A Declaration*, London, 1603.

189. *The Triall of Maist. Dorrell, A Collection of Defences against Allegations not yet suffered to receive convenient answers*, 1599, p. 79

190. Ben Jonson, *Works*, ed. C. H. Herford VI, Oxford, 1938, p. 254–69.

Chapter 24. Thomas Lister and the Guilt of Schism

191. Borthwick Institute, York, V35, 465r.

192. James J. Cartwright, *Chapters in the History of Yorkshire*, 1872, p. 149.

193. Richard Challenor, *Memoirs of Missionary Priests*, ed. E. H. Pollen, 1924; John Myerscough, *A Procession of Lancashire Martyrs*, 1958.

194. *Memorials of an Ancient House*, p. 10, 12; Dictionary of National Biography.

195. Robert Halley, *Lancashire: its Puritanism and Nonconformity*, 1869, Vol. 1, p. 124. Halley quotes as evidence of the treachery of Cardinal Allen the following from Allen's writings: 'All acts done by the queen's authority ever since she was by public sentence of the Church and See Apostolic (Bullae Pii Quinti, an. 1569) declared a heretic and an enemy of God's Church,

and excommunicated and deposed from all royal dignity, all is void by the Laws of God . . . For heresy maketh a man by all Christian laws infamous, and voideth him of all degrees and titles of honour.' In a declaratory paper issued at the time of the Armada, and signed by Allen, Queen Elizabeth was declared 'a most unjust usurper and open injurer of all nations, an infamous, accursed, excommunicate heretic, the very shame of her sex and princely name, the chief spectacle of sin and abomination in our age, the poison, calamity, and destruction of our noble Church and country, a filthy, wicked, and illiberal creature.'

Chapter 25. Margaret Pearson of Padiham

196. *TLW* 182.
197. *TLW* 151.
198. *TLW* 150.
199. *TLW* 151.
200. *TLW* 166.
201. T. Potts, *Discoverie* . . ., edited by Crossley, footnote; Richard Ainsworth, *History and Associations of Altham and Huncoat*, Accrington, 1932. Ainsworth records that Bannister's first wife was interred at Altham in December, 1611 and that in this last year of his life he had married Catherine, daughter of Edward Ashton of Chadderton. Marriage and the court-case probably hastened the old man's death.

Chapter 26. The Witches of Samlesbury

202. *TLW* 95.
203. W. Farrar and J. Brownbill (eds), *Victoria County History of England – Lancashire*, Vol. 6, 1911.
204. *Memorials of an Ancient House*, p. 205.
205. W. Farrar and J. Brownbill (eds), *op. cit.*; J. S. Leatherbarrow, *The Lancashire Elizabethan Recusants*, Chetham Soc. 110, 1947, p. 82.
206. *TLW* 86 ff.
207. *TLW* 95, 102, 103.
208. John Myerscough, *A Procession of Lancashire Martyrs*, 1958.
209. J. Webster, *The Displaying* . . ., 1677, p. 273.

Chapter 27. The Unease of Henry Towneley

210. *TLW* 65.
211. Whittaker, *History of Whalley*, p. 545; C. Haigh, *Reformation and Resistance*, p. 260.
212. Edgar Peel and Pat Southern, *The Trials of the Lancashire Witches*, p. 142.

The Surey Demoniack :

OR, AN

ACCOUNT

OF

SATANS

Strange and Dreadful Actings,
In and about the Body of

Richard Dugdale

Of *Surey*, near *Whalley* in *Lancashire* ;

And how he was Dispossest by Gods Blessing on
the Fastings and Prayers of divers Ministers and People.
The Matter of Fact attested by the Oaths of several Credible Persons, before some of His MAJESTIES
Justices of the Peace in the said County.

By John Carrington, Minister of

· L O N D O N :

Printed for *Jonathan Robinson*, at the *Golden Lyon* in St.
Paul's-Church-Yard. 1697.

213. *Dictionary of National Biography.*

Chapter 29. Coda: John Webster and Sir John Assheton

214. R. M. Jones, *Mysticism and Democracy*, 1932, p. 85 ff; In his will of 1680 Webster bequeathed 'fourty shillings to the poore of the townshipp of Grindleton in Yorkshire.' *Ibid.*, p. 19. C. Hill, *The World Turned Upside Down*, 1972; W. S. Weeks, *Dr John Webster*, no date.
215. J. Webster, *The Displaying* . . ., 1677, p.9.
216. J. Webster, *idem.*
217. K. T. Hoppen, *The Nature of the Early Royal Society*, 1976 in W. R. Owens, *Seventeenth-Century England*, p. 237 ff.
218. *TLW* 46; Whittaker, *History of Whalley*, p. 528; A Rental of February 1608/9 listed amongst the fourteen tenants of Higham Booth: Hugh Moor, John Moor of Height and John Moor of Higham, the first and the last paying amounts that would qualify them as 'gentlemen'; William Farrar, *The Court Rolls of the Honor of Clitheroe*, Vol 2, p. 404.
219. Earnest Puritan divines in the Ribble Valley continued to believe in possession by the devil. In 1689 at Surey Barn, near Whalley, the nineteen-year-old Richard Dugdale, 'the Surey Demoniak' was seized with fits. He would dance and leap 'wherein he excelled all that the spectators had seen . . . the demoniak would six or seven times together leap up so that . . . his legs might be seen shaking and quavering above the heads of the people, from which height he oft fell down on his knees, which he long shivered and travest on the ground as nimbly as other men can twinckle or sparkle their fingers, thence spring up to's high leaps again, and then falling on his feet, which seemed to reach the earth but with the gentlest and scarce perceivable touches when he made the highest leaps.' He talked in strange voices, vomited stones 'an inch and a half square' and (like William Sommers) had a lump 'which rose in the thick of his leg, about the size of a mole, and did work up like such a creature towards the chest of his body till it reached his breast, when it was as big as a man's fist.' He was often attended by six dissenting ministers, sometimes by more. His performances, which attracted crowds, were claimed by Rev Zachary Taylor to be impostures managed by those ministers, which provoked pamphleteering reminiscent of the Darrel affair a century earlier. Dugdale had started his fits in Gisburn when he was 'a hired servant with Thomas Lister of Arnoldsbigging, in the County of York, Esq.' It seems that the stories attaching to Westby/Arnoldsbigging about Jennet Preston and her associates gave shape to the boy's athletic exhibitionism. vide: John Carrington *The Surey Demoniack or an Account of Satans strange and Dreadful Actings in and about the Body of Richard Dugdale*, London 1697; Zach. Taylor, *The Surey Imposter being an Answer to the late fanatical Pamphlet entitled The Surey Demoniack*, London, 1697; *The Lancashire Levite Rebuk'd or a Farther Vindication of the Dissenters from Popery, Superstition, Ignorance and*

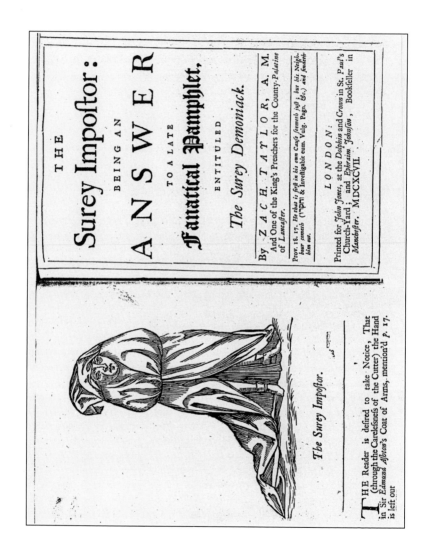

THE

Surey Impoſtor:

BEING AN

A N S W E R

TO A LATE

Fanatical Pamphlet,

ENTITULED

The Surey Demoniack.

By ZACH. TAYLOR, A. M.
And One of the King's Preachers for the County-Palatine
of Lancaſter.

Prov. 18. 17. He that is firſt in his own Cauſe ſeemeth juſt ; but his Neighbour cometh (חקר & Inveſtigabit eum. Vulg. Pagn. &c.) and ſoundeth
him out.

L O N D O N:

Printed for John Jones, at the Dolphin and Crown in St. Paul's
Church-Yard ; and Ephraim Johnſon , Bookſeller in
Mancheſter. MDCXCVII.

The Surey Impoſtor.

THE Reader is deſired to take Notice, That
(through the Careleſsneſs of the Cutter) the Hand
in Sir Edmund Aſhton's Coat of Arms, mention'd p. 17.
is left out

Knavery, unjustly Charged on them by Mr Zachary Taylor, London, 1698; Thomas Jollie, *A Vindication of the Surey Demoniack as no Imposter*, London, 1698.

Assize Records

Assize Records for the North and North-Eastern Circuits, 1607–1640 are held by the Public Record Office (ASS 1/44/1). It is a huge and disorganised mass of material. Papers and membranes are crumpled, dirty, often illegible. Searches to date have not revealed indictments mentioning Jennet Preston; indeed, it is doubtful whether there are any documents relating to the regnal years 9 and 10 of King James. The documents seem to be purely formal indictments, so elaboration cannot be expected. I am grateful to the researchers Linda McGowan of London N21 and John Dagger of Horsmonden for this information, albeit negative. Those with the palaeographic skills to read Latin legal shorthand may like to resume the search.

Bibliography

Journal of Nicholas Assheton, ed. F. R. Raines, Chetham Soc., Vol 14, 1848.

Mary Brigg, *The Early History of the Forest of Pendle*, Pendle Heritage Centre, 1989.

Champlin Burrage, *The Early English Dissenters in the Light of Recent Research 1550–1641*, Vol. II, Cambridge U.P., 1912.

James J. Cartwright, *Chapters in the History of Yorkshire – being a collection of Original Letters, Papers and Public Documents . . . Elizabeth, James I and Charles I*, Wakefield, 1872.

Richard Challenor, *Memoirs of Missionary Priests*, ed. J. H. Pollen, 1924.

Patrick Collinson, *The Elizabethan Puritan Movement*, Methuen, 1967.

John Darrel, *A True Narration of the Strange and grevous vexation by the devil, of 7. persons in Lancashire, and William Somers of Nottingham. Wherein the doctrine of possession, and dispossession of demonikes out of the word of God is particularly applyed unto Somers, and the rest of the persons controverted: together with the use we are to make of these workes of God*, 1600.

Henry Littleton Lister Denny, *Memorials of An Ancient House – A History of the Family of Lister or Lyster*, Edinburgh, 1913.

Eamon Duffy, *The Stripping of the Altars – Traditional Religion in England 1400–1580*, Yale U.P., 1992.

C. L'Estrange Ewen, *Witchcraft and Demonianism*, Heath Cranton, 1933.

Edward Fairfax, ed. William Grange, *Daemonologia: A discourse of Witchcraft. As it was acted in the family of Mr Edward Fairfax of Fuyston*, Harrogate, 1882.

William Farrar, *Court Rolls of the Honor of Clitheroe*, Edinburgh, 1912.

Joseph Gillow, *Bibliographical Dictionary of the English Catholics*, n.d.

Carlo Ginzburg, *Ecstasies – Deciphering the Witches Sabbath*, Hutchinson Radius, 1990.

Christopher Haigh, *Reformation and Resistance in Tudor Lancashire*, Cambridge U.P., 1975.

Robert Halley, *Lancashire, Its Puritanism and Nonconformity*, Vol I and II, Manchester, 1869.

G. B. Harrison (ed.), King James I, *Daemonologie*, 1597, Bodley Head Reprint, 1924.

G. B. Harrison (ed.), *The Trial of the Lancaster Witches, AD MDCXII*, Peter Davies, London, 1929. (*TLW*)

Samuel Harsnett, *A Discovery of the Fraudulent Practices of John Darrel*, 1599.

Samuel Harsnett, *A Declaration of Egregious Popish Impostures*, 1603.

Rachel A. C. Hasted, *The Pendle Witch Trial 1612*, Lancashire County Books, 1987.

Christopher Hill, *The World Turned Upside Down*, Maurice Temple Smith, 1972, Peregrine, 1984.

Christopher Hill, *Puritanism and Revolution*, Secker and Warburg, 1958, Penguin, 1990.

K. Theodore Hoppen, *The Nature of the Early Royal Society*, British Journal for the History of Science, IX, 1976 (included in W. R. Owens (ed.) above).

R. M. Jones, *Mysticism and Democracy in the English Commonwealth*, Harvard U.P. 1932.

Heinrich Kramer and Jacobus Sprenger, *Malleus Malificarum*, Tr. M. Summers. Arrow, 1971.

R. Marchant, *The Puritans and the Church Courts in the Diocese of York 1560–1642*, 1960.

J. S. Leatherbarrow, *The Lancashire Elizabethan Recusants*, Chetham Society 110, Manchester, 1947.

George More, *A True Discourse concerning the Certaine Possession and Dispossession of 7. Persons in one familie in Lancashire*, 1600.

John Mush, *The Life and Death of Margaret Clitherow*, ed. William Nicholson, 1849.

W. R. Owens (ed.), *Seventeenth-century England – A Changing Culture, Vol. 2*, Open University Press, 1980.

Edgar Peel and Pat Southern, *The Trials of the Lancashire Witches*, Hendon Publishing, Nelson, 1969.

William Perkins, *A Discourse of the Damned Art of Witchcraft*, Cambridge, 1608.

Thomas Potts, *The Wonderfull Discoverie of Witches in the Countie of Lancaster*, London 1613 (text also included in Harrison *op. cit.*, above).

F. R. Raines, *The Journal of Nicholas Assheton of Downham, in the County of Lancaster, Esq. for Part of the Year 1617, and Part of the Year Following*, Chetham Society, 1848.

James Raine (ed.), *Depositions from the Castle at York relating to Offences Committed in the Northern Counties*, Surtees Soc. Vol. XL, 1861.

Corrinne H. Rickert, *The Case of John Darrel, Minister and Exorcist*, University of Florida Monographs. Humanities. No. 9, Winter 1962.

Geoffrey Scarre, *Witchcraft and Magic in 16th- and 17th-century Europe*, Macmillan, 1987.

J. A. Sharpe, *Witchcraft in Seventeenth-century Yorkshire*, Borthwick Paper, No 81, 1992.

———, *History of the House of Stanley from the Conquest to 1776*, Preston, 1793.

Keith Thomas, *Religion and the Decline of Magic*, Weidenfeld and Nicholson, 1971, Peregrine, 1978.

H. R. Trevor-Roper, *The European Witch-craze of the Sixteenth and Seventeenth Centuries*, Pelican Books, 1978, Penguin, 1990.

P. Tyler, *The Church Courts at York and Witchcraft Prosecutions 1567–1640*, 'Northern History', Vol. IV, 1969.

D. P. Walker, *Unclean Spirits – Possession and Exorcism in France and England in the Late Sixteenth and Early Seventeenth Centuries*, Scholar Press, 1981.

John K. Walton, *Lancashire, A social history, 1558–1939*, Manchester U.P., 1987.

John Webster, *The Displaying of Supposed Witchcraft*, London 1677.

William Self Weeks, *Dr John Webster*, Clitheroe Advertiser and Times.

John White, *The Way to the True Church, wherein the Principal Motives persuading to Romanism . . . are familiarly disputed: by John White, Minister of Godsword at Eccles*, London, 1612. 4th edn, 1616.

Gladys Whittaker, *Roughlee Hall—Fact and Fiction*, Marsden Antiquarians, 1980.

T. D. Whittaker, *An History of the Original Parish of Whalley*, 1800.

T. D. Whittaker, *The History and Antiquities of the Deanery of Craven, 1805*. 3rd edn, A. W. Morant, 1878.

Index

In the seventeenth century most Lancashire family-names were spelt in several ways. I have aimed at consistency, but without wish to stifle delight at the variety.

Names in the Rental list in Appendix 2 are not all recorded in this index.

References to illustrations and family trees are indicated by an italic number.

AINSWORTH, Harrison, novelist 87
Airedale 7
ale xii, 27, 30, 33, 93, 96, 161, 181
Alker, William, of Samlesbury xiv, 136–7
Allen, Jane, née Lister 131, *132*
   William, Cardinal, xi, 131–3, 194–5, *132*
Altham, seat of the Bannisters 134, *xvi*
Altham, Sir James, judge xv, 6, 16, 61–4, 69, 163, 167, 172, 174, *2, 15, 62*
Anabaptists 48, 61–3
Anderton, James, magistrate xv
Armada, Spanish xi, 133
Arminians 127
Arnoldsbigging – see also Westby 8, 129, 131, 183, 197
Arrignement and Triall xv, 1, 6, 14, 24, 41, *2, 36*
Ashby de la Zouche 122, 125
Ashe, Richard, Counsel for the Regicides 156
Ashton, Jane, maid at Cleworth 119, 122
Assheton family of Downham 129, 168, *90*
Assheton family of Whalley 129, 168
   Sir John, of Lower Hall 152–6, 161

Nicholas, Esq. of Downham, diarist 65, 146, 190
   Richard, Esq. of Downham 91, 190
Atherton, Alexander 110
Avignon, France 57

BACON, Sir Francis 68
Baden-Württemberg 59
Baggilie, Henry 95–6
Balderston, Agnes 76
   Jennet – see also Preston, Jennet xi, 7, 76
   Nicholas 76
Baldwin, Richard, miller at Wheathead xiii, 26, 35–6
Ball 47, 86, 89
Bancroft, Richard, Bishop of London, then Archbishop of Canterbury 124, 126–7
Bannister, Nicholas Esq. of Altham xv, 19, 42, 60, 91, 134–5, 169, 171, 195, *130*
baptism, adult 125–8, 48, 106–8
Barley, Lancashire 43, 89, 179, 180
Barnes, John of Holborne, publisher 14, 163, *2, 15*

Barnoldswick 152, 159
Bath 137
Bee, Jesse, of Burton on Trent 125
begging 21, 22, 28, 34, 46
Bierley, Ellen, of Samlesbury 137–40
    Jennet, of Samlesbury 137–40
Blackburn Hundred 110, 130
Blacko 10
Blacko Hill 10, 19
Blackwell, Derbyshire 125
Blaeu, Johan, cartographer 184
bleeding of corpse 67–9, 77, 80, 168–9,
    172
Bobbin, Tim, alias of J. Collier 99
Boleyn, Anne, wife of Henry VIII 77
Bolton by Bowland 18, 184
Booker, Richard, of London 94
Booth, Jennet, of Padiham xv, 134
Boothman, Jane, of Burnley 186
Bowland, Forest of 8, 161
Bracewell xii, 70–5, 80, 153, xvi, 9
Brasenose College, Oxford 115, 118
Brearley (or Brierly), Roger, Grindle-
    tonian 106–8, 157, 192–3
Bromley, Sir Edward, judge xv, 6, 14,
    16, 61, 63, 65, 89, 149, 163, 166,
    173, 2, 15
broomstick 56
Broughton in Craven, Yorkshire 110
Browsholme 152–3, 159, 161, 153
Buckinghamshire 127
Bulcock, Jane, of Moss End xv, 45,
    51–2, 149, 180
    John, of Moss End xv, 45, 51–2,
        149, 171, 180
    (or Bullock), Henry xiii, 87, 176,
        180
Bulhole (or Bullhole) 26, 28, 29, 181,
    21, 27
Burnley 8–10, 29, 45, 186, 21
Burton-on-Trent 61, 125–6
Burton, Robert, anatomist of melan-
    choly 110
Byrom, Margret, kinswoman of the
    Starkies 120

Calvinism 111, 115–8, 122–8, 151, 157
Cambridge 94
Cambridge University 66, 111, 118,
    125, 157
cannibalism 59, 140, 140
Canon Episcopi 56
carding wool 30, 134, 181
Carr Hall xii, 84–5, 143, 177, 181, 85,
    144
Carter, Peter, schoolmaster of Whalley
    103
cat xiv, 36, 47, 87–8, 185, 158
Cathars 141
Catholics, Catholicism 82, 84, 98, 101,
    102–5, 106, 108, 119, 122, 127, 128,
    129–33, 136–42, 143, 151, 157.
    recusants 129–31, 136–7
    rituals and liturgies 42–3, 93–101,
        128, 151
Catholic Mission (or English Mission)
    104, 129, 132
Caulk, Derbyshire 122
Cecil, William, Lord Burghley 102, 130
Chadderton, Lancashire 95
Chadderton, Dr William, Bishop of
    Chester 104
charmers, see wise-men and -women
charms – see also pictures 33, 93–101,
    128
Chattox, alias of Anne Whittle xi–xv,
    3, 25–34, 36–9, 42, 45, 46–7, 49, 50,
    81, 86, 91–2, 93, 106, 110, 114, 134–
    5, 136, 149, 159–61, 169, 171, 181,
    182, 185, 33
Chelmsforth 61, 25
Cheshire 30
Christening 47–8, 82, 106, 108
circles, magic 121, 55, 122
Civil War 7–8, 148, 151, 156, 157
Cleworth (or Cleweth), near Leigh
    119–24, 193
Clideroe, Isabel de 131
Clifford family 7
Clitheroe 7–8, 11, 74, 107, 126, 135,
    153, 157, 8

Clitheroe Grammar School 157

Clitheroe, Margaret xi, 131

Coal Pit Lane (Gisburn Old Road) 10, 19, 20

Coates Hall, Barnoldswick 152–3, 159, 9

Colne, Lancashire xiv, 10, 21, 45, 46, 182, 187, 21

confessions 23–5, 28, 34, 47–8, 56, 57–8, 89–92, 185

consecrated bread 84, 103, 110

Constable – see Henry Hargreaves

copulation with devils 59, 140, 141, 157, 185, 186, 158

Covell, Thomas, gaoler and magistrate xv, 46, 49, 83, 91, 169

Coverham Abbey 50

Cowgill (Sowgill) 50, 170, 9

Craven, 8, 13, 16, 72, 76, 129, 148, 151, 161, 166–7, 173.

Cromwell, Oliver 7, 156

Cronkshaw, Anne, of Marsden 45

Crooke, Margaret, née Nutter xiv, 29, 32, 178, 181

cross, sign of 84, 96

Crowtrees 87, 21

crying out against a witch 1, 66–7, 70, 72, 75–6, 80, 168, 172

Cunningham, John, alias Dr Fian 47

Curedale 65

DALTON, Michael, author of The Countrey Justice 68, 78

Daemonologie by King James I xi, xii, 54, 56, 67, 75, 188, 64

Dandy 47, 83–6, 89

Darling, Thomas, 'The Boy of Burton' xi, 125–6, 128

Darrel, John, exorcist xi, 122–8, 141, 197, 123

Dawson, Cicilia, of Walton le Dale 65

Dee, Dr John 121

Demdike, alias of Elizabeth Southerns xi–xiv, 3, 22, 25–9, 34–42, 43, 45, 46, 48–50, 81, 83–4, 86–7, 91, 104–5, 110, 114, 159, 169, 171, 183, 185, 186, 188, 193, 23

Denham, Buckinghamshire 127

Denham, judge 65

Dentdale 51

Derby, Ferdinando, Earl of xi, 38, 75, 146, 37

    Margaret, Lady 109

    Henry, Earl of 109

Derbyshire 122, 125

Device family 134, 136, 159, 23

    Alizon xiii, xiv, xv, 21–8, 33, 34, 35, 39, 42, 45–6, 48–50, 82–3, 87, 106, 108, 149, 151, 169, 180, 181, 184, 185

    Elizabeth xii, xv, 19, 21, 22, 28, 36, 41, 45–7, 48, 49, 86, 89, 96, 149, 171, 184, 186

    James xii, xiv, xv, 19, 21, 22, 25, 34, 38, 42–54, 82–8, 89, 96–7, 99–101, 143, 145, 149, 169–71, 180, 181, 182, 184

    Jennet xii, xiv, 19, 21, 22, 41, 43, 45, 85, 89, 96, 171–3, 182

    John xii, 27, 41, 171

Devil – see familiar

Deyne, Jennet, of Newfield Edge, Middop 52

Diana, goddess 54

Dibb, Jennet, of Fewston 47

Displaying of Supposed Witchcraft by J. Webster 74, 152–3, 157–61, 185, 186, 158

Dobson, George, Vicar of Whalley xi, 103–4, 118

Dodge-sonnes 14, 17–18, 80, 166, 169, 184

Dodgsons of Padiham 18, 134–5

Dodgson, Thomas, of Bolton by Bowland xiii, 18

dog xii, xiii, xiv, 24–5, 28, 33–4, 35, 46–7, 83–6, 87, 89–91, 139, 158, 182, 185, 189, 158

Douai 129, 132

Downham, Lancashire 8, 65, xvi

Drake, William, Esq. of Barnoldswick 152–3, 161

Duckworth, John, of the Launde xii, 85

Duffy, Eamon, historian 95

Dugdale, Richard, of Surey 196–8

EAST ANGLIA 16

Eccles, Lancashire 98, 101, 120, *xvi*

Egerton, Sir Thomas, Lord Ellesmere 61

Elderson, Joan, of Newton-in-Maker-field 68

Elizabeth I, Queen 115–16, 118, 194–5

Emmanuel College, Cambridge 111

English College, Rome 104, 141

English Mission – *see* Catholic Mission

Erasmus, Desiderius 118

Erbery, William, seeker and radical prophet 107, 157

Essex 47, *25*

Essex, Robert Devereux, Third Earl of 38

Everard, John, familist and hermetic scholar 107

Ewen, C. L'Estrange, historian 56

exhumation of corpses 42, 59, 140, *140*

exorcism 110, 119, 122, 125–6, 141

FANCIE xiii, 32–4, 47, 92

familiar – *see also* dog, cat, hare, toad, foal, Fancie, Tibb, Ball 23, 24–6, 28, 32–4, 36, 46–8, 52, 54, 83–4, 85–6, 89–92, 134, 170, 172, *36*, *55*, *67*

Familism and Familists 106–8, 157, 191–2

Fawkes, Guy 49

feast, magical 91–2

Fence, Lancashire xiv, 28, 29, 33, 39, 169, 185, *21*

Fewston, Yorkshire 47

Fian, Dr – *see* John Cunningham

Fishlake 191

flying 52–7, 170, 185, 188, *53*, *55*, *67*

Florus, Br, Inquisitor 57, 59

foal 52, 54, 170, 172, 188

Foulds, Anne, of Colne 52, 182

Fox, George, Quaker 107

Foxe, John, martyrologist 115

Frankfurt 115, 118

Fylde 131

GARGRAVE, Yorkshire 94

Garnet, John, wizard 110

Gawthorpe, seat of the Shuttleworths 145, 185

Germany 59, 115, 118

Gerrard, Sir Thomas xv, 148

Gisburn 1, 7–11, 13, 18, 19, 42, 50–1, 60, 70, 72, 94, 129, 151, 152–3, 156, 159, 161, 163, 165, 166, 169, 170, 172, 196–8, *xvi*, *9*

Gisburn Parish Church (St Mary's) xiv, 7, 10–11, 13, 18, 50, 70, 78, 156, 184, *10*, *79*

Gisburn Hall 10–11, 152–3, 159, 161, *9*, *10*

Gisburn Old Road – *see* Coal Pit Lane

Gisburne Park – *see* Lower Hall, Gisburn

Glanville, Joseph FRS 159

Goldshaw (Gouldshey) Booth xi, 35, 86, 89, 170, 181, *21*, *27*, *31*

Gooderidge, Alice, of Burton on Trent 125

Good Friday xiv, 42–3, 97, 100, 101, 105, 167, 169–70, 171, 173, 187, 191

grave monument 11

Gray, Alice, of Colne 45, 52, 182

Grays Inn 156

Greenacres, John, MP, of Worston 74

Greenhead 30, 181, 182, 185, *21*, *31*, *35*

Greene, Anne, of Gargrave 94

Greenwood, Christopher, cartographer *31*

Greystone Moor 10

Grindal, Edmund, Archbishop of York 43, 102

Grindleton, Lancashire (formerly in Yorkshire) 106–8, 157, 192, 197, *xvi*, *9*

Grindletonianism 106–8, 157, 191–3
Guiseley, Yorkshire 94
Gunpowder Plot xii, 49, 146

HACKET, Dr 38
Haigh, Christopher, historian 104
Halifax xiv, 21
Halsall, Mr 38
hanging 1, 104, 121, 131, 149–51, 166, 172, *150*
hare xii, 25, 36, 84, 86, 88
Hargreaves, Blaze, of Higham 86, 182
Hargreaves, Christopher, *alias* Christopher Jackes, of Thorniholme 45
    Elizabeth, wife of Christopher 45
    Henry, of Goldshaw Booth, Constable xv, 21, 38, 42, 82, 134, 170, 180
    Hugh, of Under Pendle 45, 176, 180
    Jennet, wife of Hugh 45, 180, *44*
    John, of Goldshaw Booth 86, 89
Herodias 54
Harrison, G. B., historian 12
Harrison, George, of Cuerdale 65
Harsnett, Samuel, chaplain to Bishop Bancroft, later Archbishop of York 124, 127
Hartley, Edmund xi, 75, 119–21, 128, 141
Hartley, Michael, of Colne 52, 182
Haslingden 136
Hasted, Rachel, historian 12
Hay, Grace, of Padiham 45
healing 22, 26, 52, 87, 93–6, 101, 102, 109–10, 111–13, 193
Heber family 129, 148, *9*, *73*
    Eleanor, first wife of Thomas 72
    Jane – *see* Jane Lister née Heber
    Thomas, Esq. of Marton 3, 17, 66, 72, 114, 150, 168
Henry, Prince, eldest son of James I 146
Hewitt (Hewyt), Katherine, of Colne xv, 45, 52, 149, 171, 182
Higham Booth xiii, 27, 86, 161, 178–9, 182, 197, *21*, *31*

High Commission 124, 125–6
Hildersham, Arthur, Puritan leader, incumbent of Ashby de la Zouche 125, 126, 128
Hill, Christopher, historian 106, 107
Hockett, Mary, of Essex 47
Hoghton family 148, *130*
    Sir Richard of Hoghton Towers 129, 148, *xvi*
Holden, Alice, née Bannister, wife of Robert 134
    Ralph, son of Robert 136
    Robert, Esq. of Haslingden xiv, 114, 134, 136–41, 171, *130*
Hopkins, Matthew, witchfinder 16
Horrock Hall, near Parbold 131, *xvi*
Horrocks, Thomas, Vicar of Broughton in Craven 110
Howard, Frances, Countess of Somerset 38
Howgate, Christopher, of Pendle 45, *23*
    Elizabeth, wife of Christopher 45, *23*
Huntroyd, seat of the Starkies 119, 121, 128, *21*
Hutchinson, Anne, of Massachusetts 107

IMPOSTERS 124, 125–7, 139–42, 156, 157, 187, 194, 196–8
infanticide 17–18, 56, 59, 139–40, 141, 149
Inquisition 23–4, 56, 57–9, 111, 188
interrogation 23–4, 25–6, 34, 42, 50, 52–4, 56–7, 59

JACKES, Christopher – *see* Christopher Hargreaves
James I of England and VI of Scotland ix, 23, 47, 54, 56, 63, 67, 75, 119, 146, 163, 187, 188, *64*
Jeffreys, Thomas, cartographer 51, *9*
Jesuits 127
Jews 141
Joan of Arc 56
Johnson, Margret 187

Johnson, William of the Grange 152, 161
Johnson, Ben, playwright 128

KILDWICK, Yorkshire 157
Knyvet, Thomas, Lord Eskrick 49, 187
Kramer (or Institor), Heinrich, Inquisitor 56, 188
Kylden, Stephen, of Southwark 37

LAMBERT, John, Major General 156
Lancashire 7, 95, 98, 102, 104, 110, 132, 183–4, *31*
Lancaster 134, 183, *15, 39*
    Castle and Gaol xiv, 29, 35, 39, 45–6, 49, 83, 91, 104, 134, 150, 169, *15, 39*
    Assizes xv, 3, 7, 8, 21, 39, 61, 63, 65, 89, 121, 134, 173, 183, *15*
Lathom, Lancashire, seat of the earls of Derby 38, 75, *xvi*
Latimer, Hugh, bishop 110
Laund, The 32, 85, 178, 181–2, 185, *21, 31*
Law, Abraham, son of John xiv, 21–2
    John, pedlar xiv, 21–2, 24, 193
Lawrence, John 49
league with the Devil 23, 24, 28, 33–5, 83–4, 111, 151, 157, 185
Legate, Bartholomew, Familist martyr 61–3
Leicester, Earl of 38
Leigh, Lancashire 119, 192, *121*
Leigh, William, Rector of Standish 146, 148
Lichfield 63, 118
Lister family, of Westby 131, 133, 139, 148, 153–6, 183, 197, *9, 13, 71, 154–5*
    Alice, née Hoghton xi, 129
    Effamia, née de Westbye 183
    Jane, née Greenacre, wife of Thomas senior 74, 77, 78, 80
    Jane, né Heber, wife of Thomas junior xii, 72, 75, 156
    John 156

Kathrine (later Kathrine Assheton) 156
    Leonard, of Cowgill 50–1, 78, 80, 170–1, *9*
    Mary, née Deane 156
    Thomas senior xi, xii, 1, 7, 12–14, 17, 66–7, 69, 70–2, 74, 75–7, 78, 129, 149, 153, 166, 167–8, 172, *15*
    Thomas junior xi, xii, xiv, 12, 13–14, 17–19, 45, 50–1, 66–7, 68, 70, 72, 75, 77, 79–81, 82, 91, 114, 129, 133, 149–50, 156, 166–7, 168–73
    Thomas, Captain 156
    Rosamund, wife of Thomas Southworth 139
    William xiv
Loftus, Anne, wife of Leonard Lister 50
Lombard Street, London 157
London 1, 2, 3, 6, 14, 115, 137, 157
Loomeshaw's wife, of Burnley 186
Louvaine 132
Lower Hall, Gisburn, later known as Gisburne Park 8, 152–6, 159, 161, *9*
Lutherans 126, 127

MADNESS – *see also* possession 33–4, 35, 52
Malham 156
Malkin Tower xiv, 14, 19–20, 22, 26, 35, 38, 41, 86, 87, 91–2, 149–50, 171, *9, 21, 31*
    Assembly xiv, 3, 12–14, 17, 19–20, 41–6, 48–54, 56–7, 60, 80, 82, 87, 89, 105, 167, 169–73, 187
Malleus Maleficarum 23, 56, 188
Manchester 137
Manchester College 115, 122, 137
mare 134, 155–6
Marsden (now called Nelson) 45
Marsden, Henry, Esq. of Gisburn 10–11
    Henry, Esq. of Gisburn, MP 10, 152–3, 161, *10*
Marshalsea 133, 143

Marton, Yorkshire 17, 66, 70, 72, *9*
Mary I, Queen 115, 118, 131
Massachusetts 107
Matthew, Henry, of Guiseley 94
Middleton School 115
Middop 10, 52
milk 26, 28, 36, 181
Milton, Lancashire (formerly Yorkshire) 157, *xvi*
Milton, Henry, of Rough Lee 86, 89, 176, 179.
Moore, Hugh, of Pendle xii, 28, 182
 Hugh, of Higham 197
 John, of Higham xiii, 27–8, 33, 93, 161, 182, 197
 John junior xiii, 28, 33, 161
 Sir Jonas, FRS 152, 159–61, 182, *160*
More, George, exorcist 122, 124, 127, 141
More, Henry, FRS 159
Mortlock, Elizabeth, of Cambridgeshire 94
Moss End 45, 180
Mouldinge, Elena, of Hoghton 65
Murton, John 115

NEW FLEET PRISON, Manchester 137
Newchurch in Pendle xii, xiv, 42, 46, 83, 84, 101, 102–4, *xvi*, *21*
Newfield Edge, Middop 51–2
News from Scotland 47–8
Newsholme 18, 129
Newton in Makerfield 68
Nieuport 133
night-flying – *see* flying
Nottingham 126, 128
Nowell family, of Read 148, 190, *117*
 Alexander, Dean of St Paul's xii, 115–18, 132, 143, *166*
 Katherine, née Murton 115
 Laurence, Dean of Lichfield 118
 Roger, Esq., of Read, grandfather of his namesake 115
 Roger, of Read xii, xiv, xv, 3, 19, 21–6, 28, 29–34, 35–6, 38–9, 42–

5, 48–54, 56, 59–60, 75, 80, 82–3, 86, 87, 91, 93, 96, 99, 110–1, 114, 115, 118, 119, 124, 128, 134, 143, 150–1, 168–9, 171, 186, 188
Nutter family 185, *30*
 Alice, of Rough Lee xv, 45, 86–7, 104, 149, 179, 182
 Anne, daughter of Anthony xiii, 27, 33, 181
 Anthony 27, 33, 177, 181
 Christopher, of Greenhead, son of Robert the elder xi, xv, 29, 36, 181, 186
 Fr Ellis, priest 104, 182
 Fr John, priest xi, 104, 133, 182
 John, of Higham Booth xiv, 29, 33, 181
 John, of Bulhole xii, 26, 28, 177, 181, *27*
 John junior, of Bulhole xii, 28
 Marie, wife of Robert 36
 Miles 45, 87, 176, 179
 Richard, or Dick 45, 179
 Robert the elder, of Greenhead 30
 Robert xi, xv, 29–32, 36, 181, 182, 186
 Fr Robert, *alias* Rowley, priest xii, 104, 182

ORMSKIRK, Lancashire 38, 110, *xvi*
Owtinge, Thomas, Vicar of Bracewell 72
Oxford University 104, 115, 118, 125, 131, 156
Oxhey Place, Watford *62*

PADIHAM xv, 18, 45, 134–5, 183, *21*
Papal Bulls 56, 133, 188, 194
Parbold, Lancashire 131
Parker, Thomas, of Browsholme 152–3, 161
Parr, John, of Cleworth 119
Paythorne 18
Pearson, Margaret, of Padiham xv, 18, 134–5, 183

Peel, Edgar, and Southern, Pat, authors
    of *The Trials of the Lancashire Witches*
    12, 82, 96, 185, 187
Pell, John, FRS 152
Pendle Forest 16, 169, 170–1, 175–82,
    185, *8*, *31*
Pendle Hill 8, 102, 107, 151, 161, *74*,
    130
Pendle Water 185, *21*
Perkins, William, theologian xii, 23, 25,
    38, 66–7, 109, 110–14, 118, 128,
    192–3, *112*
Petty, William, FRS 152
Philip, King of Spain 132
pictures xii, 27, 36–9, 42, 80, 84–8, 110,
    161
Pilkington, James, Bishop of Durham 103
pillory xv, 135, 183, *135*
Pope Innocent VIII 188
Pope Pius V 133, 194
possession, alleged: Starkies 119–24, 193–
    4; Katherine Wright 125; Thomas
    Darling 125–6; William Sommers
    126, 193–4; Grace Sowerbutts 139–
    41; Richard Dugdale 197; Jennet
    Deyne 52; in Denham 122; satirised
    by Jonson 128; scepticism of Harsnet
    127; and of Webster 142, 194
Potts, Thomas, Clerk ot the Court xv,
    1–6, 12–15, 17, 19, 35, 41, 45, 57,
    66–7, 76–7, 87, 141, 143, 151, 184,
    187, *2*, *15*
Pratt, William, second husband of Alice
    Lister 129
Prentis, Joan, of Essex *25*
Preston, Lancashire, Battle of 8
Preston, Henry, father of William 7
    Jennet xi, xiv, xv, 1–20, 41–2, 45–6,
        49–51, 52–4, 60, 61, 66–7, 68–9,
        70–2, 74, 76–7, 78–81, 82, 114,
        128, 149–51, 152, 159, 161, 163–
        74, 197, *2*, *15*
    William, husband of Jennet xi, 7,
        149, 165, 173
Puritanism and Protestantism 4, 43, 48,

    110–11, 114, 115–18, 122, 124, 125–
    8, 133, 136, 146–8, 151, 197

QUAKERS 107

RAILING – *see* crying out
Ranters 191–2
Read, seat of the Nowells xiv, 3, 21,
    23, 28, 110, 115, *xvi*, *21*
Redferne, Anne xi, xii, xiv, xv, 29–32,
    36, 39, 45, 49–50, 86, 149, 169, 181,
    186, *33*
    Marie, daughter of Thomas and
        Anne xii, 86, *33*
    Thomas, husband of Anne xii, 30,
        32, 86, *33*
Reedley Hollow 104, *21*, *31*
Regino, Abbot of Prüm 54
Ribble, River 7–8, 129, 136, 139, 151,
    130
Ribblesdale Arms 156
Rigby, John, of Horrock Hall xii, 131
Rimington 8, 183–4
Robinson, Agnes 80
    Anne 1, 66–9, 70, 75, 77, 80, 168–9
    alias Swyer, Christopher, of Barley
        43, 176, 180, 187
    Edmund, of Wheatley Lane 187
    James, former lodger at Greenhead
        xii, xiv, 29–30, 178, 181
    alias Swyer, James, of Barley 89, 187
    alias Swyer, John, of Barley xii, xiv,
        43, 86, 89, 176, 180, 187
    John, of Rough Lee xiii, 24, 46
Robey, Isabel, of Windle xv, 67, 149,
    183
Rombalds Moor (Romles Moor) 60, 170
Rossall 131, *xvi*
Rough Lee xiii, 24, 45, 46, 86, 87, 89,
    175–6, 179–80, *21*
Royal Society 152, 159

SABBATHS 23, 42, 56–9, 60, 150, 151,
    157, 187, 188, *67*
Samlesbury xv, 136–42, 183, *xvi*

Church 140
Hall 136–7, 141, *130*, *137*
Lower Hall 139, *139*
witchcraft trial 136–42
Sandes, William, Mayor of Lancaster xv, 83
Sandys, Edwin, Archbishop of York, xi, 131
Sawley (Salley) 8, 11
Sawley Grange 152, 159, *9*
Saxton, Christopher, cartographer 183, *xvi*
Scot, Reginald 68, 110
Scott, Sir Walter 191–2
Seekers, 48, 61–3, 106–8
Seller, alleged to be father of Elizabeth Device's child 41, 187
Settle, Yorkshire 7
Shakespeare, William 67–8, *37*
shape-changing 52, 54, 140, 170
Shelford 57
Sherburn family, of Stonyhurst 129, 148
Sir Richard of Stonyhurst 137, 143, *130*
Sheriff of Lancashire xii, 115, 136
Shuttleworth family, of Gawthorpe 148, *147*
Sir Richard 29, 146, 179, 185
Col. Richard 145–6, 157, 175, 179
Singleton, John, of Samlesbury xv
Skipton, Yorkshire 7, 60
Slaidburn, Lancashire (formerly Yorkshire) 148
Smithfield, London 63
Snowhill, Gisburn 10
Somers, William, of Nottingham 126, 128, *123*
Somerset 68
Southerns, Elizabeth – *see* Demdike
Southwark 37, 131
Southworth family 129, 136–9, 148, *137*, *138*
Christopher, priest, son of Sir John 139, 141
Jane, wife of John xiv, 136–41, 143

Sir John 136–9, 141, 143, *130*
John, son of Thomas 137
Thomas, son of Sir John 137–9
Sowerbutts, Grace xv, 46, 139–41
Sowgill – *see* Cowgill
spells – *see* charms
Spenser, Edmund, poet 99
Sprenger, Jakob, Inquisitor 56, 188
St Mary's Hall, Oxford 131
St Paul's Cathedral, London 115
Standish, Lancashire 146
Stanguidge, Old 57
Stanley, William 133
Stansby, W., printer 6, 163, *2*, *15*
Starkie family, of Huntroyd and Cleworth 126, 128, 141, 148, 151, 193, *120*, *123*
Anne, née Parr, wife of Nicholas 119, *120*
Ann, daughter of Nicholas xi, 119–22
Edmund, father of Nicholas 119
John, son of Nicholas xi, 75, 119–22
Laurence, father of Edmond 119
Nicholas 119–21
stone-pit 35
Stonyhurst, seat of the Sherburns 137, 145, *xvi*, *130*
Strasbourg 115, 118
stroke or seizure 21–2, 35
Strype's *Annals* 136
sucking 24, 25, 35, 46, 91, 185, 186, *158*
Surey, near Whalley 197
Swyer, *alias* Robinson – *see* Robinson

TATTERSON, John, of Gargrave 94
Taylor, Zachery, clergyman 197, *198*
teeth xii, 41
Tempest family 129, 148
Sir Richard 72
Thompson, Agnis, associate of Dr Fian 47
Thorniholme 45, *21*
Thornton in Craven, Yorkshire 139
Thorpe, Margaret, of Fewston 47

Tibb xi, 35–6, 46, 92, 186
toad 134
torture 38, 47–8, 56, 59, 91, 131, 134, 190
Towneley family 129, 148, *130*, *145*
    Ann, wife of Henry xii, 84–5, 143, 181
    Henry of Carr Hall 84, 143–8, 181, *144*
    Sir John, of Towneley Hall 118, 143, 179, 181, *130*, *145*
Towneley Hall 143, *xvi*, *130*, *146*
Trawden, Lancashire 182
Trevor-Roper, Hugh, historian 141
Turnpike Trust 10
Twiston, Lancashire 184
Tyburn 104
Tyldesley, Lancashire 192, *xvi*, *121*

UNDER PENDLE 45, 180, *44*
unguent from dead babies 56, 59, 87, 140
Up Holland, Lancashire 110

VOMITING 38, 125, 126, 194, 197

WALES 30
Walshman, Thomas, of Samlesbury 139
Walsingham, Sir Francis 109, 139
Walton, Sir Issac, author of *The Compleat Angler* 115
Walton le Dale, Lancashire 65
Watford *62*
Webster, Dr John, of Clitheroe 68, 74, 102, 107, 126, 142, 152–3, 156–61, 185, 186, 188, 190, 194, 197
Weets Hill 10
Wennington Old Hall 11
West Riding 8, 152
Westby Hall, Gisburn 1, 8, 13–14, 50, 70, 75–6, 78, 131, 167, 170, 183, 197, *13*, *83*
Weston, William, Jesuit xi, 127, 141
Whalley, Lancashire 102–4, 121, 135, 136, 197, *104*

Whalley Abbey, seat of the Asshetons of Whalley 153, 156
Wheathead Mill (or Weethead) xiii, 26
Wheatley Lane 187
White, John, minister of Eccles xiii, 98, 101, 102
White, Margaret, of Fewston 47
White Lee, Higham 161, *21*
White Moor 187
Whittaker, Gladys, historian 87, 187
Whittaker, William, Regius Professor 118
Whittle, Anne – *see* Chattox
    Elizabeth, daughter of Chattox xii, 27, 28, *33*
Wightman, Edward, Familist martyr 61–3
Wilsey, James, of Pendle 41, 169
Windle, Lancashire xv, 149, 183
Winstanley, Elizabeth 110
Winthrop, John, first governor of Massachusetts 107
Wisbeach Castle 104, 141
wise-women and wise-men 3, 22, 23–4, 60, 80, 93–6, 102, 109–14, 119, 151
witch-hunts 16, 59
witch-marks 24, 91, 190
Wolfenbüttel 59
Wolton, John, Bishop of Exeter 118
Wood, Isabel, mistress of Sir Richard Sherburn 137
Worston, Lancashire 74
Wonderfull Discoverie, The xv, 3, 6, 12, 14, 24, 41, 49, *15*
Wright, Katherine, of Blackwell 125
Wynckley, Thomas 65

YORK 11, 103, 151, 163
    Assizes xiv, xv, 1, 3, 12, 14, 16, 17, 19, 46, 49–50, 61, 63, 66, 70, 74, 149, 163, 165, 166–70, 199, *2*, *15*
    Church Courts 94, 103, 106, 110
Yorkshire 7–8, 94, 106, 152